DATE DUE

Social Psychology
and Organizational Behaviour

Social Psychology
and Organizational Behaviour

Edited by

Michael Gruneberg
University College of Swansea

and

Toby Wall
University of Sheffield

JOHN WILEY & SONS
Chichester · New York · Brisbane · Toronto · Singapore

Library of Congress Cataloging in Publication Data:
Main entry under title:

Social psychology and organizational behaviour.
   1. Organizational behaviour—Addresses, essays, lectures.
   2. Psychology, Industrial—Addresses, essays, lectures.
   3. Social psychology—Addresses, essays, lectures.
   I. Gruneberg, Michael M. II. Wall, Toby D.
HD58.7.S64 1984   158.7   83-19871

ISBN 0 471 10326 8 (U.S.)

British Library Cataloguing in Publication Data:
Social psychology and organizational behaviour
   1. Organizational behaviour
   I. Gruneberg, Michael   II. Wall, Toby
302.3′5   HD58.7

ISBN 0 471 10326 8

Typeset by C. R. Barber & Partners (Highlands) Ltd, Fort William, Scotland and printed by St Edmundsbury Press, Bury St Edmunds, Suffolk

List of Contributors

DR MICHAEL GRUNEBERG, *Department of Psychology, University College of Swansea, University of Wales, Singleton Park, Swansea, SA2 8PP, U.K.*

DAVID GUEST, *London School of Economics and Political Studies, Houghton Street, Aldwych, London, WC2 2AE, U.K.*

DR JEAN HARTLEY, *Social Science Research Council Industrial Relations Research Unit, University of Warwick, Coventry, CV4 7AL, U.K.*

DR DIAN-MARIE HOSKINS, *University of Aston Management Centre, University of Aston, Nelson Building, Gosta Green, Birmingham, B4 7DU, U.K.*

PROFESSOR ABRAHAM KORMAN, *Baruch College, The City University of New York, 17 Lexington Avenue, New York, NY10010, U.S.A.*

PROFESSOR EDWIN LOCKE, *College of Business and Management, University of Maryland, College Park, Maryland, U.S.A.*

PROFESSOR ROGER MANSFIELD, *Department of Business Administration and Accountancy, University of Wales Institute of Science and Technology, Cardiff, Wales, U.K.*

DR IAN MORLEY, *Department of Psychology, University of Warwick, Coventry, CV4 7AL, U.K.*

DR GORDON O'BRIEN, *Department of Psychology, School of Social Sciences, The Flinders University of South Australia, Bedford Park, South Australia 5042, Australia.*

PROFESSOR DONALD VREDENBURGH, *Baruch College, The City University of New York, 17 Lexington Avenue, New York, NY10010, U.S.A.*

DR TOBY WALL, *Medical Research Council and Social Science Research Council Social and Applied Psychology Unit, University of Sheffield, Sheffield, S10 2TN, U.K.*

PROFESSOR PHILIP YETTON, *Australian Graduate School of Management, University of South Wales, PO Box 1, New South Wales, Sydney 2033, Australia.*

v

Contents

Social Psychology and Organizational Behaviour
Edited by M. Gruneberg and T. Wall
© 1984 John Wiley & Sons Ltd

Chapter 1

Introduction

Toby Wall and Michael Gruneberg

The aim of this book is to introduce students to social psychological approaches to the understanding of organizational behaviour. It is directed towards both undergraduate and graduate students new to the area—those pursuing taught courses, or research, concerned with people in work environments. These areas of study will typically come under such titles as industrial, occupational, organizational, or applied social psychology, and organizational behaviour, or management studies. A social psychological perspective, while not commensurate with these overlapping areas of inquiry, is a central element within each. This book is intended to reflect this common core.

In order to meet our objective we asked established academics currently involved in both teaching and research to outline the state of the subject within their field of expertise. The assembled group of contributors has an international flavour. Two members are from Australia, three from the United States, and five from the United Kingdom. Together, they provide an authoritative account of important social psychological contributions to the study of the relationship between people and their work.

AN HISTORICAL PERSPECTIVE

A useful way of outlining the nature of current social psychological approaches within organizational behaviour is to take an historical perspective. This enables one to identify not only the substantive issues which characterize the area, but also the reasons for their inclusion. It thus provides a vehicle for introducing the content of the present volume.

While different authors highlight alternative points of departure for psychological interest in paid employment, all are agreed this effectively began shortly after the turn of the century. For Ferguson (1962) the book by Scott in 1903 entitled *The Theory of Advertising* represents the first clear example of the application of psychology to business matters. Others, however, point to Taylor's *Principles of Scientific Management* (1911) or Munsterberg's text

Psychology and Industrial Efficiency (1913) as the springboards for a new area of study and application. It was certainly soon after these publications that work in the area gained momentum. During the First World War psychologists became active in the selection and training of recruits. In 1917 the *Journal of Applied Psychology* was first published in the United States. In the United Kingdom Myers' book *Mind and Work* was released in 1920; *Occupational Psychology* (now known as the *Journal of Occupational Psychology*) made its appearance in 1926; and in the same decade the Medical Research Council inaugurated the Industrial Fatigue Research Board (later called the Industrial Health Research Board) which undertook a programme of field studies relating work repetitiveness to performance.

None of the above contributions, however, represents a clear social psychological approach. This did not emerge as a force in its own right until around the 1930s. In this decade the work of Hoppock (1935), on job satisfaction, placed the measurement of job attitudes and empirical examination of their determinants and correlates squarely on the map. Undoubtedly the greatest formative influence, however, was that provided by the work of Elton Mayo and his colleagues at the Hawthorne Works of the Western Electric Company which came to fruition in the 1930s (see Mayo, 1933; Roethlisberger and Dickson, 1939). For Blum and Naylor (1968) this represents:

'. . . the most significant series of studies ever carried out in industry in terms of the impact they had on the growth and development of industrial psychology. They provided the foundation and impetus for the expansion of industrial psychology beyond the realm of selection, placement and working conditions into the study of motivation, morale and human relations' (Blum and Naylor, 1968, p. 18).

It is worth considering these studies in slightly greater detail.

The Hawthorne Studies actually began in 1924 with a series of experiments to examine the effects of illumination intensity on work performance. In an initial study productivity was found to fluctuate independently from illumination levels. In subsequent better controlled investigations performance was found to improve with increased light intensity in experimental groups—but so did performance in control groups. The investigators then decided to systematically decrease levels of illumination, but found that performance again improved. The investigators thus had little option but to abandon the hypothesis that level of illumination would positively affect productivity. Clearly, other more powerful factors were at work.

In 1927 the company joined forces with scientists from the Harvard School of Business Administration and several more investigations were carried out. Here again the focus was on varying work conditions, but several alternatives were examined. These included a performance related payment scheme, rest pauses and working hours. Almost without exception each change in work conditions, whether for better or worse, was followed by some increase in performance. Even a return to initial work conditions, a 48 hour, five-and-a-half day week with no rest pauses, did not cause a decrement in work output. Once again, the investigators had to accept that a number of work conditions they presumed would affect performance were of no demonstrable importance in that respect. But now they had a new problem. How were they to account for the observed changes in output?

It was in addressing this question that social factors in work were brought into consideration, and a social psychological perspective was explicitly formulated. The investigators noted that the process of conducting experiments on work conditions removed employees from their normal work environment, set them apart and intensified their interaction. In practice, the experiments had resulted in a complex of additional changes. Supervision had become less directive, the operatives were more able to determine their own work pace, they became involved in decision-making and developed their own norms, work methods and values. It was perhaps these unintended consequences of the investigations which accounted for the otherwise perplexing pattern of results obtained. With commendable persistence the researchers continued their investigations adopting the new perspective. They undertook a programme of interviews with over 21,000 employees explicitly focussed on their attitudes towards work. From this they found that the content and style of personal relationships, with both peers and superiors, was an important work factor, and that individuals benefited solely as a result of being interviewed. Another study in the 'Bank Wiring Observation Room' served to cement the investigators' view of the importance of social aspects of the work. Here they observed in considerable detail the social pressures developed by groups to regulate performance.

We shall not further describe the Hawthorne Studies here as they are well presented by several authors and are discussed elsewhere in this book (Chapter 3). We should note however that although these investigations are not without their critics (see, for example, Landsberger, 1958; Bramel and Friend, 1981), there is little dispute concerning their formative influence over psychological research into work organizations. In particular they drew attention to supervisory and leadership style, group structure and processes, employee involvement in decision-making, and job attitudes and satisfaction as salient aspects of individual work experiences. In effect, the Hawthorne Studies served to delineate a social psychological perspective to organizational behaviour upon which others could and did build.

Before leaving these investigations mention should also be made of one further legacy. In conjunction with subsequent critical evaluation of the studies, there emerged the notion of the 'Hawthorne Effect'. This refers to the possibility the improvement in work attitudes and performance, or more generally changes in these and other respects, may be occasioned merely by conducting a study, rather than by the specific manipulations carried out. This emphasizes the point that research in organizations is a social event in itself with consequences for the outcome and interpretation of change.

It would not be unreasonable to argue that the two decades or so which followed the Hawthorne Studies represent a period of consolidation during which investigators extended their research into the effects of leadership style, group processes, and job attitudes. The Ohio State Leadership Studies (e.g., Stogdill and Coons, 1957) and the Michigan Leadership Studies (e.g., Katz, Maccoby, and Morse, 1950) exemplify subsequent work concerned with supervisory and managerial behaviour. This allowed more wide-ranging and prescriptive contributions to organization practice such as those offered by Likert (1959), McGregor (1960), and Blake and Mouton (1964). Consideration of work groups also came to the fore, well supported by Homans' contributions as described in his books *The Human Group* (1950) and *Social Behaviour: Its Elementary Forms* (1961). And the study of work attitudes developed at a considerable pace, requiring Herzberg, Mausner, Peterson, and Capwell (1957) to consider nearly 1,800 references in their comprehensive review of job satisfaction research. These topics, invigorated by recent empirical research findings, remain today as central components of the social psychological approach to organizational behaviour. However, the field is now much more broadly conceived as a result of developments in the 1960s which we shall now briefly consider.

In the mid-1960s several psychologists began to argue for a more inclusive approach to the study of work behaviour. Much as the Hawthorne Studies heralded the addition of a 'social dimension' to research, so did a number of publications identify the further need to add an organizational perspective. Particularly influential in encouraging this orientation were books by Bass (1965) and Schein (1965) entitled *Organizational Psychology*, Katz and Kahn's (1966) volume *The Social Psychology of Organizations*, and Pugh's (1966) position paper 'Modern organization theory: a psychological and sociological study'.

The theme underlying these initiatives is well expressed by Kahn and his co-authors (1964):

> 'Knowledge can best be advanced by research which attempts to deal simultaneously with data at different levels of abstraction—individual, group and organization. This is a difficult task and not uniformly satisfactory. It is nevertheless a core requirement for the understanding of human organizations. Organizations are reducible to individual acts, yet they are lawfully and in part understandable only at the level of collective behaviour' (Kahn, Wolfe, Quinn, Snoek and Rosenthal, 1964, pp. 397–398).

Similarly, Katz and Kahn, in the Preface to the second edition of their book (1978) state:

> 'That social psychological principles can be applied to all forms of collective organized effort is now acknowledged in many disciplines. Industrial psychology

has moved towards becoming organizational psychology and not only studies people in many organizational settings, but on occasion recognizes organizational or system variables in shaping that behaviour' (Katz and Kahn, 1978, p. iii).

This new perspective was reflected in the introduction of a new journal, *Organizational Behavior and Human Performance*, in 1966; and by the fact that, in 1973, Division 14 of the American Psychological Association, previously called the Division of Industrial Psychology, modified its title to the Division of Industrial and Organizational Psychology.

It was in this way that to the focus on individual and small group behaviour and the emphasis on leadership, group decision-making, and job attitudes, was added a concern for organizational characteristics as reflected in such constructs as bureaucracy, organizational structure, organizational climate, and organizational development. More important than a list of constituent concepts, however, is the emergence of the idea that characteristics ranging from indices of size to types of industrial relations systems provide legitimate and manageable foci for empirical and theoretical enquiry. Moreover, the orientation helps to break down interdisciplinary barriers so that concepts and levels of analyses offered by sociology, political science, organizational science, and economics may be brought to bear on given problems where they help in the fuller understanding of social behaviour within organizations.

THE CHAPTERS TO FOLLOW

Within the context of this book the dual heritage of social psychological approaches to organizational behaviour is clearly in evidence. Together the chapters which follow cover both those topics clearly marked out by the seminal Hawthorne Studies and reflect the broader perspective encouraged by the later incorporation of an organizational perspective.

More specifically the next chapter (Chapter 2), by Phil Yetton, addresses the question of leadership. It traces the history of the area from trait approaches, through behavioural or leadership style 'theories', to modern contingency models. With respect to the latter attention is paid to trait-contingency (Fiedler's LPC model), behaviour-contingency (House's path-goal approach), decision-contingency (Vroom and Yetton's model), and subordinate relationship-contingency (Graen's dyad model) formulations.

In Chapter 3 Gordon O'Brien considers the various factors which affect group productivity. These include leadership style (thus providing a link with the previous chapter), group cohesiveness, goal-setting, inter-member compatibility, communication networks, and power structures. Among the issues raised by O'Brien is that of group decision-making. This is taken up by Ian Morley and Dian Hoskins in Chapter 4 from a very different perspective. Taking a systems view their contribution focusses on how decision-making is affected by organizational structure and internal political influences.

Edwin Locke, in Chapter 5, introduces research into job satisfaction. There he considers the conceptual foundations and psychological bases of job satisfaction, its expected relationship with work performance and withdrawal behaviour (e.g., absence and labour turnover) and the relevance of a range of factors as determinants of job satisfaction—such as work content, pay, promotion, work conditions, and participation.

In Chapter 6 Roger Mansfield, drawing on a variety of disciplinary sources, introduces the concepts of formal and informal organizational structure and considers alternative approaches to characterizing these. He then moves on to describe research on the determinants of alternative organizational structures and the effects of the latter on employee attitudes and behaviour.

Historically, one of the weaknesses of social psychological approaches to work organization has been its avoidance of industrial relations issues in general and conflict in particular. Yet these are two important aspects of working life. In Chapter 7 Jean Hartley addresses these topics principally through a focus on strikes in terms of their causes, processes and outcomes.

Chapter 8, by David Guest, considers psychological contributions to organizational development and change. A criticism sometimes levelled at psychologists is that while they acquire knowledge relevant to applied problems they do not carry it through into practice. In this chapter the author highlights the practical implications and use of major theoretical approaches, outlines alternative methods of introducing change, and discusses contemporary integrative frameworks stemming from interest in organizational development, the quality of working life movement and employee participation.

In the final chapter Abe Korman and Don Vredenburgh discuss the conceptual, theoretical, and ethical foundations of research in work organizations. An initial consideration of the development of theory leads into an analysis of the scientific status of the social psychological approaches to organizational behaviour. Here methodological and applied questions are paramount. The authors then raise some of the ethical issues which have occurred and must inevitably arise in research of this nature. Throughout, the authors are both analytical and descriptive with respect to the field as it has developed to date, and are also prescriptive in looking to the future.

In summary, this book aims to give the student a basic grounding in a number of central areas which relate social psychology to organizational behaviour. These include areas such as industrial relations, organizational climate, and ethical and historical perspectives which are often absent from present day books on organizational behaviour. In our selection of contributions, too, we have sought to given an international perspective to a subject so often treated in terms of one cultural boundary whether North American, British, or European.

REFERENCES

Bass, B. M. (1965) *Organizational Psychology*, Allyn and Bacon, Boston.

Blake, R. R., and Mouton, J. S. (1964) *The Managerial Grid*, Gulf, Houston, Texas.

Blum, M. L., and Naylor, J. C. (1968) *Industrial Psychology*, Harper and Row, London.

Bramel, D., and Friend, R. (1981) Hawthorne, the myth of the docile worker and class bias in psychology. *American Psychologist*, **36,** 867–878.

Ferguson, L. W. (1962) *The Heritage of Industrial Psychology*, Finlay Press, Hartford, Conn.

Herzberg, F., Mausner, B., Peterson, R. O., and Capwell, D. F. (1957) *Job Attitudes: Review of Research and Opinion*, Psychological Services of Pittsburgh, Pittsburgh.

Homans, G. C. (1950) *The Human Group*, Harcourt Brace, New York.

Homans, G. C. (1961) *Social Behavior: Its Elementary Forms*, Harcourt, Brace and World, New York.

Hoppock, R. (1935) *Job Satisfaction*, Harper and Row, New York.

Kahn, R. L., Wolfe, D. M., Quinn, R. P., Snoek, J. E., and Rosenthal, R. A. (1964) *Organizational Stress: Studies in Role Conflict and Ambiguity*, Wiley, New York.

Katz, D., and Kahn, R. L. (1966) *The Social Psychology of Organizations*, Wiley, New York.

Katz, D., and Kahn, R. L. (1978) *The Social Psychology of Organizations, 2nd edition*, Wiley, New York.

Katz, D., Maccoby, N., and Morse, N. C. (1950) *Productivity, Supervision and Morale in an Office Situation*, Survey Research Centre, University of Michigan, Ann Arbor.

Landsberger, H. A. (1958) *Hawthorne Revisited*, Cornell University Press, Ithaca.

Likert, R. (1959) Motivational approach to management development. *Harvard Business Review*, **37,** 75–87.

Mayo, E. (1933) *The Human Problems of Industrial Civilization*, Macmillan, New York.

McGregor, D. (1960) *The Human Side of Enterprise*, McGraw-Hill, New York.

Munsterberg, H. (1913) *Psychology and Industrial Efficiency*, Houghton Mifflin, Boston.

Myers, C. S. (1920) *Mind and Work*, University of London Press, London.

Pugh, D. S. (1966) Modern organization theory: A psychological and sociological study. *Psychological Bulletin*, **66,** 235–251.

Roethlisberger, F. J., and Dickson, W. J. (1939) *Management and the Worker*, Harvard University Press, Cambridge, Mass.

Schein, E. H. (1965) *Organizational Psychology*, Prentice-Hall, New York.

Scott, W. D. (1903) *The Theory of Advertising*, Small, Maynard and Company, Boston.

Stogdill, R. M., and Coons, A. E. (1957) *Leader Behavior: Its Description and Measurement*, Ohio State University, Bureau of Business Research, Research Monograph No. 88.

Taylor, F. W. (1911) *Scientific Management*, Harper, New York.

Social Psychology and Organizational Behaviour
Edited by M. Gruneberg and T. Wall
© 1984 John Wiley & Sons Ltd

Chapter 2

Leadership and Supervision

P. YETTON

The First World War and Crimean War were led by officers who were '*born to rule*'; and fought by soldiers whose role has been classically described as follows—'Theirs not to reason why. Theirs but to do and die'.

This chapter is about the alternatives to heredity as the basis of leadership, and to authoritarianism as the dominant form of managerial control. Its structure follows the historical pattern of research, which itself reflects the sequence of questions that Western society has asked since the First World War about the appropriate distribution of power in institutions.

Central to that general debate has been the specific question of participative versus autocratic management. It is this recurrent issue of the social structure of decision making which is the focus of this chapter. The discussion is limited in this way to provide coherence to a topic which has filled many books as authors have tried to explain why one president, executive, manager, or administrator is more successful than another.

More specifically the aim of this chapter is to provide understanding of: (i) early approaches to leadership, namely trait theory and behavioural models; and (ii) current contingency approaches as represented by Fiedler's LPC Model, Path–Goal theory, the Vroom–Yetton Model, and Graen's Dyad Model. Throughout comment will be made on each of these approaches, on their respective merits, weaknesses and implications for practice. The chapter begins, however, with some illustrations of managerial decision-making which serve as a reference point throughout the remainder of the text.

SOME INTRODUCTORY ILLUSTRATIONS

All of us have observed leader behaviour varying from autocratic to democratic to laissez-faire. An autocratic decision style is one in which the manager retains the decision-making rights to him or herself, is task orientated, gives orders to his or her subordinates, and for which communication is typically one-way and downwards. The manager is the initiator of all salient actions. In contrast, in a laissez-faire decision style, the manager imposes few, if any, controls on subordinates. Decisions are left to subordinates and it is they who are the principle initiators of actions. A continuum between these two extremes is presented in Figure 1.

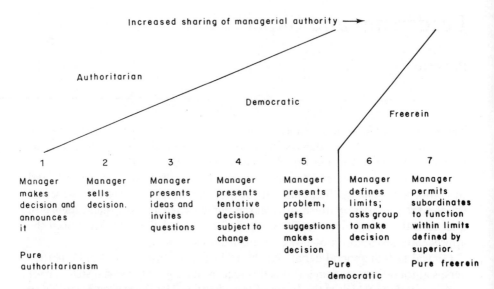

Figure 1.   A continuum of leader behaviour and leadership styles. Adapted from Tannenbaum, R., and Schmidt, W. H. (1958). How to choose a leadership pattern, *Harvard Business Review*, **March–April 1958,** 96

Let us begin by listing four cases in which different styles identified in Figure 1 are illustrated. By returning to and re-examining these cases throughout the chapter, they will provide a relatively concrete application and integration of the theories discussed.

Case A: Market research consultant

Kent Department Stores asks a market research agency for a cost estimate for a quote on a corporate image survey in Coventry where they opened a new store twelve months ago. Field work and computer cost estimates have already been obtained from the field force co-ordinator and computer bureau, respectively. It would fit easily into the current project schedule. *The consultant reviews all the information and submits a quote: autocratic.*

Case B: Buying controller Davids Ltd

Davids Ltd is a small department store chain. It is the responsiblity of the fashion buying controller to finalize the fashion direction and budgets for next spring. The dress, suits, coats, separates, and sportswear buyers are in general agreement. All that is required is to make slight adjustments to achieve over-all balance within the total fashion budget. *The buying controller negotiates agreement with each buyer: individual consultation.*

Case C: Product manager Crutch Jeans
Crutch Jeans U.K. is an off-shoot from the U.S. parent which was formed to exploit the fashion end of the punk jean market. It is time to finalize the product line for next season. Five new styles have been field tested against the existing six style product line, and detailed costings are available on all options. The problem is whether to expand the product to seven rather than six styles and which to select. *The product manager calls a meeting of sales manager, designer, production manager, and accountant, he shares the problem with them, and listens to their arguments and advice before making the decision: group consultation.*

Case D: Fashion manager
Five product managers responsible for men's shirts, women's shirts, swimwear, sportswear, and jean tops report to the merchandise manager. While they have company cars, they do not park in the covered car park. This is reserved for senior management. Recent building extensions have made available three additional covered spaces which have been assigned to the product managers. How should they be allocated? *The manager calls a meeting in which his product managers work out a satisfactory assignment: democratic group.*

EARLY APPROACHES

A simple trait or personality model of leadership may explain the differences in style described above in terms of the manager's personality. The consultant might have a higher need for dominance than the merchandise manager. Alternatively, within a behavioural model the link between personality and behaviour would be relaxed. The fashion buyer may be described as high on initiating structure behaviour and the merchandise manager as high on consideration behaviour. To explain both descriptively (what happened) and normatively (what should have happened), the early trait and behavioural models assume differences between managers.

TRAIT THEORY

Between the First and Second World Wars, researchers attempted to answer the question of how leaders differed from followers. If heredity could not be relied on as a selection mechanism, could personality and/or other individual trait tests provide alternatives? Such strategies implicitly or explicitly assumed differences in individual performance to result from pre-existing trait differences (Figure 2).

Figure 2.   Trait models of leadership

Stogdill (1976) reviews an impressive range of trait studies. However, it is the number of such studies and not the consistency of their findings which is impressive. Factors which discriminated between leaders and followers in one study typically failed to replicate in subsequent research. Jenkins (1947) and Gibb (1969) present major reviews of the literature and find no universal trait or set of traits common among leaders and their subordinates. On the other hand, Stogdill (1976) reports evidence that leaders and followers differ with respect to their intelligence, need for power, dependability, sense of responsibility, social participativeness, and the socio-economic status of their parents.

In a recent major replication, Ghiselli (1971) reports that compared with ineffective managers, effective managers score higher on intelligence, self-assurance, supervisory ability, need for occupational achievement, decisiveness, and need for self-actualization and lower on need for security. He also reports effectiveness to be independent of need for power, socio-economic background, need for money, maturity, and relative masculinity/femininity orientation.

There appears to be agreement that effective managers have above average scores on intelligence, self confidence, need for job success, and initiative. The literature says nothing about the additivity or substitutability of the various characteristics. The implication is that it is better to be high on all. Of course, if we try to select someone in the top 10% on five independent dimensions such as those above, we have restricted the domain of potential candidates to one in 100,000 from the total population. In addition, the choice may be further restricted by other requirements. For example, he or she should be an accountant between 30 and 40 years old!

Of course, these dimensions may not be independent. It is likely that self-confidence and initiative are as much outcomes of past successes as they are independent predictors of future success. In addition, the high need for power among managers may reflect assumptions made by those appointing managers to senior positions rather than any causal relation between it and performance. Evans (1979), using a crude classification system, summarizes Stogdill's (1976) review as follows:

Appointed leaders:
   Twelve of 23 studies found intelligence higher for leaders.
   Five of 23 studies found social skills higher for leaders.
Emergent leaders:
   20 of 40 studies found intelligence higher for leaders.
   22 of 40 studies found social skills higher for leaders.

This pattern is consistent with the author's recent experience in examining three years of performance appraisals for 45 senior managers in one company. In no case was a manager graded as currently promotable if he or she did not score well above average in technical knowledge, but over 50% of the currently promotable managers were scored adequate or below on interpersonal skills!

After a massive research effort, we seem to be confident of little more than intelligence being positively related to managerial success. In a technologically-based industrial society this must come as little surprise to most. However, our major gain is probably the lack of any findings. To be able to conclude that personality does not dominate managerial performance is of great importance. Researchers are thereby freed to look elsewhere for the determinants of effective managerial behaviour.

Behavioural Models

After the First World War, the search for a theory of leadership sought personality and other individual difference correlates of managerial performance. After the Second World War, the research focus shifted to behavioural differences and the human relations school of management emerged. This asserted that increased participation leads to increased morale which then generates high performance. After all, had not the forces of democracy been shown to triumph over the autocratic forces of fascism?

We are all familiar with stories of leadership portrayed in the cinema, whether it is John Wayne winning the war single-handed or Luke Skywalker defeating the Empire. The leader of the good guys is usually inexperienced, his/her troops are outgunned and outnumbered, and they begin by losing. Finally, as survival is threatened, the leader takes advice from his experienced NCO or other mentor, and begins to treat his troops as individuals. The unit develops tremendous morale, and defeats the enemy who lose because they act rigidly and stupidly. Given the social acceptability of this form of leadership it was rational to prove scientifically that effective leaders participated with and were considerate of their subordinates/followers.

The basic behavioural model is presented in Figure 3. Research consistently reports positive correlations between participative styles of decision taking and subordinates' satisfaction (see for example review by House and Baetz, 1979). While the relationships between satisfaction and participation is consistently strong, the relationship with performance is both variable and weak. It would therefore be a poor guide to managerial behaviour and/or training.

Figure 3. Behavioural models

There are two other major research themes in the behavioural literature. One was developed at Ohio State University and the other at Michigan University in the U.S.A. At Ohio, Halpin and Winer (1957) factor analysed over 1,500 items descriptive of managerial behaviour and identified four principal factors. Two of these, *consideration* and *initiating structure*, accounted for the majority of the explained variance.

Consideration is the empathy a manager shows for subordinates' emotional needs, and the warmth, support, and respect he or she shows for them. The shift from low to high consideration in the John Wayne war film is always very obvious, and is immediately followed by a rise in morale. In contrast, initiating structure reflects the level of organization and structuring of subordinates' actions by the manager. The shift in the typical film from low to high initiating structure is less obvious and the research findings less consistent than for the parallel consideration shift (Stogdill, 1976).

Again there is an extensive body of research findings. For example, Halpin (1957) reports a positive correlation between initiating structure and performance. Korman (1966) presents a positive relationship between consideration and subordinates' satisfaction and a negative one between turnover and consideration.

The above and other similar findings were summarized by Blake and Mouton (1964) in their Managerial Grid, according to which effective managers are high in both consideration and initiating structure. The leader benefits from the advantages associated with a high score on each dimension. The high consideration characteristic would offset any tendency for the high initiating structure behaviour to generate high grievance rates. Fleishman and Harris (1962) report that managers high on initiating structure tend to generate both high performance and high grievance rates among their subordinates. However, those who are also high on consideration avoid the high grievance rates.

Whereas the Ohio group began by attempting to identify the major dimensions of leader behaviour, the Michigan team classified managers as effective or ineffective and then attempted to isolate leader behaviour which differentiated between them. Their findings are summarized in Table 1.

Table 1.   Michigan Model

	Effective managers	Ineffective managers
I	Concerned about subordinates	Task focused
II	General supervision	Close supervision

In an early study Katz, Maccoby and Morse (1950) report that high performance managers tend to be person-centred as opposed to production-centred. They provide general rather than close supervision, and differentiate their own from their subordinates' roles. The first two findings were subsequently replicated by Katz, Maccoby, Gurin, and Floor (1951). They found no evidence for the effectiveness of role differentiation. The findings for consideration versus task and general versus close supervision have been replicated frequently (Stogdill, 1976).

Does Table 1 present the basis for an adequate theory? Unfortunately, the general conclusion is no. The early research at Ohio was preoccupied with developing instruments to measure consideration and initiating structure. Their existence encouraged replication and facilitated cross validation. The chance of finding any inconsistencies which existed was therefore high. In contrast, the Michigan research classification was derived from in-depth interviews. Errors in variables across studies are likely and few studies could be and were replicated. As such the consistency of their results is more apparent than real.

The three sets of research findings can be integrated at a very general level. Participation is likely to map into general supervision and high initiating structure.* A participative style would also be likely to emphasize people and consideration towards subordinates. At this level of generalization, the three models are equivalent and all appear plausible.

Two major reservations limit this integration. First, the level of participation in the cases above may be a property of the four jobs rather than of the leadership strategy. If similar problems occur within, rather than between jobs, then the within manager's style variance would dominate the between job variance. That is, an individual manager could act autocratically on Monday morning and participatively in the afternoon. This shift may be large relative to any average difference in participation comparing his or her behaviour with that of a colleague. This is the pattern reported by Vroom and Yetton (1973). Similar arguments could be made with respect to the other variables, in which case, while the theory would be valid, it would explain little of importance.

The second major reservation is the lack of longitudinal studies establishing causality. The few such studies reported tend to suggest that low performance leads to both low morale and close supervision (Lawler and Porter, 1972). It may be that style as measured above is as much an outcome as it is a cause of performance and satisfaction. Of course, causality was not a problem for the personality theorists who simply assumed that personality caused behaviour rather than itself being formed by the leadership experience. We will return to this issue later as it is also of major concern in the review of current theories.

Comment on the Early Approaches

The answers we get nearly always depend on the questions we ask. Even with

*An examination of the items in a typical initiating structure questionnaire suggest that while high scores would tend to weight onto general supervision, a few items (telling subordinates what to do) would weight on to close supervision.

similar questions, a different frame of reference can substantially alter the answers or, at least, their interpretation. This is the case here. Let us re-examine the four illustrative cases described earlier.

For a reader who assumed a personality or individual differences frame of reference for leadership, it is natural to expect that four different managers were described. After all, there are four different jobs and four very different leadership styles. In fact, all refer to a single manager and were taken from her employment history when interviewed for the position of managing director for a major fashion company. She is not atypical. Table 2 presents the style choices made by 35 managers when asked how they would act in each of the four situations. On three of the cases, they report a high degree of consistency both with each other and the actual manager involved. The exception is the parking lot problem (Case D, p. 11).

Table 2.   Leadership style choices of 35 managers

	Autocratic	Individual consultation	Group consultation	Democratic group
Research consultant	33*	2	0	0
Buying controller	5	23*	6	1
Product manager	3	6	26*	0
Fashion manager	13	5	3	14*

*Mary Derbyshire's choice

It is easy to see, from an examination of the four illustrative cases, that participation and performance can only be weakly linked within a personality or behavioural main effect model. Our successful applicant for the managing director's job, Mary Derbyshire, varies her behaviour from highly autocratic to highly participative. This is consistent with the patterns for the other managers. Only in the parking lot problem do we observe a wide variation in autocratic and participative managerial behaviours. A general relationship between participation and performance takes no account of the variation in style variance across situations.

How do we explain Mary's apparently inconsistent participative behaviour? Just as the behavioural models questioned the link between personality and behaviour, the recent theories challenge the assumption that an individual has a single dominant leadership style. Instead, he or she is fitted (Fiedler, 1967) or fits his or her style (Path–Goal: House and Mitchell, 1974) to the situation. Vroom and Yetton (1973) also fit the manager's style to the situation, but distinguish situations in terms of different problems within the manager's role. They define situations in terms of the characteristics of problems which the manager confronts. Graen also disaggregates, in his case, across different subordinates rather than across problems (Dansereau, Graen, and Haga, 1975). By relaxing different assumptions, each of these theories attempts to resolve inconsistent findings apparent in the simple personality and behavioural main effect models.

CURRENT APPROACHES

The human relations school of management was finally buried by the management community with Richard Nixon and the Vietnam War. The general belief in the obvious rightness of being considerate to subordinates and others engendered by the Second World War had been dissipated. The shift in both the management and academic community was towards contingent models in which the situational context both does and should influence both behaviour and its outcomes.

This next generation of models is significantly more complex than the earlier ones. In addition, unlike the trait and behavioural models discussed above, the contingency models discussed here have very different internal structures. There is no single, all embracing contingency model. Different assumptions are relaxed in each of Fiedler's, Path–Goal, Vroom–Yetton's and Graen's models. Indeed, these models are often presented not only as competing but as mutually exclusive. If one is validated, the others are wrong. Because most researchers defend one model at the expense of the others, the relative importance of the phenomena they address is inadequately discussed in the literature. In fact, they attempt to explain different phenomena. As far as this author knows, there is no single empirical comparative study of these theories.

Fiedler's (1967) theory is the earliest and the most extensively researched. Three situational factors, *leader member relations, task structure,* and *leader position power* determine the favourability of the situation for managers high or low on the Least Preferred Coworker (LPC) trait. It holds that low LPC managers perform best in situations of either high or low favourableness, where as high LPC managers fit situations of medium favourableness. This is a trait–contingency model with an initial emphasis on the selection of managers to match the situation followed by some situation engineering and manager training to correct mismatches. It fits within the person–situation interaction paradigm.

Path-Goal makes the influence of leader behaviour, initiating structure and consideration, dependent on the degree of structure present in the situation (House and Mitchell, 1974). This is a behaviour–contingency model. Both this and Fiedler's theory average across leader behaviours in a particular role. The different styles a manager uses on different problems and in his/her interactions with different subordinates are ignored.

Both Vroom–Yetton and Graen disaggregate manager behaviour. Vroom and

Yetton (1973) show that variation in style for an individual manager is greater than the difference between managers. They identify seven situational dimensions which both should and do influence the level of subordinate participation in decision-making. Graen differentiates between subordinates instead of problems (Dansereau, Graen, and Haga, 1975). Managers act differently towards different subordinates. Members of the IN-group are consulted like colleagues, whereas members of the OUT-group are treated as hired workers and told what to do.

Each of the four models is considered in greater detail next.

Fiedler's LPC Model

Fiedler's LPC model was the first sustained attempt to develop a contingent model of leadership (Fiedler, 1967). Others such as Tannenbaum and Schmidt (1958) had advocated situation based models but Fiedler's was the first such systematic empirical investigation. His model has three situational factors which define the degree of situational favourableness for the leader.

Leaders are differentiated by their LPC score. The meaning of LPC and its behavioural correlates are still a matter of conjecture and some controversy. A

Pleasant	8	7	6	5	4	3	2	1	Unpleasant	_____
Friendly	8	7	6	5	4	3	2	1	Unfriendly	_____
Rejecting	1	2	3	4	5	6	7	8	Accepting	_____
Tense	1	2	3	4	5	6	7	8	Relaxed	_____
Distant	1	2	3	4	5	6	7	8	Close	_____
Cold	1	2	3	4	5	6	7	8	Warm	_____
Supportive	8	7	6	5	4	3	2	1	Hostile	_____
Boring	1	2	3	4	5	6	7	8	Interesting	_____
Quarrelsome	1	2	3	4	5	6	7	8	Harmonious	_____
Gloomy	1	2	3	4	5	6	7	8	Cheerful	_____
Open	8	7	6	5	4	3	2	1	Guarded	_____
Backbiting	1	2	3	4	5	6	7	8	Loyal	_____
Untrustworthy	1	2	3	4	5	6	7	8	Trustworthy	_____
Considerate	8	7	6	5	4	3	2	1	Inconsiderate	_____
Nasty	1	2	3	4	5	6	7	8	Nice	_____
Agreeable	8	7	6	5	4	3	2	1	Disagreeable	_____
Insincere	1	2	3	4	5	6	7	8	Sincere	_____
Kind	8	7	6	5	4	3	2	1	Unkind	_____
									Total score	======

Figure 4. Least preferred coworkers (LPC) scale

manager's score is his or her average score on the 16 item scale in Figure 4. A manager with a low score sees his least preferred coworker in a generally poor light. In contrast, a manager with a high score differentiates between performance and individual differences among his work colleagues.

In their initial studies, Fiedler and his associates found correlations between LPC scores and managerial performance ranging from +0.8 to −0.8 (Fiedler, 1967). This is typical of the trait research findings discussed above. Instead of rejecting LPC as a leadership trait, Fiedler examined why successful board chairmen were high LPC, whereas, the best open hearth supervisors were low LPC. Situational favourableness was found to moderate the LPC/performance relationship. Fiedler argues that under high situational favourableness subordinates accept being directed. A low LPC or task-orientated manager fits such a situation. In the converse situation, with everything stacked against the leader, he or she must intervene decisively and direct subordinates' actions. Here again a low LPC task focussed manager is needed. On the other hand, when the situation is moderately favourable, a high LPC or person-centred management style is required to work through the issues involved. These results are presented in Figure 5 which reports the correlation between performance and LPC under different conditions of situational favourableness. (Note that correlations vary from strongly positive to strongly negative.)

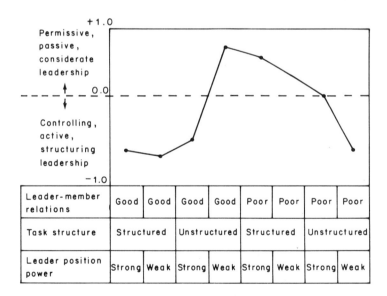

Figure 5. Fiedler's LPC model. Correlation between performance and LPC under different conditions of situational favourableness. Reproduced with permission from Fiedler, F. E. (1972). The effects of leadership training and experience: a contingency model interpretation, *Administrative Science Quarterly*, **December 1972**, 455

This theory is inductive in that it was developed to account for the variance in correlations observed between LPC and manager performance. Naturally, it explains much of the variance in this relationship reported in the initial research. The validation studies report contradictory results. For example, Graen, Orris, and Alvares (1971) in a laboratory experiment failed to replicate the earlier findings. This study was undertaken after Graen, Alvares, Orris, and Martella (1970) re-analysed Fiedler's initial results and questioned his interpretation. The controversy has raged ever since. Chemers and Rice (1974) review the literature and conclude the theory is valid, whereas, Ashour (1973) argues it is false. Recently, Schrieheim and Kerr (1977) and Fiedler (1977) reviewed the evidence. The former came down against the theory, the latter, not surprisingly, in favour.

The problem in all the reviews is how to aggregate across different studies. Recently developments in meta analysis have resolved some of these issues. In meta analysis the studies to be reviewed are treated as a sample of the possible studies which could be done. Variations in results are compared to the variance expected given sampling error, measurement reliability, range restriction and other sample characteristics. Using this technique, Strube and Garcia (1982) find strong evidence in support of the theory. The exceptions are Octants II and III (the second and third from the left in Figure 5). They also note that the majority of studies are of Octants I, III, and V. In Octant I with very high situational favourableness a task focussed manager is needed is run an efficient operation with few problems. In Octant V with poor leader member relations but otherwise a favourable situation, a person-centred manager is needed. As already noted, the results for Octant III are inconclusive.

Assuming that the theory is valid, how could it be used? Selection and placement are obvious options, however, there are two major difficulties. One is that managers may fake their LPC score. The other is that leader–member relations need to be predicted before the manager is appointed. For internal promotion under relatively stable conditions this might be possible. However, if the situation is Octant V with poor leader–member relations due to the previous manager's behaviour, the new high LPC (person-centred) manager might improve the situation and create an Octant I situation in which he or she is a mismatch. If the future situational favourableness is a function of present leader behaviour, there is a major validity threat to the theory.

If an error in selection is made and a mismatch is appointed, what action should be taken? Initially Fiedler favoured engineering the situation to fit the person. However, in practice this option may be limited. For example, an increase in position power may be unacceptable to his or her colleagues, or more generally within the over-all power structure of the organization. Conversely, where a decrease is called for, the manager may not find it acceptable. Similarly, any change in the level of task structure may require major alterations in responsibilities and the associated information and other decision making and implementing technologies. These could result in mismatches elsewhere.

More recently, Fiedler has advocated training to resolve mismatches. Typically, this is in reference to a mismatch due to the presence of low task structure. This is resolved by training the manager in the skills necessary to get on top of the problems and structure the work situation. This moves us in a direction in which the contingency conditions are themselves a function of managerial behaviour.

While meta analysis has established general support for the theory, the discussion above raises some important reservations about its application. The interactions between both engineering and training solutions to mismatches and matters of system design and efficiency warrant careful examination. Most importantly, the behavioural correlates of LPC under different conditions of favourableness need to be established. Fiedler provides no direct evidence that high LPC managers are person-centred or low LPC managers task-centred. Yet much of the arguments supporting the theory rest on this assumption.

Path–Goal Theory

Fiedler's theory is a trait-contingency model. The situation determines the effectiveness of the trait. The Path–Goal model is a behavioural–contingency model. The inconsistencies in the behavioural model discussed above are assumed to be a function of the situation. Both high and low initiating structure and consideration are deemed to be appropriate depending on the situation (see Figure 6).

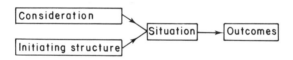

Figure 6. Path–Goal model

The underlying theory is an expectancy model. The manager satisfies his or her subordinates to the extent that they find their work experience intrinsically or extrinsically rewarding. The manager's behaviour is motivating in the degree to which he or she makes those rewards contingent on task performance. Effective leadership involves the joint event of anticipated satisfactions by subordinates perceived by them as contingent on organization performance.

This is the basic structure of any expectancy model. While the above statement appears simple, its operationalization has led to many very complex models. Both subordinates' utility functions (value of a reward) and their risk preferences and other determinants of subjective probabilities are complex issues. For example Schuler (1976) shows that only when the task is well structured and non-ego involving, do subordinate personalities moderate the style–satisfaction–performance relationship.

This relationship is likely to be sensitive not only to personality and other individual differences among subordinates, but also to management team dynamics and organization structural characteristics. For example, Miles and Petty (1977) report that organization size moderates the basic model. In small government agencies, the correlation between initiating structure and subordinates' satisfaction is positive, and negative for large agencies. In contrast, the correlation between consideration and satisfaction is higher for large rather than small agencies.

A leadership theory in which the moderators for secondary hypotheses span personality and organization theory suffers from a lack of specification. The problem with the Path–Goal model is that it is simply too general. Rather than being a theory about leadership, it is the application of the general expectancy model to the area of leadership. All the problems experienced with expectancy models elsewhere are then encountered in the context of leadership. Even House (House, Filley, and Kerr, 1976) reviews the evidence and concludes that the theory is not sufficiently developed and well-specified to be used as a prescriptive theory.

Vroom–Yetton Model

Like Fiedler's theory, the Vroom–Yetton model is essentially a diagnostic one. Unlike Fiedler, Vroom and Yetton assume that managers can vary their style from situation to situation (see Figure 7). The model is concerned with deriving and implementing a solution to a recognized problem. Thus the model is different from Fiedler's in two major ways. First, the situational characteristics are properties of specific decisions confronting the manager, rather than being general characteristics of the manager's position or role. (The Path–Goal model, like Fiedler's, generates behaviour at the role level.) Second, the leader is assumed to have a flexible style. He or she may use all the styles employed in the four illustrative cases, as did Mary Derbyshire. It could be appropriate for a

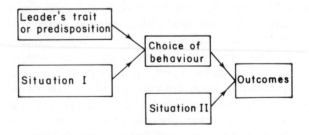

Figure 7.   Vroom–Yetton model of leadership

manager to be autocratic Monday morning and participative in the afternoon because the problems are different.

Vroom and Yetton identify five different leadership styles which span a continuum from autocratic to participative (see Figure 8). These are similar to those proposed earlier by Tannenbaum and Schmidt (1958) (see Figure 1) and Heller (1971). Seven problem characteristics define the situation (see Figure 9). A problem's situational characteristics define a feasible set of styles which is used to generate a solution which meets the necessary acceptance and quality constraints. The feasible set may contain up to five styles. The normative model is presented in Figure 9. To apply it, the manager begins at the left-hand side and asks himself or herself the first question: 'Is there a quality requirement such that one solution is likely to be more rational than another?' If the answer is no, the manager follows the upper route, if the answer is yes, he or she follows the lower route. Whenever a box is encountered the corresponding question above is asked. This is repeated until a terminal node is reached. Each node is labelled with the styles which satisfy that type of problem.

AI You solve the problem or make the decision yourself, using information available to you at the time.

AII You obtain the necessary information from your subordinates, then decide the solution to the problem yourself. You may or may not tell your subordinates what the problem is in getting the information from them. The role played by your subordinates in making the decision is clearly one of providing the necessary information to you, rather than generating or evaluating alternative solutions.

CI You share the problem with the relevant *subordinates individually*, getting their ideas and suggestions without bringing them together as a group. Then *you* make the decision, which may or may not reflect your subordinates' influence.

CII You share the problem with your subordinates *as a group*, obtaining their collective ideas and suggestions. Then you make the decision, which may or may not reflect your subordinates' influence.

GII You share the problem with your subordinates as a group. Together you generate and evaluate alternatives and attempt to reach agreement (consensus) on a solution. Your role is much like that of chairman. You do not try to influence the group to adopt 'your' solution, and you are willing to accept and implement any solution which has the support of the entire group.

Figure 8.   Leadership styles

The structure of the decision tree in Figure 9 incorporates seven rules. Three protect the quality of the decision and four protect its acceptance by subordinates. Any particular rule states that under given circumstances, a subset of the five styles should be eliminated from the set of styles considered feasible.

These are avoided because they involve a potential risk to quality and/or acceptance. The rules are presented in Figure 10.

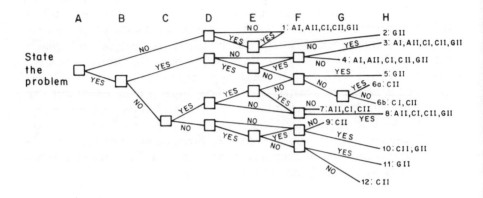

Figure 9. Vroom–Yetton normative model
Decision-process flow chart for group problems (feasible set)

A. Is there a quality requirement such that one solution is likely to be more rational than another?
B. Do I have sufficient information to make a high-quality decision?
C. Is the problem structured?
D. Is acceptance of decision by subordinates critical to effective implementation?
E. If I were to make the decision by myself, is it reasonably certain that it would be accepted by my subordinates?
F. Do subordinates share the organizational goals to be attained in solving this problem?
G. Is conflict among subordinates likely in preferred solutions? (This question is irrelevant to individual problems.)
H. Do subordinates have sufficient information to make a high-quality decision?

The decision tree format makes two features very obvious. First, there is not necessarily a single best style for a problem. In some instances any of the five styles would do while in others the model recommends a single best decision method. Where more than one style is feasible, additional criteria for restricting the choice are suggested. These include, for example, minimizing the managerial resources involved in the decision, or developing the subordinates' understanding of the problem.

Rules protecting quality requirements

The leader information rule
If the quality of the decision is important and the leader does not possess enough information or expertise to solve the problem by himself, then AI is eliminated from the feasible set.

The goal congruence rule
If the quality of the decision is important and subordinates are not likely to pursue the organizational goals in their efforts to solve this problem, then GII is eliminated from the feasible set.

The unstructured problem rule
In decisions in which the quality of the decision is important, if the leader lacks the necessary information or expertise to solve the problem by himself, and if the problem is unstructured, the method of solving the problem should provide for interaction among subordinates likely to possess relevant information. Accordingly, AI, AII, and CI are eliminated from the feasible set.

The acceptance rule
If the acceptance of the rule by subordinates is critical to effective implementation and if it is not certain that an autocratic decision will be accepted, AI and AII are eliminated from the feasible set.

The conflict rule
If the acceptance of the decision is critical, an autocratic decision is not certain to be accepted and disagreement among subordinates in methods of attaining the organizational goal is likely, the methods used in solving the problem should enable those in disagreement to resolve their differences with full knowledge of the problem. Accordingly, under these conditions, AI, AII, and CI, which permit no interaction among subordinates and therefore provide no opportunity for those in conflict to resolve their differences, are eliminated from the feasible set. Their use runs the risk of leaving some of the subordinates with less than the needed commitment to the final decision.

The fairness rule
If the quality of the decision is unimportant, but acceptance of the decision is critical, and not certain to result from an autocratic decision, it is important that the decision process used generate the needed acceptance. The decision process used should permit the subordinates to interact with one another and AI, AII, CI, and CII are eliminated from the feasible set.

The acceptance priority rule
If acceptance is critical, not certain to result from an autocratic decision and if subordinate(s) is(are) motivated to pursue the organizational goals represented in the problem, then methods which provide equal partnership in the decision-making process can provide greater acceptance without risking decision quality. Accordingly, AI, AII, CI, and CII are eliminated from the feasible set.

Figure 10. Vroom–Yetton model rules

Second, it is also immediately apparent from the tree that if a manager makes incorrect judgements about the answers to any of the seven situational questions, then the style recommended by the model may be inappropriate. For example, an incorrect judgement as to the likelihood that subordinates would accept and be committed to a given decision could lead to the model prescribing an autocratic process (AI) rather than a participative style (GII). Examining managers' codings of standard cases and both managers' and their subordinates' codings of on-line problems, Yetton (1980) concludes that perceptual errors in judgements are not a major problem for the implementation of the theory.

Vroom and Jago (1978) report a test of the normative theory using managers' reports of recalled problems. Each manager was asked to recall and describe two problems, one of which was successfully managed, the other unsuccessfully. After identifying their problems, the managers were trained in the use of the model. They were asked to compare the style they actually used with that prescribed by the decision tree. When the styles used agreed with the model, the outcomes were more frequently successful (68%) than unsuccessful (32%). When the styles were in violation of the model, the outcomes were most frequently unsuccessful (78%) than successful (22%).

While this evidence appears to be strong, there is a major weakness. Self reports tend to be biased (Bass, 1957). This is supported by differences in managers' self-report style and similar judgements by their subordinates (Jago and Vroom, 1975). However, the latter data refer to expected behaviour on hypothetical questions and not to recalled behaviour from actual situations.

House, Filley, and Kerr (1976) question the parsimony of the model and the capacity of the average manager to use such a complex strategy. Following this line, Field (1979) presents a simplified version of the model. However, to do this he increases the average level of participation for a range of problems which would substantially raise the cost of the strategy. The trade-off of simplicity for higher costs may be inappropriate. Certainly, with over 5,000 managers in the U.S.A., Europe and Australia trained in the original model, few have complained that it is too complex. Indeed, in personalizing the model many increase its complexity.

As well as proposing a normative model describing how managers should act, Vroom and Yetton investigated how they do in fact behave. They found that managers were more participative on problems with a quality requirement, or where they lack some of the relevant information or expertise, or which are unstructured, than on problems without one or more of those characteristics. Managers are also more participative if acceptance of the decision by subordinates is important and when acceptance is unlikely to exist for an autocratic decision taken by themselves. If acceptance is important, and the subordinates share the manager's goals, and there is no conflict among subordinates, managers are again more participative than if any or all of these conditions are not satisfied.

A comparison of these descriptive findings reveals that, with one exception, the normative and descriptive patterns of behaviour have the same sign but the variance in behaviour within the descriptive model is less than within the normative. That is, when the normative model says a manager should be very participative, he does tend to act participatively as indicated by the model but not to the degree prescribed. Similarly, when the model advocates autocratic behaviour, managers are typically autocratic but are slightly less so than is suggested by the normative model.

The exception to this general pattern is the typical manager's avoidance of highly participative styles when conflict among his subordinates is strong. In contrast, the Vroom and Yetton normative model advocates participative styles when, in addition to the presence of conflict, it is also necessary to develop the subordinates' commitment to the resultant decision in order to safeguard its effective implementation. While investigating possible differences among managers' responses to situational variables, Jago (1978) found some evidence for a manager-situation interaction with respect to conflict. While the typical manager is averse to conflict, there are perhaps a quarter of managers who are not. These appear to be comfortable in using participative decision modes even when a high level of conflict is present. Vroom and Yetton (1973) speculate that such interactions may be just as important as determinants of behaviour as the direct situational effects. Jago's recent research seems to confirm this (Jago, 1978). No major changes in theoretical framework are required to take account of any such individual situation interactions.

Whereas application is problematic with both Fiedler's and the Path–Goal theory this is not so for the Vroom–Yetton model. The five styles are already in most managers' repertoires and upgrading their skills in this area simply requires the application of existing training technologies. In addition, managers can make judgements about problem characteristics. So, improving a manager's choice of style is only a matter of learning to apply the rules combined with training in group dynamics and problem solving, with an emphasis on coping with conflict.

Graen's Dyad Model

Whereas Vroom and Yetton disaggregate across problem situations, Graen's dyad theory disaggregates across subordinates (Dansereau, Graen, and Haga, 1975). Instead of an emphasis on subordinates as potential team members, Graen's theory explicitly assumes managers do not act in the same undifferentiated way towards all subordinates. In particular, subordinates are divided into IN- and OUT-group members. The IN-group members are allowed access to more information, given more discretion, and have more influence, than members of the OUT-group.

Graen and his associates describe the relationships between managers and subordinates in terms of task interactions to the exclusion of social processes.

The supervisor gives members of his or her IN-group information on a 'want to know' basis, influence through participative decision making, and task support. The manager's relationship with these favoured subordinates depends little on the formal authority portrayed in an organization chart. Rather than subordinates, they are 'trusted assistants' or colleagues. These subordinates reciprocate with greater expenditure of time and effort than formally required. Conversely, other subordinates are treated as 'ordinary workers'. For them, communication is formal, access to information is restricted to a 'need to know' basis, and they carry out their manager's instructions. They experience a formal contractual relationship with their manager.

Crouch and Yetton (1982) elaborate the basic dyad model to include social relationships. Following Homans (1950), they argue that work group members who have more frequent task contact form social relationships. Over time, stable cliques develop. The pattern is presented in Figure 11.

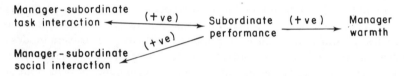

Figure 11.   Manager–subordinate dyad

These results challenge two basic assumptions central to current leadership theories. These are social/task independence and subordinate homogeneity. Instead, the levels of manager–subordinate task and social contact, manager warmth, and subordinate performance are found to be highly interdependent. These results have substantial implications for the Fiedler, Path–Goal and Vroom–Yetton theories.

Comments on the Contingency Models

In the introduction to this section, it was noted that the contingency models described above are typically treated as if they are competing, even mutually exclusive, rather than complementary. In contrast, it is assumed here that the four models explain different phenomena.

Let us begin by exploring the overlap between Graen's dyad and the Vroom–Yetton models. To integrate this with the Vroom–Yetton model, Crouch and Yetton (1982) show that it is sufficient to assume that the IN- and OUT-groups experience a different mix of problems. The IN-group is both allocated responsibility for a high proportion of the complex problems experienced by the work group and encouraged to redefine and expand problems at their own discretion. In contrast, OUT-group members' responsibilities are well structured and they are given little discretion in problem redefinition. Given these two different problem mixes, the Vroom–Yetton model would descriptively predict and normatively advocate a participative highly involved task and social structure for the IN-group; and an autocratic relationship between the manager and the OUT-group.

This identifies two important qualifications which should be made to the Vroom–Yetton model. One is that problem characteristics are not dictated by an autonomous environment but are frequently under the control of the manager. The other is that problem characteristics are frequently a function of subordinates' abilities and predispositions towards participative decision taking, properties which differ across subordinates. For example, those with weak performance records should and would have tasks structured for them. With them, the manager would act in an authoritative manner.

Crouch and Yetton (1982) extend this analysis to the Path–Goal model. Members of the IN-group participate with their manager and experience his or her behaviour as supportive. They would code their manager as high in consideration. Conversely, the OUT-group would score their manager as low. It follows that variance in subordinates' coding of their manager's level of consideration should not be treated as error.

Furthermore, assume high performing groups have a high proportion of IN-group members and vice versa for poor groups. Then, there would be a positive relationship between consideration and performance across groups. For example, Lowin and Craig, (1968) found that high subordinate performance leads to increased considerate manager behaviour. This is a complete reversal of the Path–Goal model. Considerate manager behaviour is a joint outcome with, rather than a determinant of, high performance.

The research findings for the relationship between initiating structure and performance within the Path–Goal model are less consistent than those in relation to consideration. This may be so because when subordinates experience the same level of *initiating structure*, its form may be very different. For the IN-group, the manager helps members to structure up complex and ill-defined problems. The group codes the manager high on initiating structure. OUT-group members may also rate their manager high on initiating structure but this is the result of close supervision rather than in joint problem solving.

Finally, Fiedler's theory assumes *situational favourableness* as defined by *task structure, leader-subordinate relations,* and *leader position power* to be independent of the manager's style. The above speculation suggests that these three characteristics are as much outcomes as determinants of leader effectiveness. Furthermore, the IN-groups tend to be characterized by low structure and good leader member relations, while the OUT-group are the converse. As such, leader–member match and mismatch occurs within the same work team. Only for the limited case of relatively undifferentiated groups is Fiedler's theory unconfounded. An examination of group differentiation may account for the inconsistent findings in that literature.

The above discussion implicitly argues that there is a general theory for which the four contingency models described above are special cases. Each explain some of the observed leader behaviour and group performance. The inconsistencies reported in the literature should then be interpreted not as evidence against one of the theories, but of its incompleteness. The formulation of such a theory requires two shifts in leadership research. One is to treat the theories as potentially complementary rather than competitive. The other is to conduct research simultaneously on at least two and, preferably, all four theories. In the interim, the practising manager or academic consultant should simply apply each model and review carefully any dissimilar recommendations, in the light of his or her own experience.

A MORE GENERAL PERSPECTIVE: WHAT IS MISSING FROM CURRENT APPROACHES?

The contingency theories resolve some of the problems associated with the earlier trait and behavioural models. However, as Kuhn (1962) comments, a paradigm shift retains most but not all of the explanatory power of the rejected paradigm. Nearly always something is lost. This is the case with leadership theory. Below four areas of loss are considered.

Individual Differences

Trait theories were concerned not only with personality but all individual differences. As noted earlier, intelligence is positively correlated with managerial performance. Certainly, Mary Derbyshire is of above average intelligence, performing at the top of both her undergraduate and MBA classes. Even with no account for industry, staff/line, and other differentials, research reports positive correlations between MBA grade point average and managerial performance.

Of course, most people would accept that subordinate ability is a major determinant of work group performance. Yet of the contingency theories, only Graen addresses the issue of subordinate ability. For Vroom and Yetton, it is the style rather than the members selected for that style which is central to their theory. Similarly, Path–Goal and Fiedler make little reference to ability differentials. This probably reflects the emphasis on group process rather than member ability in the small group literature since the Second World War.

Prior to that war, the greater emphasis was on ability rather than group dynamics. Recently, there is a developing literature which reemphasizes the importance of member ability (Einhorn, Hogarth, and Klempner, 1977; Laughlin, Kerr, Davis, Halff, and Marcinak, 1975). In particular, Yetton and Bottger (1982) show that group composition effects are likely to dominate process gains and losses.

It may be that individual differences among managers and, perhaps more

importantly among their subordinates, are an important determinar.
group performance. For example, it is likely that a high need for power ι
managers combined with a low need for power by their subordinates lea
high risk of 'group think'. This is described by Janis and Mann (1977) as a pr   ss
in which subordinates censor their own criticisms. This results in a spurious
consensus around their perception of their leader's preference. Little real
problem solving takes place and a poor decision may be accepted.

On a very different tack, it appears that females are better than males at
interpreting non-verbal cues. It may be that there are a number of individual
differences which are more important than the recent literature acknowledges.
Subordinates' characteristics, or those interacting with their manager's profile,
may have important consequences for performance. Certainly, this is believed by
a wide cross section of managers.

One individual difference has been purposely excluded from the discussion so
far. This is charisma. There is no doubt that some leaders including Jesus Christ,
Gandhi, Mao Tse Tung, Patton, Stalin and de Gaulle, held a very strong
magnetic attraction for their followers. While the existence of charismatic
leadership is not in doubt, its nature is not understood and does not fit within any
of the patterns described here.

Interpersonal Trust

Just as the rejection of the trait paradigm in favour of behavioural models of
leadership may have led to an inappropriate de-emphasis of individual
differences, so did the subsequent shift to contingent models tend to lose sight of
the importance of interpersonal trust. While the behavioural models measured
and researched initiating structure and consideration, the underlying philosophy
of the human relations movement emphasized trust and openness
(Golembiewski and McConkie, 1975).

Again returning to Mary Derbyshire, we find that on more than one occasion
when she moved jobs, one of her subordinates followed her to the new
organization. A major factor in this was the subordinate's trust that Mary would
be open, honest with, and not exploitative. In contrast, low trust generates
defensiveness and team disintegration which effectively blocks both learning and
problem solving (Gibb, 1969). Gibb argues that trust facilitates increased
feedback and more effective communication which jointly generate increased
performance.

The contingency models do not reject the importance of trust. Rather, the
development and maintenance of high interpersonal trust simply ceases to be a
central focus. In Fiedler's theory, leader member relations are a contextual factor
rather than an important outcome of the manager's behaviour. The other three
contingent models are essentially diagnostic. In general, they lack an effective

implementation strategy. The development of interpersonal trust between manager and subordinates is central to any such strategy.

Goal Setting

Leadership theories are concerned with getting things done, as are theories of work motivation. Both involve the identification of, and commitment to, goals. Goal theory (not to be confused with the Path–Goal model, though there is overlap) rests on a simple assumption. The greater the magnitude and specificity of a goal, the greater its impact on behaviour. Of course, goals can be impossible. The objectives, while difficult, should be achievable. Research on the goal setting techniques shows impressive results with employees ranging from waiters and truck drivers to research scientists and managers, (Locke, Shaw, Saari, and Latham, 1981).

The basic steps are as follows. Required performance behaviours are specified in detail, levels of performance are agreed (or imposed), feedback on performance is given regularly and goal attainment is rewarded. It should be noted in the context of participative leadership theories that in goal setting, participation leads to greater performance than imposed standards only in so far as participation leads to the setting of more difficult goals. The basic model introduces structure and direction into work activity, monitors progress, and rewards it. Here, there is a link with the early Michigan studies of close versus general supervision. The intention and effect of setting performance behaviours is to prevent the manager from constantly reciting them to subordinates. Rather the discussion and thinking generated by the process of identifying required performance behaviours, especially under co-operative conditions, is to socialize the subordinate into acceptance of role requirements. When such norms are internalized, the manager's supervisory style would tend to be general rather than close. Within the framework agreed, the subordinates assume responsibility for task completion.

CONCLUDING REMARKS

This 'review' of the leadership literature attempts to show how and why the questions asked by both managers and researchers have changed over time. Through new questions we learn more about leadership but forget some of the things we knew. In conclusion, it might be interesting to sketch this author's view of 'where we are' and 'where we are going'.

Where we are is learning to discriminate among the needs of different situations: across roles for Fiedler and Path–Goal; across problems for Vroom–Yetton; and across subordinates for Graen. While doing this, we need to remember the importance of ability (selection and training) and interpersonal trust contained in the early trait and human relations theories, respectively.

Given our strong socialization towards democracy and egalitarianism, this capacity to discriminate among colleagues and subordinates will not come easily.

Where we are going is to examine the current theories as complementary rather than competing. This will facilitate an interpretation across existing theories. It will require the development of a theory of followership to integrate subordinates' and managers' behaviour in a single leadership model. The initial directions for this are indicated in the elaborations by Crouch and Yetton (1982) on Graen's dyad model. Within this perspective, the inconsistent findings, particularly with respect to Fiedler and Path–Goal, would be treated not as evidence against those theories but as evidence of their incompleteness. Factors treated as fixed in one theory, for example leader member relations in Fiedler's theory, would be treated as the outcomes from Path–Goal or Vroom–Yetton. The resultant integration is likely to be at least an order of magnitude more complex than the current contingency models.

However, the greatest challenge to theory is not the above. Rather, it is the need to extend the range of leader behaviour which is the subject of research and theory development. The literature has been dominated by a concern with, for example, participation and consideration, which are a limited subset of leader behaviour. The domain of leadership is much wider. This can be seen if we simply observe managers' actions.

REFERENCES

Ashour, A. S. (1973) Further discussions of Fiedler's contingency model of leadership effectiveness, *Organizational Behaviour and Human Performance*, **9**, 369–376.

Bass, B. M. (1957) Leadership opinions and related characteristics of salesmen and sales managers, in Stogdill, R. M., and Coons, A. E. (eds.), *Leader Behaviour: Its Description and Measurement*, Ohio State University, Bureau of Business Studies, Columbus, Ohio.

Blake, R. R., and Mouton, J. S. (1964) *The Managerial Grid*, Gulf Publishing Co., Houston, Texas.

Chemers, M. J., and Rice, R. W. (1974) A theoretical and empirical examination of Fiedler's contingency model of leadership effectiveness, in Hunt, J. G., and Larson, L. L. (eds.) *Contingency Approaches to Leadership*, Southern Illinois University Press, Carbondale, Illinois.

Crouch, A. C., and Yetton, P. W. (1982) Manager-subordinate relationships in vertical dyad linkages, *AGSM Working Paper No. 82-001*, **February 1982.**

Dansereau, F., Graen, G., and Haga, W. S. (1975) A Vertical Dyad linkage approach to leadership within formal organizations: A Longitudinal Investigation of the Role Making Process, *Organization Behaviour and Human Performance*, **13**, 46–78.

Einhorn, H. J., Hogarth, R. M., and Klempner, E. (1977) Quality of group judgment, *Psychological Bulletin*, **84**, 158–172.

Evans, M. G. (1979) Leadership, in Kerr, S. (ed.), *Organizational Behaviour*, Grid Publishing, Columbus, Ohio, pp. 207–240.

Fiedler, F. E. (1967) *A Theory of Leadership Effectiveness*, McGraw-Hill, New York.

Fiedler, F. E. (1976) The leadership game: matching the man to the situation, *Organisational Dynamics*, **Winter, 1976,** 6–16.

Fiedler, F. E. (1977) Validation and extension of the contingency model of leadership effectiveness: a review of empirical findings, *Psychological Bulletin*, **26**, 128–148.

Field, R. H. G. (1979) A critique of the Vroom–Yetton contingency model of leadership behaviour, *Academy of Management Review*, **4(2)**, 249–258.

Fleishman, E. A., and Harris, E. E. (1962) Patterns of leadership behaviour related to employ grievances and turnover, *Personal Psychology*, **15**, 43–56.

Ghiselli, E. E. (1971) *Exploration in Managerial Talent*, Goodyear, Santa Monica.

Gibb, C. A. (1969) Leadership, in Lindzery, G., and Aronson, E. (eds.), *The Handbook of Social Psychology* (2nd Edn.), Addison–Wesley, Reading, pp. 205–282.

Golembiewski, R. T., and McConkie, M. (1975) The centrality of interpersonal trust in group processes, in Cooper, C. L. (eds.), *Theories of Group Processes*, John Wiley, London, 1975.

Graen, G., Alvares, K., Orris, J. B., and Martella, J. A. (1970) Contingency model of leadership effectiveness: antecedent and evidential results, *Psychological Bulletin*, **74**, 285–296.

Graen, G., Orris, J. B., and Alvares, K. (1971) Contingency model of leadership effectiveness: some experimental results, *Journal of Applied Psychology*, **55**, 196–201.

Halpin, A. W. (1957) The leader behaviour and effectiveness of aircraft commanders, in Stogdill, R. M., and Coons, A. E. (eds.), *Leader Behaviour: Its Description and Measurement*, Ohio State University, Bureau of Business Research, Columbus, Ohio.

Halpin, A. W., and Winer, B. J. (1957) A factorial study of leader behaviour descriptions, in Stogdill, R. M., and Coons, A. E. (eds.), *Leader Behaviour: Its Description and Measurement*, Ohio State University, Bureau of Business Research, Columbus, Ohio.

Heller, F. A. (1971) *Managerial Decision-Making*, Tavistock, London.

Homans, G. (1950) *The Human Group*, Harcourt, Brace, and Jovanovich, New York.

House, R. J. (1971) A path goal of leader effectiveness, *Administrative Science Quarterly*, **16**, 321–338.

House, R. J. (1973) A path goal theory of leader effectiveness, in Fleishman, E. A., and Hunt, J. G. (eds.), *Current Developments in the Study of Leadership*, Southern Illinois University Press, Carbondale, Illinois.

House, R. J. (1977) A 1976 theory of leader effectiveness, in Hunt, J. G., and Larson, L. L. (eds.), *Leadership: The Cutting Edge*, Southern Illinois University Press, Carbondale, Illinois, pp. 189–207.

House, R. J., and Baetz, M. L. (1979) Leadership: some empirical generalizations and new research directions, in Staw, B. M. (ed.), *Research in Organizational Behaviour*, JAL Press, Greenwich, Connecticut, pp. 341–423.

House, R. J., Filley, A. C., and Kerr, S. (1976) Relation of leader consideration and initiating structure to R and D subordinates' satisfaction, *Administrative Science Quarterly*, **16**, 19–30.

House, R. J., and Mitchell, T. R. (1974) Path goal theory of leadership, *Journal of Contemporary Business*, **5**, 81–97.

Jago, A. G. (1978) Configural cue utilization in implicit models of leader behaviour, *Organizational Behaviour and Human Performance*, **22**, 474–496.

Jago, A. G., and Vroom, V. H. (1975) Perceptions of leadership style: superior and subordinate descriptions of decision making behaviour, in Hunt, J. G., and Larson, L. L. (eds.), *Leadership Behaviour*, Kent State University Press, Kent, Ohio, 103–120.

Janis, I., and Mann, L. (1977) *Decision making: A Psychological Analysis of Conflict Choice and Commitment*, Free Press, New York.

Jenkins, W. O. (1947) A review of leadership studies with particular reference to military problems, *Psychological Bulletin*, **44**, 54–79.

Katz, D., Maccoby, N., Gurin, G., and Floor, L. (1951) *Productivity, Supervision, and*

Morale among Railroad Workers, University of Michigan, Institute of Social Research, Ann Arbor.

Katz, D., Maccoby, N., and Morse, N. (1950) *Productivity, Supervision, and Morale in an Office Situation*, University of Michigan, Institute for Social Research, Ann Arbor.

Korman, A. K. (1966) Consideration, initiating structure, and organizational criteria: a review, *Personnel Psychology*, **19**, 349–361.

Kuhn, T. S. (1962) *The Structure of Scientific Revolution*, University of Chicago Press, Chicago.

Laughlin, P. L., Kerr, N. L., Davis, J. H., Halff, H. M., and Marcinak, K. A. (1975) Group size, member ability and social schemes on an interactive task, *Journal of Personality and Social Psychology*, **31**, 522–535.

Lawler, E. E., III, and Porter, L. W. (1972) The Effect of Performance on Satisfaction, in Bass, B. M., and Deep, S. D. (eds.), *Studies in Organizational Psychology*, Allyn and Bacon, Boston.

Locke, E. A., Shaw, K. N., Saari, L. M., and Latham, G. (1981) Goal setting and task performance: 1969–1980, *Psychological Bulletin*, **90**, 125–152.

Lowin, A., and Craig, J. R. (1968) The influence of level of performance on managerial style: an experimental object lesson in the ambiguity of correlation data, *Organization Behaviour and Human Performance*, **3**, 440–458.

Miles, D. H., and Petty, M. M. (1977) Leader effectiveness in small bureaucracies, *Academy of Management Journal*, **20(2)**, 238–250.

Schrieheim, C. A., and Kerr, S. (1977) RIP LPC: a response to Fiedler, in Hunt, J. G., and Larson, L. L. (eds.), *Leadership: The Cutting Edge*, Southern Illinois University Press, Carbondale, Illinois, pp. 51–56.

Schuler, R. S. (1976) Participation with supervisor and subordinate authoritarianism: a path goal theory reconciliation, *Administrative Science Quarterly*, **21**, 320–325.

Stogdill, R. M. (1976) *Handbook of Leadership*, Free Press, Glencoe, Illinois.

Strube, M. J., and Garcia, J. E. (1982) A meta-analytic investigation of Fiedler's contingency model of leadership effectiveness, *Psychological Bulletin*, **90(2)**, 307–321.

Tannenbaum, R., and Schmidt, W. (1958) How to choose a leadership pattern, *Harvard Business Review*, **36(2)**, 95–102.

Vroom, V. H., and Jago, A. G. (1978) On the validity of the Vroom–Yetton Model, *Journal of Applied Psychology*, **63**, 151–162.

Vroom, V. H., and Yetton, P. W. (1973) *Leadership and Decision Making*, University of Pittsburgh Press, Pittsburgh.

Yetton, P. W. (1980) Managers' subjective perception of their work situation with regard to the application of Vroom–Yetton leadership model, *Technical Report No. 1*, Australian Graduate School of Management, University of New South Wales.

Yetton, P. W., and Bottger, P. C. (1982) Individual versus group problem solving: an empirical test of a best member strategy, *Organization Behaviour and Human Performance*, **29**, 307–321.

Social Psychology and Organizational Behaviour
Edited by M. Gruneberg and T. Wall
© 1984 John Wiley & Sons Ltd

Chapter 3

Group Productivity

G. E. O'BRIEN

TWO SEMINAL STUDIES OF GROUPS

The Hawthorne Studies

Observation of workers assembling telephone equipment, schoolboys making masks, and housewives making decisions about meat purchases have provided data and theory that have greatly influenced the development of work group psychology. Hence, it is important to consider these early studies briefly in order to understand some of the strengths and weaknesses of group theory. The studies on telephone equipment employees were conducted at the Hawthorne works of the Western Electric Company in Chicago from 1927–1932. The studies were originally started by the company as an investigation of the effects of fatigue and illumination on group performance. When the productivity of test groups increased in a manner unrelated to manipulations of the physical environment, a group of Harvard investigators from the Graduate School of Business Administration was called in. The group was led and influenced by an Australian psychologist, Elton Mayo. Mayo's earlier writing and charismatic personality had promoted the importance of interpersonal relationships as a predictor of work relationships, and it was felt that he might unravel an explanation for this puzzling 'Hawthorne' effect. The subsequent studies were reported by Roethlisberger and Dickson (1939), and Whitehead (1938). Their significance for work groups was publicized by Mayo (1933) and Roethlisberger (1941).

The studies are lengthy and complex but the most important projects involved:

1. Observation of a small group of girls in the relay test room.
2. Extensive interviews with factory employees.
3. Observation of a group of men in the bank-wiring room.

In the first stage a group of five girls were selected to assemble telephone relays under the scrutiny of a trained observer. The girls were selected on the basis of their experience and personal compatibility. The task was an individual one involving the connection of 35 different parts to form a relay module. It is important to note that there was no task interdependence. They formed what was later described as a co-acting group with no co-ordination of tasks across girls or any collaboration between girls on the sub-tasks involved. This relay assembly group worked in a special room and, over a period of two years, imposed changes were made in task complexity, work hours, style of supervision, and pay rate. The pay rate differed from that they had previously experienced in that they were paid on the basis of their own group's performance and not on the basis of factory output. Initially, they received this new pay rate and also were given friendly supervision in that they were encouraged to express their opinions about aspects of work arrangements. A 30% increase in productivity was reported. When another group of girls was selected and paid at the new rate an increase of 13% in productivity was reported but this decreased by 16% when the preferred pay system was withdrawn. Another experiment with girls splitting mica in a co-acting task system showed a 16% increase in productivity over 14 months followed by a steady decline.

The next project was an extensive interview study of over 1,600 skilled and unskilled workers in order to provide information that could be used for the training of supervisors and the improvement of working conditions. Initially, the interviewers used a structured list of questions asking about employees attitudes to physical work factors and company policy. However, employees tended to wander off in their responses, talking about 'irrelevant' topics such as their family and social life. Interviewers then used what is now called 'non-directive interviewing'. The employees talked about anything they wanted with an attentive, non-critical interviewer. It was found that this method of personnel counselling allowed employees to express their complaints and sentiments about working. Often it was reported that the employees did not really want action to be taken on their complaints or that employees thought that management had been responsive in making changes when none had actually occurred. The process of interviewing had altered sentiments about work by allowing employees to discuss their feelings and emotions in a way that linked their personal history, the social situation at work and their experience within interviews.

The third major project was the observation of 14 male operators in a bank-wiring room. The task was one involving task interdependence or co-ordination as the wiring of complicated telephone switchboards required a sequenced set of operations involving nine wiremen, three soldermen, and two inspectors. Thus the work rate of a given worker was affected by the work rate of at least two other workers. Although there was a group wage incentive scheme, the employees held a rigid informal rule or norm about the number of connections that they should perform. Ridicule and social isolation were the lot of those who worked too hard—'rate-busters'—or too little—'chiselers'. This was observed by the construction of what is now known as sociometric matrices—the patterns of informal liking and communication relationships. There were also two other strong norms—you should not say anything detrimental about fellow employees to supervisors and you also should not act distantly or officiously towards other employees.

The reporters of the Hawthorne Studies considered many alternative explanations for the behaviour that they observed. Their preferred interpretation was that employees had strong social needs or sentiments that could be productively expressed within the solidarity or cohesiveness of their work group. Trained managers, skilled in human relations, should understand this informal network and use it to develop group loyalty and identity which, in turn, would result in higher productivity. These studies are often cited as classic studies, despite recognition of their methodological shortcomings. It is frequently said that they identified the importance of group cohesiveness, group norms, and participative group structures for determining productivity and job satisfaction. This is despite many critical analyses of the studies that demonstrated that strict causal inference was not possible because the groups were small in number, there were no control groups, productivity measures were questionable and studies were conducted at different times. Thus, they did not control for unknown changes in economic and social conditions (Landsberger, 1958; Rose, 1978).

The most radical criticism of the Hawthorne Studies and their interpreters has been made by Carey (1967) who used the published reports to document employee resistance to the relay experiments. Some girls showed poor discipline and did not work hard and this led to harsh directive supervision and eventually to the replacement of these girls with others known to be more co-operative with management. Bramel and Friend (1981) provide further documentation of this resistance to managerial procedures that were considered manipulative. The most plausible explanation of the relay group productivity increases, however, is not the power of management to use imposed sanctions for poor work but the use of a group incentive scheme. Considerate supervision appeared to be associated, at times, with positive work attitudes but the main factor associated with changes in productivity was the pay rate. Increases in productivity occurred when it was one of the factors introduced and productivity declined when the preferred pay system was withdrawn even though the supervisors remained considerate. Carey was led to ask why the Hawthorne writers and subsequent writers in organizational psychology have made a selective interpretation of the results. He argues that industrial psychology has always tended to adopt theories that are congenial to managerial values. Access to organizations depends on managerial approval and thus it is understandable that the interventions made should show how productivity and profits would be increased without threatening managerial authority or the distribution of major resources—power and money.

These criticisms should alert the student of work groups to the role of the researcher and how theories and interpretations might be biased by personal and social values (cf. Hartley, Chapter 7). Analyses of his criticisms shows that

Carey's own values appear to lend an unwarranted dogmatism to his conclusions. Other interpretations of the dominance of the 'human relations' explanations are possible by considering the training and background of the leader of the human relations approach to group performance. Before coming to the United States from Australia, Mayo who was a professor of psychology, had provided an analysis of democracy and political beliefs using a clinical approach (Mayo, 1919). This provided evidence that he was predisposed to analyse social organization in terms of social harmony rather than in terms of group or class conflict. His clinical orientation was also shown in his application of personal therapy to the treatment of shell-shocked soldiers. Hence, when he started directing the analyses of the Hawthorne results he already was concerned to demonstrate the conditions under which social harmony and productivity could be maximized. Being a psychologist by training he concentrated on individualistic explanations of sentiments, attitudes, and restriction of output. He quoted other psychologists to support his interpretations. He felt indebted to Piaget for the development of non-directive interviewing and acknowledged the influence of Janet, Jung, and Freud in his interpretation of dissatisfaction and low productivity. To some extent, he saw lack of employee co-operation as an instance of obsessional thinking. The details of his explanations are not important. What is important is that this individualistic approach led him to neglect structural variables such as power and task variables as determinants of group performance. For example, he never considered varying the group task structure so that the skills of the employees could be better utilized. Roethlisberger did actually report that there were variations in skill-utilization in the bank-wiring group. In this co-ordinated structure, it was possible that restriction of output was partly due to the brighter workers realizing that their efforts were limited by the performance of the least able member. They actually did find that the poorest performer was the most intelligent and high on dexterity. The best performer was relatively unintelligent and poor on manual dexterity. Hence it was possible that limited opportunities for skill-utilization were due to the co-ordinated structure which led to corresponding deficits in employee motivation.

The psychological interpretation of the Hawthorne Studies can thus be partly understood in terms of the individualistic background of psychological theory. Certainly Mayo had much more contact with managers than with employees, but he was not motivated to please managers and become a servant of the powerful. Rather he wanted to change them so that they used human relations to promote both individual and social harmony.

Lewin's studies

This role for the work psychologist was also implicit in the research and theory of

Kurt Lewin, who was responsible for another set of studies that have had a seminal effect on modern group psychology. Lewin was a German psychologist whose work in the United States was partly motivated by a desire to demonstrate the superiority of democratic social organization to authoritarian social organization. He also tried to show how individual behaviour could only be understood in terms of a total social situation or field (Lewin, 1939). Although he did manipulate the physical environment, his theories were subjective in that he believed that an individual responded in terms of his own personal representation or perception of the social field. His group studies examined the role of group structure as determinants of productivity, aggression, and attitudes. His most detailed experiment showed that the performance of a group varied as a function of leadership structure (Lewin, Lippitt, and White, 1939).

With groups composed of members from a boys' club in Iowa, he systematically varied the style of adult leaders. Democratic groups were those where the leader involved boys in planning activities and fully explained the basis of his standards of blame and praise. Autocratic groups had leaders who directed activities and kept their standards of praise and blame to themselves. Laissez-faire groups had leaders who did little unless asked to by the members. The results have been commonly reported as showing that democratic groups were more productive in their major goal of making papermache masks than both autocratic and laissez-faire groups. They also, it is claimed, show that satisfaction and group cohesiveness was highest in the democratic groups. The other well-quoted study by Lewin compared discussion and lecture method's of changing the attitudes of women towards the purchase of unpopular cuts of meat. In the discussion groups women were encouraged to express their preferences in a supportive atmosphere, given information about the relative nutritional value of various cuts and asked to make a public statement about their preferences after the discussion period. The same information was given to the lecture groups and no discussion or public commitment was required of them.

The group leadership study actually found that productivity, as measured by quantity, was highest in autocratic groups although quality was best in democratic groups. It is reported that reactions of group members varied and the degree of hostility and satisfaction expressed was partly a function of prior group structures and socialization experiences. Both studies are cited as sources of the participating approach to group management but it is an approach that uses participation in a way that distinguishes it from influences. The democratic and discussion groups did not allow the members to adopt policies or arrangements of their own choosing. They were certainly encouraged to express their views but they all were required or requested to follow the recommendations of their leaders. There was certainly no joint decision making. Attitudes changed, according to Lewin, in a manner which resembled the process of changing the shape of ice. Participation led to unfreezing of attitudes and the consideration of alternative attitudes and behaviours. Information imparted by those with higher power and status helped resolve the problem of choosing alternatives and their final choice was a refreezing engineered by the act of public commitment. This process was successfully applied by Lewinian students who used the participatory, 'democratic' style of management to overcome resistance to task changes in a pyjama factory (Coch and French, 1948).

The similarities between Lewin's and Mayo's theories can be made explicit.

1. Both are psychological in that they explain group processes in terms of individual factors such as attitudes and social needs.
2. They do not seriously consider behaviour as being explainable in terms of objective structure or monetary rewards.
3. They endorse a social harmony view of the work group that considers hostility, aggression, and conflict as dysfunctional.
4. Their data actually describe structural relationships such as power, task allocation and task co-operation but these are not recognized as explanatory variables. The only structure that is given serious attention is the informal structure.

These themes have persisted in group research. In the next section a brief review will be made of the numerous 'psychological' or individualistic theories of group productivity.

GROUP PRODUCTIVITY AS A FUNCTION OF MEMBER RESOURCES

The psychological approaches to group productivity have concentrated on predicting group performance using variables that describe both the individual attributes of individuals and the informal relationships that occur among group members. These approaches are consistent with the historical tradition formed by the human relations group and field theorists. The main attributes that have been studied include leadership style, motivation, ability, and work related needs. The informal relationships that have been identified as predictors of group performance include interpersonal attraction, cohesiveness and personal compatibility. The research has investigated the extent to which common sense ideas about group processes are justified. If we asked the proverbial person in the street what makes a productive work group or a successful football team, he would probably answer by saying that you had to have the right people who could work together under good leadership. The right people could be those with sufficient ability and motivation. Good leadership would be direction that helped the group to organize its efforts and maintain good interpersonal relationships. Each of these personal and interpersonal factors will be considered in turn.

Leadership Style

The studies on leadership subsequent to the Hawthorne Studies and Lewin's democratic leadership studies continued to investigate two styles of leadership that contrasted person-oriented (democratic, employee-centred) and task-oriented (autocratic, production-oriented) styles. The leadership research is discussed more fully in Chapter 2. At this point it is possible to summarize what is known about the relationship between leadership and group performance. The early research found that whether or not a leader was considerate and person-oriented or structuring and task-oriented bore no consistent relationship to group productivity. Some studies showed that group productivity was better with person-oriented leaders while others found that task-oriented or directive leaders were better. This embarrassing inconsistency in research results appeared to be due partly to the use of differing measures of leadership style and behaviour but mainly to the fact that groups varied across studies in their tasks, formal structure, and member relationships.

This lead to the development of the contingency approach to leadership effectiveness. Fiedler's contingency model of leadership had the great virtue of redirecting research by framing the leadership question in a different way (Fiedler, 1964, 1978).

Instead of asking, which style of leadership is more effective?, the question was: 'How does the group situation determine the relative effectiveness of leadership styles?'. Fiedler's model of leadership describes situations in terms of their favourability for the leader. The concept of favourability can be understood by translating it to mean 'opportunities for leader influence over task procedures' (O'Brien, 1969). The three main factors that Fiedler postulated as determinants of leader influence were:

1. Leader–member informal relations. Was he/she liked?
2. Position–power. Did he have legitimate power over rewards and sanctions?
3. Task–structure. Was the task structured or unstructured?

The leader was in a situation of high potential influence if he enjoyed good interpersonal relationships, had high position power and the task was structured. By varying those situational components into either good or poor interpersonal relationships, high or low power, and structured or unstructured tasks, eight different situations can be generated that vary in leader potential influence. Fiedler found that person-oriented leaders did best in situations of intermediate favourability whereas task-oriented leaders did best in situations of high or low favourability.

This finding has been repeated in a large number of studies (Strube and Garcia, 1981). At present the interpretation of these findings and the appropriateness of the measures of leadership style is a matter of debate. However, the main point about leadership effectiveness has been missed. Although this theory includes structural group variables, it does not yet show how leadership style actually contributes to group productivity. This is attributable to an omission of a theory of group performance. It is a theory that compares the effectiveness of two leadership styles in situations that vary in structure. It does not go on to establish the way in which leadership style and group structure affect productivity. This point can be illustrated by reference to studies that compared leadership style and group structure as determinants of group productivity (Hewett, O'Brien, and Hornik, 1974; O'Brien and Kabanoff, 1981). In these studies, the task organization and interpersonal compatibility of the group were varied.

It was found that the type of task organization used accounted for most variance in group productivity (29%–54%). Leadership style, either directly or in combination with situational variables, accounted for less than 3%.

The general implication is that structural variables account for much more variance in group productivity than do measures of the stable motivational and behavioural dispositions of leaders. Although Fiedler has not yet generated a theory of group performance that can show how certain leader behaviours can facilitate or impede group performance, he has recognized that group structure can provide 'screens' that prevent the utilization of leader abilities (Fiedler and Leister, 1977).

If a theory of group performance was available that identified the optimal group structure for performing a given type of task, then one could predict that a leader would be most successful if he or she made decisions that led to the highest utilization of member abilities within the structure that maximized performance.

Effective leadership requires that the leader adopt the optimal structure for performing a task. The effective leader would also identify the task relevant abilities of group members and allocate them to tasks in such a manner as to maximize group productivity. A third leader function would be to resolve interpersonal conflict and personal stress by showing them how co-operative effort leads to the acquisition of desired personal outcomes. The leadership theory required is approximated by the Vroom and Yetton (1973) theory discussed in Chapter 2 which describes leader performance in terms of decision strategies and not in terms of leader personality. Further research still needs to supply a theory of organizational performance and this is probably the reason why this theory is better at predicting group acceptance of decisions than predicting group productivity (Vroom and Jago, 1978).

Group Cohesiveness

Both the Hawthorne Studies and Lewin's small group research suggested that high performance groups were those where members felt highly attracted to the group. Such groups are said to have high solidarity or cohesiveness. One reason why cohesive groups could be more productive is that members wish to remain as valued co-workers and thus are more responsive to group pressure. If the group aims at high productivity—a high performance norm—then group pressure towards this norm should be more effective in cohesive groups than in groups lacking in cohesion. However, if the group norm is towards restricted productivity—as was the case in the bank-wiring study—then the degree of cohesion should be negatively related to performance. This effect was found in an early study (Shachter, Ellertson, McBride, and Gregory, 1951). Reviews of subsequent studies have shown that the relationship between group performance and cohesion is complex and depends on the group goal, task structure, and the dispersion of abilities within the group (Lott and Lott, 1965). If, for example, the group valued good interpersonal relationships more than a high quality product, then a group may avoid strategies or issues that are liable to threaten good personal relationships (see Chapter 4).

Effort: Expectancy Approaches

Another approach to predicting work group performance is based on the simple idea that group performance will be higher as the amount of effort expended by group members increases. The theory has been mainly used to predict individual performance but its application to work groups implicitly assumes that group effort is obtained by adding individual levels of effort. The amount of effort expended is predicted using individual or subjective variables. Firstly, it is assumed that the amount of effort expended depends on the extent to which the members expects that effort is likely to lead to successful performance. Secondly, the amount of effort expended should be proportional to the attractiveness or valence of group outcomes (e.g. pay, sense of achievement, fatigue). Thirdly, effort should be proportional to the degree to which the individual believes that job performance is instrumental in achieving the outcomes. As Guest notes (Chapter 8), the expectancy approach, while of some value, has severe limitations as a theory of motivation in relation to performance.

Goal Setting

A large number of studies have shown that group goal setting can have a positive effect on group performance provided that the goals are specific and moderately difficult. Many of these studies were conducted by Locke and his associates and the results have been integrated in a comprehensive review (Locke, Shaw, Saari, and Latham, 1981). Goal setting is an objective procedure but it is here considered to be an individual variable because its effects are explained in motivational terms. The history of the concept has individualistic origins in Lewin's concept of level of aspiration although the effect of group aspiration levels were investigated by Zander (1971). Goal setting was also a central part of the theory of management by objectives (Odiorne, 1978). The positive effects of goal setting appear to be quite robust in that 90% of studies comparing individuals and groups with specific and challenging goals with individuals and groups with either easy, 'do your best' goals, or no goals, showed that specific and challenging goals produced highest performance. Locke, Shaw, Saari, and Latham (1981) consider four possible mechanisms to explain these results. Specific and difficult goal setting could induce higher member performance through directing attention and action, mobilizing effort, increasing persistence, or motivating the member to adopt efficient task strategies. The conditions under which one or all of these mechanisms apply is a present research goal in goal-setting theory.

Group Feedback

Another objective variable that can affect group performance is type of feedback. Like goal-setting, it is classified as an individual variable because feedback effects are commonly explained in cognitive and motivational terms. The literature on group feedback is reviewed by Nadler (1979). It appears that feedback has greater effect on the attitudes of members toward the group (e.g., attraction, involvement) than on productivity. However, feedback to the group as a whole is likely to be most effective when the task requires a reasonable amount of co-operative effort. If the group does not have a collaborative division of labour and group performance depends on the sum of individual performance, then feedback to individuals appears more effective than feedback to the total group.

Pay

Pay is an objective reward that has been shown to have strong effects on individual and group performance (Lawler, 1971). The motivational effects of pay appear quite complex because pay may not mean just money to buy essential food, clothing, and shelter. Employees also can see pay as important for the satisfaction of their needs for esteem, autonomy, and self-actualization. The importance of money as a motivator of high group member performance has been stressed by Locke, Feren, McCaleb, Shaw, and Denny (1980) who, in a review of the relative performance effects of money, goal setting, job enrichment, and participative decision-making, found that money was a much more powerful motivator of high performance than the other variables.

Compatibility

The theory of group productivity advanced by Schutz (1955, 1958) maintained that the productivity of a group was largely determined by the degree of personal compatibility that existed between group members. He specified three major needs that were important to measure when assessing compatibility. These needs were identified as:

1. The need for affection and intimate close relationships.
2. The need for control over activities and people.
3. The need for inclusion. This need refers to the strength of the desire for being part of a group.

Each of these need areas is assumed to be composed of two aspects—the person's desire to express the need and the person's desire to receive its expression from others. Although Schutz suggested that there were several kinds of compatibility, he considered that 'interchange compatibility' was most important in group situations. Operationally, an individual's desired amount of interchange in a given need area is measured by the sum of his 'expressed' and 'wanted' scores for that need area. A group is compatible if there is little difference between the members' required amount of interchange across their needs for affection, control, and inclusion. Conversely, incompatibility occurs when there is a large discrepancy across group members in their desired levels of affection, control, and inclusion.

Schutz's early studies showed that compatible groups are generally more productive than incompatible groups. Incompatibility tended to increase the number of task irrelevant behaviours in a group such as conflict, attention-seeking, and withdrawal. Later studies have found some additional support for Schutz's theory. Hewett, O'Brien, and Hornik (1974) found that small groups working on a construction task were more productive when members were compatible than when they were incompatible. The importance of compatibility seems to depend partly on the amount of interaction in a group. Schutz did predict that the effect of compatability upon productivity would be greater when the 'interchange requirements' of the group task were high. Some support for this was obtained from an analysis of his own data and from a study that varied the collaboration requirements of a group task (O'Brien, Hewett, and Hornik, 1972).

THE COMBINATION OF INDIVIDUAL ABILITIES IN GROUPS

The German experimentalist tradition of the nineteenth and early twentieth century helped shape a line of research on small groups that has focussed on two main problems:

1. Do individuals work better alone or in the presence of others?
2. Is the co-operative effort of a set of individuals working in a group more productive than individuals working alone?

One of the earliest investigators of the first problem was Triplett (1898) who found that a majority of his child subjects wound fishing reels faster when in competition with others than when they wound alone. He attributed gains in performance to increased stimulation of the co-acting, competitive situation. This study also found that some children performed worse and this was explained in terms of over-stimulation. In this design the effects of competition and co-acting were confounded and later studies found that co-action without competition could help improve performance in some situations but depress it in others. The general positive effect of the presence of others was termed 'social facilitation'. The research since then has supported an arousal theory of social facilitation which states that working in the presence of others can improve performance on simple, well-learned tasks because individuals have higher arousal levels in co-acting situations than in isolated ones. If the task is difficult and involves learning of novel responses then increased arousal results in poorer performance (McGrath, 1976; Zajonc, 1966).

This line of research suggests that the mere presence of others in work groups can have an arousal effect that can either help or depress group performance. The effects of arousal and stress on co-acting groups has not led to much research on the effects of stress in interacting groups, although McGrath presents a theory that shows how the performance of baseball teams can be predicted from its past performance, the difficulty of its opponents and the level of arousal of team members (McGrath, 1976).

The second problem in this experimental social psychology tradition has attracted a great deal more research and reviews are available in a number of sources (Hill, 1982; Shaw, 1976; Steiner, 1972). The general finding is that groups generally are less productive than a set of individuals but not always. It again depends on the nature of the task and the way in which the group is organized.

In predicting the level of group performance most of the theories in this area have used some rule of combination of member abilities or knowledge in order to predict group performance. For example, some theories have predicted that group performance is a function of the abilities and resources of the most expert member. This is a model that can be useful if there is a single task that can, in principle, be solved by an individual working alone. Obviously groups are likely to be superior to a given individual, because, as size increases there is a greater chance of there being an individual of high ability in the group. This finding is not particularly useful for understanding group performance because it says nothing about the effects of group organization.

If a group is not compared to an individual but to a set of individuals who have an equivalent distribution of abilities to those in the group then the problem is more interesting and relevant. The classification of comparison groups would be:

A n individuals working alone.

B n individuals co-acting—working independently on the problem in the presence of others.

C n individuals working in an unstructured group.

Comparison of A and B has been the focus of social facilitation studies. In studies comparing individual's (A) with unstructured groups (C) it has sometimes been found that groups are superior to individuals. For some creative tasks where individuals or groups have to produce novel associations or ideas, groups can be superior. For example, 'brainstorming' groups (Osborn, 1957) might be asked to produce novel ideas in a fixed period of time. The groups can build on ideas suggested by others but they are specifically instructed not to evaluate or criticize any ideas. Some studies (e.g., Meadow, Parnes, and Reese, 1959) have found that creativity is higher in such groups than that of the summed contribution of individuals working alone. A common explanation is termed 'pooling'. Hearing or seeing the contributions of others stimulates a member so that he responds not only to his other mental associations, but also to the associations of others. As the task is typically fairly simple, social facilitation effects are probably present as well. With tasks that involve complicated calculations or manipulations the group can also be more effective because members of a group can check mistakes better than individuals alone.

Generally, groups are less effective than individuals. This is so for a number of reasons.

1. Groups initially have to spend time working on task strategies.
2. The strategy adopted may not be the optimal way of distributing member abilities.
3. Even if reasonable effective task allocations are made, the process of individual interaction may lead to interpersonal communication difficulties. The style of communication may lead to conflict and loss of motivation. Dominant individuals may be perceived as talking too much or trying to impose their ideas on members. Even if members are compatible, the process of communicating may involve time that detracts from the time maximally available for direct task activity.

These are the kind of difficulties that depress group performance and have been termed 'process losses' (Steiner, 1972). Steiner's general formulation of group productivity is then:

$$\text{Actual productivity} = \text{potential productivity} - \text{process losses.}$$

The research considered so far has studied groups performing simple tasks that could be done, in principle, by any one member.

Such tasks are called unitary by Steiner (1972) whereas divisible tasks are capable of being broken up into sub-tasks so that the final product is completed only after the sub-tasks have been completed in some specified order. This distinction is not very precise because it depends on some criteria that will allow one to specify an indivisible task element. For example, the task of a jury may be considered unitary because each individual has to decide if the defendant is guilty or not guilty and this judgement is one that ultimately the juror has to make alone. Yet the task of making a judgement can itself be divided into sub-tasks. The judgement might depend on the assessment firstly, of the evidence favouring a guilty verdict and secondly, the evidence favouring a not-guilty verdict. This illustrates a fundamental difficulty in task analysis. There is no objective criteria for specifying a task 'unit' and often a group task can be divided in many ways depending on the researcher's theory of the task process.

It is possible, however, to divide group organizations into those where all group members co-operate by sharing the whole task (collaboration) and from those where groups specify subtasks or have them imposed. The form of co-operation that occurs then is one of co-ordination as there are specified time relationships governing the performance of the sub-tasks. This distinction between collaborative and co-ordinated task structures will be discussed more fully later when we consider structural determinants of group performance.

Much of the small group literature has dealt with collaborative groups where all members work together on the group task. The first research problem is predicting how individual resources (e.g., abilities, knowledge, judgements) are combined to form a group product. With decision tasks, where groups have to make a final choice between a limited number of alternatives, there are quite a number of complex theories that attempt to predict how group members combine their individual judgements. The work of Davis (Davis, 1973; Stasser and Davis, 1981) has identified the rules of combination, or social decision rules, that groups such as juries use in making a decision. These theories do not deal with structural variables and make fairly simple assumptions about the group process that will occur, e.g., individuals will seek to comply with expectations of others and the strength of these compliance pressures is directly related to the number of individuals who share judgements that are different to those of the individual. The models are able to predict the probability of a group reaching a given decision on the basis of information about the distribution of individual preferences prior to interaction. At present these theories have not directly addressed the problem of how differences within a group (e.g., power, communication) affect decisions and thus have little to say about how structural features affect decision quality. For certain problem solving tasks, this probability approach has been able to make some statement about the degree of group success. If groups decide to use a hierarchical method of combining information whereby greater weight is given to the inputs of the most expert, then they are superior to groups which use an egalitarian combination method— where everyone, regardless of ability, is able to make an equal input.

The second research problem with collaborative groups also involved an individualistic approach. Steiner (1972) developed models to predict the effect of size upon group productivity. Steiner maintained that the actual function depended upon task type. Disjunctive tasks are those where the group performance is determined largely by the competence of the most gifted member. The potential productivity for these groups increases with size but the rate of increase in productivity decreases with size. As size increases, the net increment obtained by adding a new member becomes smaller. With conjunctive tasks, group potential productivity is determined by the least able member and, as size increases, Steiner claims that potential productivity will decrease.

The difficulty with this approach is that it does not allow one to clearly distinguish between the abilities required by the task and the allocation of tasks to individuals. What Steiner calls a conjunctive task is typically one that involves an assembly line method for doing the task. Here, faulty work by one member can spoil the whole product. For such co-ordinated task structures, the principle of productivity is 'a chain is only as good as its weakest link'. If the group decided to let all members do all of the tasks and sub-tasks then group productivity would be proportional to the ability of the most competent member *provided* the group allows the most competent person to do the task. The main point here is that a given task may be either disjunctive or conjunctive depending on the organization that is used. By classifying tasks in this way Steiner fails to ask the important question—how may the organization of tasks between members affect productivity?

STRUCTURAL DETERMINANTS OF GROUP PERFORMANCE

A group is not just a set of persons. It is a set of persons working on a set of sub-tasks in order to achieve a common goal. A set of individuals without a common goal is an aggregate or collection. In order to achieve the group goal a group has rules about how the members of the group should contribute. This means that there is a division of labour. Different positions are allocated various sub-tasks and these sub-tasks are generally ordered by time or precedence relationships. Some sub-tasks have to be done first before other sub-tasks can be started. Hence, a concept of group structure must include a description of the division of labour and a description of sub-task relationships. It should also refer to the authority or control system that a group uses to ensure that members work according to a definite plan.

This definition of a group indicates that there are a number of elements of group structure. How are these elements combined? A structure, generally defined, is a set of rules or relationships that order a set of elements. Hence, the problem of defining group structure involves firstly, specifying the elements of the group and secondly, specifying the main relationships that order these elements. The previous paragraph mentioned three elements of a group structure. These are persons, positions, and tasks. These elements are central concepts of a theory of social structure called structural role theory (SRT) (Oeser and Harary, 1962, 1964; Oeser and O'Brien, 1967). This formulation is derived from Weber's analysis of bureaucratic organizations (Weber, 1947) and Lewin's concept of a social field. SRT then identifies a number of relationships that connect persons, positions, and tasks. Informal relationships are relationships between persons and include specific relationships such as liking, communication, and personal compatibility. If a specific informal relationship exists between two persons (h_1, h_2) then it can be represented in a simple graph by a line from h_1 to h_2. If the direction of the relationship is specified the graph is called a digraph. For example, in Figure 1 the line connecting h_1 to h_2 has an arrow indicating that h_1 likes h_2. If the relationship is reciprocal and h_2 also likes h_1 then this is represented by a line going from h_2 to h_1. The formal structure of a group is described by four main relationships. These relationships are:

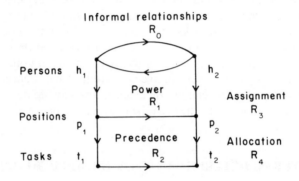

Figure 1. Basic elements and relationships of group structure

1. Assignment relations between persons and positions (persons are assigned to different positions).
2. Authority or formal power relations between positions and positions (some positions may have formal power or control over other positions).
3. Allocation relations between positions and tasks (certain tasks are allocated to different positions).
4. Precedence relations between tasks and tasks (some tasks have to be performed before others).

Figure 2 represents a simple group structure that contains two persons (h_1, h_2), two positions (p_1, p_2) and two sub-tasks (t_1, t_2); h_1 likes h_2, h_1 and h_2 are each assigned to one position and position p_1 has authority over p_2. The group task is achieved by performing t_1 and t_2 with t_1 being performed before t_2. Position p_1 is allocated t_1 but both positions share t_2. This method of representing structures can be applied to more complex groups as long as the elements and relations can be identified. The structure can be represented graphically as well as in matrix

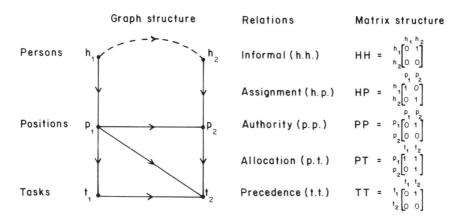

Figure 2.   A two person, two position, and two task group depicted in both graphical and matrix form

form. A matrix is an array of numbers and each pattern of relationships between elements can be also shown in a matrix. For example, the liking relationships between h_1 and h_2 can be represented as a HH matrix, thus

$$
HH = \begin{array}{c} h_1 \\ h_2 \end{array} \begin{bmatrix} h_1 & h_2 \\ 0 & 1 \\ 0 & 0 \end{bmatrix}
$$

The entry $h_1 h_2$ is 1 because there is a liking relationship from h_1 to h_2. A zero entry $h_2 h_1$ indicates that there is no relationship going from h_2 to h_1. The matrix can deal with positive or negative relationships simply by making the numbers positive for liking or negative for disliking. Other components of the total structure are represented by other matrices (HP, PP, PT, TT) and these are shown in Figure 2. Matrix representations can be very useful for representing complex structures. The matrices that describe the structure of group relationships can be used to derive more complex group properties. Using simple matrix algebra, the SRT matrices have been used to obtain measures of group co-operation (O'Brien, 1968), influence (O'Brien, Biglan, and Penna, 1972), and participation (O'Brien and Gross, 1981).

This framework for describing group structure is also useful for organizing research on structural determinants of group productivity. Most research has concentrated on only one or two relationships at a time without attempting to relate the total graph or field to group process and productivity. A brief review of the main areas of structural research can thus classify the research in terms of the particular relation that is varied. Two informal relationships, cohesiveness and compatibility, have already been considered. Cohesiveness and compatibility were placed in the section on individual determinants of group performance. Communication network theory has relied less on individual explanations and so is included in this section.

Communication Networks

A large number of studies have endeavoured to ascertain the communication patterns that facilitate or impede group performance. Communication is a central aspect of group processes as information must be transmitted, commands given, policies discussed, and feelings expressed. Hence, it is not hard to justify the importance of communication studies. The earliest studies on communication networks were done by Bavelas (1950) whose research paradigm has dominated the field. Bavelas imposed various communication channels on small groups and studied their effects on group process and productivity. His theoretical approach was complex and was derived from Lewin's field approach in that it sought to examine group behaviour as a function of a set of connected communication channels. Later studies were more empirical and sought to establish generalizations about the effects of communication networks before erecting explanatory theories. For example, Leavitt (1951) studied the effect of the communication channels depicted in Figure 3 upon the performance of five man groups. The group's task was to discover the symbol that was held by all group members. Initially, all members had been given symbols written on cards (e.g., square, asterisk). These had been distributed in such a way that only one symbol was commonly held. The subjects were seated around a circular table but screened from each other by vertical partitions. A central box allowed subjects to communicate with each other by message cards. By opening or closing different slots the communication structure could be varied.

Leavitt investigated the effects of the various networks on problem solution time, accuracy, leader emergence and task satisfaction. Results showed that the 'common-symbol' problem was solved fastest by the Wheel and Y structures and slowest for the Chain and Circle structures. However, subjects generally enjoyed the Chain and Circle structures more than they did the Y and Wheel structures. This study and subsequent ones have tried to explain the effects of different networks in terms of a concept of centrality. One reason why the Wheel and Y structures were more effective was due to the existence of a central position that was able to organize and integrate messages effectively.

Members' satisfaction with the task was greatest as their relative centrality increased. However, the summed centrality of persons did not predict group performance very well so other indices such as peripherality (Leavitt, 1951) and independence (Shaw, 1964) were developed. The communication network literature has been reviewed and integrated by a number of authors (Glanzer and

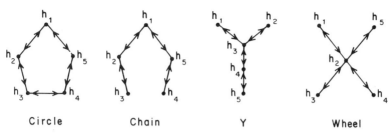

Figure 3. Communication networks used in Leavitt's (1951) study

Glaser, 1959; 1961; Shaw, 1964, 1978). The field is in a state of decline at present partly because the large number of studies have not been amenable to a coherent theoretical integration. Whether or not a given communication network is productive depends on many structural variables (e.g., task complexity) and individual variables (e.g., personality, ability). The studies are important, however, because they do show that structural variables can have a strong effect on group productivity and they did lead to an appreciation of the value of matrices for measuring structural properties.

The area is being revived to some extent by the development of telecommunications. Many organizations use telephones or closed-circuit-television to connect personnel in different geographical locations. This has led to some research on the relative effectiveness of face-to-face groups and mediated communication groups on decision making and problem solving. The literature is reviewed by Williams (1977). In these studies an extra variable is being added to describe the communication network. This is the form of communication—face-to-face, telephone, or audio-visual. It appears that group decisions made by telephone are just as effective as decisions made when members are physically together—provided that the problem is fairly routine and the members know each other. Surprisingly, it has been found, so far, that audio-visual media are not as effective as first suspected. The visual component of audio-visual communication does not seem to add very much when compared to communication by sound alone. Much research still needs to be done on establishing the relative effectiveness of the structure of communication networks within a given media. At present, this seems a very promising area of communication research as large organizations are increasing their use of telephones and television in order to minimize the cost of transporting people to one conference location.

Collaboration and Co-ordination

A number of studies have shown that the division of tasks within a group significantly affects interpersonal behaviour and group productivity. These studies have been conducted in different kinds of organizations including manufacturing companies (Davis, 1966; Rice, 1953, 1958; Woodward, 1965), mining groups (Trist and Bamforth, 1951), and temporary laboratory groups (Hewett, O'Brien, and Hornik, 1974; Ilgen and O'Brien, 1974; Kabanoff and O'Brien, 1979a, b; O'Brien and Ilgen, 1968; O'Brien, Hewett, and Hornik, 1972; O'Brien and Owens, 1969; Shiflett, 1972). In many of these studies the analysis of the formal work organization has been carried out at a qualitative level. The task allocations, for example, have been simply categorized as being co-acting versus interacting, co-ordinated versus unco-ordinated, or interdependent versus independent. These terms all refer to possible forms of co-operation. In order to further the analysis of co-operation it is desirable to distinguish between the two major forms of co-operation and provide a method for measuring the degree to which these forms exist in a given structure.

The amount of co-operation in a group is defined as the extent to which group members integrate their efforts. This integration can be achieved in two ways. The first form is collaboration. This occurs when tasks are shared between positions in a group. A typical planning or policy committee shares all tasks and has high collaboration. A group of salespersons in a shop generally do not collaborate, for each salesperson serves his or her own customers. The second way in which a group may co-operate is by dividing the group goal into sub-tasks that are ordered by definite precedence relationships. Sub-tasks are then allocated to the various positions. This form of co-operation is used in manufacturing industries that have assembly line technologies. Group members co-operate not by sharing tasks (collaboration) but by co-ordinating their sub-tasks so that the work flow is smooth and continuous. The two forms of co-operation are termed collaboration and co-ordination (O'Brien, 1968; Witz and O'Brien, 1971). The two forms are distinguished for reasons of clarification and any organization or group frequently has a division of labour that is partly collaborative and partly co-ordinated. Although the concept of division of labour has a long history in sociology where it is generally attributed to Durkheim (1947), the concept has been relatively neglected in organizational psychology.

Some hints about its potential importance were given in the earlier discussion of the Hawthorne Studies. It was suggested that the different processes observed in the relay and bank-wiring groups could have been partly due to the different forms of formal co-operation employed in the two groups. One programme of research, however, has endeavoured to establish the effects of collaboration and co-ordination on small group productivity. The basic design involved imposing structures that varied in collaboration and co-ordination upon small groups matched in ability, interpersonal relations, and power structure.

The organizations used in the Kabanoff and O'Brien (1979) study are shown in Figure 4. Using a balanced task order, all four organizations worked on three problem solving, three discussion, and three creative tasks. In organization 1 (co-acting), each member had sole responsibility for one task and was the only person

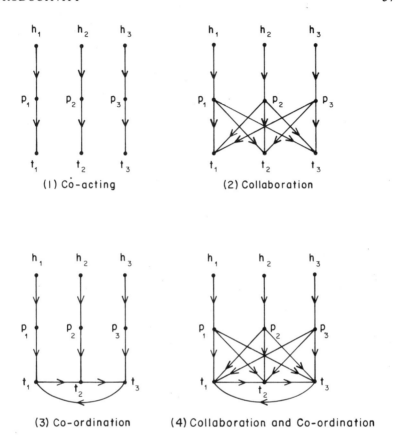

Figure 4.   Collaboration and co-ordination structures used in Kabanoff and O'Brien's (1979a, b) small group productivity experiments

to work on it. There was no co-ordination or collaboration. In organization 2, all members were required to work together on each problem. This involved collaboration but no co-ordination. Organization 3 involved co-ordination only. Each member began working on one task and after one-third of the time passed it on to another group member and began working on a task begun by another group member. A second exchange occurred after two-thirds of the total allocated time. Organization 4 was a mixture of collaboration and co-ordination. For the first one-third of the time members discussed all tasks and then followed organization 3 for the remaining time.

Both collaboration and co-ordination had significant and independent effects on group productivity across all three task types. Groups involving co-ordination were superior to groups without any co-ordination while groups utilizing collaborative structures were inferior in performance to those using structures without any collaboration. These results were generally found to be consistent with those obtained by O'Brien and Ilgen (1968) for creative tasks and by Hewett, O'Brien, and Hornik (1974) for manipulative tasks. The inferior performance of collaborative groups was partly due to the shorter length of their written product. However, when productivity scores on written tasks were adjusted by correcting for product length, collaboration still led to inferior performance.

The results can be explained in two ways. Firstly, collaborative structures involve more time on resolving conflicts (Ilgen and O'Brien, 1974) and thus have less time available for production and evaluation of ideas. Collaborative groups also lead to some inhibition on the part of some members. Having lower self-worth or dominance they fail to contribute ideas that may be of high quality (Kelly and Thibaut, 1969). Secondly, co-ordination ensures that every person makes a contribution. It also provides greater opportunity, in written tasks, for individuals to separate the process of idea production from the process of evaluation (Vroom, Grant, and Cotton, 1969). For creative tasks, it facilitates a pooling effect, in that co-ordinated groups had higher performance than co-acting groups (O'Brien and Ilgen, 1968). Circulated drafts allowed individuals to become stimulated by ideas of other members without it being dissipated by on-going distractions from other members (Madsen and Finger, 1978). Finally, co-ordination may be an effective way to reduce pressures towards conformity that exist in face-to-face collaborative groups (Hoffman, 1965).

The positive effects of co-ordination and the negative effects of too much collaboration have been also demonstrated in some recent studies of group judgement and decision-making. These studies are not accompanied by a structural theory of group process but they involve practical techniques for improving the quality of group outputs by introducing task co-ordination and reducing collaboration. The techniques are:

1. Nominal group techniques (Delbecq, Van der Ven and Gustafson, 1975);
2. Delphi methods (Linstone and Turoff, 1975); and
3. Social judgement analysis (Hammond, Rohrbaugh, Mumpower and Adelman, 1977).

An early study compared judgements made by individuals, unstructured interacting groups, nominal groups and Delphi groups (Gustafson, Shukla, Delbecq, and Walster, 1973). The four different organizations for making judgements can be represented schematically.

Individual estimation	E_I
Interacting group	$T \rightarrow E_G$
Nominal group	$E_I \rightarrow T \rightarrow E_G$
Delphi group	$E_I \rightarrow F \rightarrow E_G$

where E is the stage (or substage) of individual (E_I) or group (E_G) estimation. T is a stage of talking where groups may generate, evaluate and integrate ideas. F is a feedback stage where there was no talking, but each member received information about other members' estimates.

The groups were required to make judgements about the probable sex of a person, given information about physical characteristics such as height and weight. The nominal groups produced more accurate group estimates than the average of individual estimates. It was also superior to the unstructured interacting group. The Delphi groups performed worst. The superiority of the nominal group was attributed to the separation of generating and evaluating stages. The talking stage allowed the group to focus on individual estimates generated during the initial stage. They discussed reasons for differences and then integrated their ideas into a preferred group estimate. The authors stressed the importance of face-to-face interaction in the talking stage as they explained the relatively poor performance of the Delphi group in terms of the 'distorting' effect of written feedback.

Some later studies have questioned the generality of these results because the task was so simple. Proponents of social judgement analysis also have argued that an even better method of making judgements and decisions would be one where members are required to evaluate not just the various member estimates but also the rules that members use in making these estimates. An experiment comparing social judgement analysis and the Delphi technique was conducted by Rohrbaugh (1979). Small groups (five or six persons) were required to develop a rule for admitting students to an educational institution using variables unrelated to academic ability. All members were initially given the scores of a sample of applicants on five variables. These were:

V_1 Expectations of later social success.
V_2 Expectations about academic achievement.
V_3 Expectations about personal independence.
V_4 Attitudes toward premarital sex.
V_5 Attributed personal importance of motion pictures.

The researcher had previously estimated the relative importance of these five different measures for predicting subsequent academic performance using a validation sample. The prediction equation obtained was of the form:

$$P = aV_1 + bV_2 + cV_3 + dV_4 + eV_5.$$
(academic
performance)

where the magnitude of the constants (a–e) reflected the relative importance of the associated variable. Hence the experimenter had a standard for comparing accuracy of group predictions. The experimenter initially asked all subjects to predict academic performance of a set of individuals using their personality profiles. He then constructed groups that contained individuals with dissimilar selection policy rules. Half of these groups were randomly allocated to the social judgement analysis organization and half to the Delphi organization. The social judgement group members were each given their own policy formula and those of other group members. They were told to examine their differences and interact until they reached an agreed policy. The Delphi group members were shown the relative weights (constants a→e) they gave to predictors and the scores on each variable associated with either the estimated highest and lowest grade. All members received their own and other group members' weights. Individuals were then asked to estimate new weights and this was repeated twice when presumably there was group consensus.

Both procedures produced final group estimates that were superior to initial average accuracy. They were of the same degree of accuracy as that achieved by the second most proficient member of the group. Although there were no significant differences in group accuracy between procedures, the social judgement groups reduced member disagreement more. This was found by comparing the final group policy with that privately endorsed by individuals at the end of the meeting. The conclusion made was that the social judgement analysis produced greater consensus because they had more complete 'cognitive' maps of the process required in decision making. This appears to be attributable to the more detailed information they received from the experimenter and not to the relative superiority of discussion to the voting procedure. From the point of view of co-operation structure studies, both techniques led to relatively high levels of decision accuracy because they allowed, through co-ordination, the separation of generative and evaluating stages.

A similar experiment was performed comparing social judgement analysis to the nominal group procedure (Rohrbaugh, 1981). This time the group task was to predict the finishing order of horses in a race given information about:

1. Post position.
2. Speed rating.
3. Yearly winnings.
4. Form guide selections.

The nominal group were not given the form of the prediction formula, just the weights generated by initial member estimates. They then discussed the weights of group members and finally voted on the preferred group weightings. Both techniques improved on the average initial member weighting and were equally effective. It appeared that both methods were again useful in reducing group process losses due to factors such as personal domination of unstructured discussions by a few members, wasted time on tangential ideas and social pressures to conform to majority decisions.

Power Structures

The literature on the effect of formal power structures upon group productivity is very scarce. The reasons for this and the significance of its neglect is discussed by Cartwright (1965). It is sufficient here to indicate that one of the major features of an organization is the system of formal authority. Some people are given positions which grant to them a right to influence and control the behaviour of others. The effect of this formal power structure must be incorporated into a theory of group process if such a theory aims to claim applicability for the 'real' world. This is not to assert that power does not appear as a variable in group studies. Most experimental studies of groups deal with a specific power structure—one where all members have equal formal power. These studies, therefore, are unable to make assertions about the effects of varying power structures. Some studies have studied control structures in organizations using perceptions of power (Tannenbaum, 1968) but have not examined in detail the correspondence between perceived and objective legitimate power. Quite a few studies have looked at power structures in interaction with other variables. For example, Fiedler (1978) investigated group effectiveness as a function of leader style and leader position power.

A few studies appear to have examined power structures. Lewin, Lippitt, and White (1939) found that autocratic leaders had more productive groups than democratic leaders when a quantity criterion was used. Democratic groups were superior on a quality criterion. The word 'appears' is used deliberately because both types of group structures had similar formal power structures. They both had one appointed leader and the power status of members was equal. What did vary was the style of decision making used by the formal leader. There was little evidence that the democratic or participative style actually involved members having real influence over the decisions made by the group. Certainly the application of this experimental paradigm to a pyjama factory (Coch and French, 1948) was a study of participative decision-making. In order to overcome employee resistance to changes in work methods, some were allowed to discuss their objections while others were simply told what they had to do in an autocratic manner. A close reading of this study makes it apparent that the same managerial policies were adopted in both participative and autocratic procedures (Carey, 1977). The observed superiority of participative groups could not be attributed to power sharing. Much of the subsequent literature on participative decision-making cannot be considered as studies on power equalizations because no clear distinction is made between actual influence and participation in decisions through opinion giving, objection raising, suggestions (O'Brien, Biglan, and Penna, 1972). Participation may be an effective method of improving group productivity (Locke and Schweiger, 1979) but it is best understood as a motivational technique and not a method of distributing power. This point has also been made by Mulder (1977) who argues that participation can, unintentionally, be a method of increasing, rather than decreasing, power differences. The use of participative decision making without changing the group power structure (the PP matrix) is often associated with improvements in job satisfaction. This literature is reviewed by Wall and Lischeron (1977) who describe studies where it does and does not lead to satisfaction. The preceding comments suggest that participation is neither an effective method of improving group productivity or group member satisfaction when participation is not associated with perceptions of changes in the power structure or when members are not rewarded for increased participation through sharing the benefits of higher group productivity. When sharing in rewards occurs *and* when individuals believe, even if it is a misperception, that participation leads to increased power, then substantial increments in productivity can occur. This seems to have happened in communal work groups in China. These groups also endured an unknown amount of coercive leadership but many of the elements of Chinese 'mass line leadership' bear striking resemblances to Lewinian participative management (Barlow, 1981).

INTEGRATION OF INDIVIDUAL AND STRUCTURAL VARIABLES

So far, this review of the determinants of group performance has shown that a large number of variables determine group productivity. The variables may be divided into two classes. One class includes variables that describe the characteristics of individuals in a group. Individual abilities, motivations, personality, level of aspiration, and task perceptions have all been found, in certain situations, to be predictors of group performance. The typical social psychological theory of groups has endeavoured to show how group outputs are a function of combined individual attributes. This approach has had limited success because research has regularly found that results need to be qualified by reference to the type of task and type of situation. This introduced a second class of variables describing the type of group tasks and the structure of the group. Structural approaches to group productivity have been less popular. When they are used they are also incomplete. The effects of a given structure upon productivity depends on the characteristics of the members who operate within the structure. It is clear that major advances in a knowledge of group productivity depends on the development of theories that integrate the individual and structural level. Social psychologists have always been aware of this need. Lewin (1939) in his well known formula, stressed that the task of psychology was to predict human behaviour (B) as a joint function of the person (P) and the total situation or environment.

$$B = f(P, E)$$

Later on, Allport (1962) in reflecting on the lack of progress made towards this aim, stated that the 'master problem' of social psychology was to develop theories which showed how individual and social structures interacted.

Part of the problem is the ingrained individualism that was discussed earlier in the context of the Hawthorne Studies. Another reason is the difficulty involved in obtaining clear and quantitative methods of describing group and organizational structures. A more charitable and optimistic outlook is to explain the current stage of group psychology as one of identifying predictors. Once we have found most of the factors that can affect group outputs we can then start the task of combining the factors to form interactional theories. At least there are some signs that this interactional stage has started.

There are a few integrative theories of work group performance that utilize both individual and structural variables. One theory that promises to do this is socio-technical theory (Emery and Thorsrud, 1969; Emery and Trist, 1960; Rice, 1953, 1958; Trist and Bamforth, 1951). This theory is discussed in detail in Chapter 8. One of the basic postulates of this theory is that the formal and informal structure of a work group should match the task system. However, the task system should not be the main basis or reason for designing the form of group structure. Rather the task and the group structure should allow employees to satisfy their individual needs for challenge, learning, autonomy (or 'elbow room'), social support and recognition, and a desirable future. This basic principle of socio-technical theory is one that has been termed the 'human value' principle (Cherns, 1976).

Although the theory originally promised a conceptual scheme to show how various group structures could match a variety of technologies and a variety of social needs, more recent formulations have concentrated on specifying one preferred group structure—the semi-autonomous group—and one universal set of needs. The theory of semi-autonomous groups has become more or less formalized (Herbst, 1962). The group structure prescribed is one where groups of employees have responsibility for a 'whole' series of sub-tasks and are able to switch their task allocations because they learn to become skilled at a variety of tasks. Although this form of organization has been shown to be associated with improvements in group performance and job satisfaction the 'boundary conditions' under which it will or will not be effective have yet to be established. An attempt to do this was made by Hackman and Oldham (1980) who proposed a formula for estimating the effectiveness of semi-autonomous groups. The formula is:

Over-all group effectiveness
$$= S_1 \text{ (level of effort of members)}$$
$$+ S_2 \text{ (amount of knowledge or skill of members)}$$
$$+ S_3 \text{ (appropriateness of task performance strategies)}$$

The coefficients, S_1, S_2, and S_3, are 'saliency' coefficients. The level of skill of members, for example, may not be salient or important if the group is performing an unskilled task such as collecting rubbish or performing simple clerical tasks. The level of effort is considered to be proportional to the amount of variety, task identity, task significance, autonomy, and job feedback (Hackman and Oldham, 1975). These 'desirable' task attributes are very similar to those proposed by earlier socio-technical theorists although they were derived from other sources (Hackman and Oldham, 1975; Turner and Lawrence, 1965). Unfortunately, this formula cannot be used as a predictive model because (i) no method is provided for estimating saliency coefficients; (ii) the perceived task attributes do not predict productivity well (O'Brien, 1982; Roberts and Glick, 1981) although they do correlate positively with job satisfaction; (iii) the degree of correspondence between perceived and objective task attributes is relatively low (Roberts and Glick, 1981); and (iv) no information is provided about task strategies that are appropriate for groups with a specific task structure. Approaches that prescribe semi-autonomous groups require more empirical analysis and theoretical refinement before they can be accepted as panaceas to cure low group productivity (Blackler, 1982).

The most detailed analysis of the Norwegian semi-autonomous group concluded that performance effects have not yet been properly established and where objective increments on performance do occur they appear to be due more to the operation of group pay systems than the degree of congruence between structure, task, and social needs (Carey, 1977).

Although socio-technical theory has not made a detailed, precise analysis of group and individual structures, it has oriented many researchers away from preoccupation with individuals. Perhaps its major contribution has been to point out that work groups of the future are going to have changing goals and hence need flexible work structures (Kozan, 1982). It is an empirical question to determine how many work groups really need to change or adapt structures continuously in order to deal with a turbulent environment that produces changing group goals. The view expressed in this chapter assumes that most work groups have stable goals that require regular patterns of structure and behaviour. Future evidence may prove this assumption untenable.

CONCLUSION

We have come a long way since the Hawthorne research and the Lewinian group climate studies. Nevertheless, the influence of these seminal studies is apparent in current theories of group productivity. Not only is this influence apparent in the choice of variables (e.g., cohesiveness, goal setting, leadership style), but also in the use of both field studies in natural settings and laboratory experimentation. This alternation between the field and the laboratory has been fruitful in the past and is likely to be precondition of progress in the future. Observation of groups in organizations can lead to the identification of variables associated with productivity and these variables, once clearly defined, can be manipulated in laboratory experiments in order to test specific hypotheses. Hypotheses can, of course, be tested in field situations where there are good 'quasi-experimental' designs (Cook and Campbell, 1979) but the strongest causal inferences can be made in laboratory experiments. The major problem with laboratory experimentation is whether the results are generalizable to field groups. Some authors (e.g., Payne and Cooper, 1981) claim that the relevance of laboratory groups to understanding on-going work groups has not been demonstrated. This is a problem termed 'external validity' (Campbell and Stanley, 1966). There is no foolproof method of ensuring high external validity but it is achievable to the degree that the variables studied in laboratory groups include variables that determine the performance of field groups. Thus, the division of labour in field groups can partly be understood by laboratory experiments on collaboration and co-ordination because collaboration and co-ordination are variables that were defined after observation of field groups. Qualifications about laboratory experiments also have to be balanced by qualifications about field studies. Studies that concentrated on unskilled employees performing routine, assembly-line tasks may produce results that cannot be generalized to groups where the employees are skilled and the tasks challenging. This point was made quite strongly in a recent study (Dipboye and Flanagan, 1979) that found that the external validity of field studies in organizational psychology was no better than the external validity of laboratory experiments.

This chapter concentrated on group productivity. There are other important measures of group performance that have been omitted. These include acceptance of group strategies by group members, the time taken to achieve given productivity levels, and the ability of the group to adapt to changes in structure and goals. The achievement of high levels of any one of these outputs may be quite incompatible with short term productivity. Typically, the practical choice of group structure is guided by some trade-off rule that seeks to maximize two or more of these measures of group performance. The omission of indirect measures of group performance does not mean that they are considered unimportant. In a limited space it was only possible to deal with the major index of group efficiency. It is hoped that the complexity of group productivity research has been integrated, to some extent, by showing how various studies can be classified as individualistic, structural or interactional. Real and substantive integration is a continuing challenge. The major conclusion of this chapter is that integration will only be achieved by interactional theories that explain how group structure and member resources jointly determine productivity.

REFERENCES

Allport, F. H. (1962) A structuronomic conception of behavior: Individual and collective. I. Structural theory and the master problem of social psychology. *Journal of Abnormal and Social Psychology*, **64**, 3–30.

Barlow, J. A. (1981) Mass line leadership and thought reform in China. *American Psychologist*, **36**, 300–309.

Bavelas, A. (1950) Communication patterns in task-oriented groups. *Journal of the Acoustical Society of America*, **22**, 725–730.

Blackler, F. (1982) Job redesign and social policies, in Kelly, J. E. and Clegg, C. W. (eds.), *Autonomy and Control at the Workplace*. Croom Helm, London.

Bramel, D., and Friend, R. (1981) Hawthorne, the myth of the docile worker, and class bias in psychology. *American Psychologist*, **36**, 867–878.

Campbell, D. T., and Stanley, J. C. (1966) *Experimental and Quasi-experimental Designs for Research*. Rand McNally, Chicago.

Carey, A. (1967) The Hawthorne studies: A radical criticism. *American Sociological Review*, **32**, 404–416.

Carey, A. (1976) Industrial psychology and sociology in Australia, in Boreham, P., Pemberton, A., and Wilson, P. (eds.), *The Professions in Australia*. University of Queensland Press, St. Lucia, Queensland.

Carey, A. (1977) Norwegian experiments on democracy at work: A critique and a contribution to reflexive sociology. *Australian and New Zealand Journal of Sociology*, **15**, 13–23.

Cartwright, D. (1965) Influence, leadership, control, in March, J. G. (ed.), *Handbook of Organizations*. Rand McNally, Chicago.

Cherns, A. B. (1976) The principles of sociotechnical design. *Human Relations*, **29**, 783–792.

Coch, L., and French, J. R. P. (1948) Overcoming resistance to change. *Human Relations*, **1**, 3–19.

Cook, T. D., and Campbell, D. T. (1979) *Quasi-experimentation: Design and analysis issues for Field Settings*. Rand McNally, Chicago.

Davis, J. H. (1973) Group decision and social interaction: A theory of decision schemes. *Psychological Review*, **80**, 97–125.

Davis, L. E. (1966) The design of jobs. *Industrial Relations*, **6**, 21–45.

Delbecq, A. L., Van der Ven, A. H., and Gustafson, D. H. (1975) *Group techniques for program planning*. Scott Foresman, Glenview, Illinois.

Dipboye, R. L., and Flanagan, M. F. (1979) Research settings in industrial and organizational psychology: Are the findings in the field more generalizable than in the laboratory? *American Psychologist*, **34**, 141–150.

Durkheim, E. (1947) *The division of labor in society*. The Free Press, New York.

Emery, F. E., and Thorsrud, E. (1969) *Form and content in industrial democracy*. Tavistock, London.

Emery, F. E., and Trist, E. L. (1960) Socio-technical systems, in Churchman, C. W., and Verhulst, M. (eds.), *Management sciences, models and techniques*, Volume 2. Pergamon Press, London.

Fiedler, F. E. (1964) A contingency model of leadership, in Berkowitz, L. *Advances in experimental social psychology*, Volume 1. Academic Press, New York.

Fiedler, F. E. (1978) The contingency model and the dynamics of the leadership process, in Berkowitz, L. (ed.), *Advances in experimental social psychology*, Volume II. Academic Press, New York.

Fiedler, F. E., and Leister, A. F. (1977) Leader intelligence and task performance: a test of a multiple screen model. *Organizational Behavior and Human Performance*, **20**, 1–14.

Glanzer, M., and Glaser, R. (1959) Techniques for the study of group structure and behavior: I. Analysis of structure. *Psychological Bulletin*, **56**, 317–332.

Glanzer, M., and Glaser, R. (1961) Techniques for the study of group structure and behavior: II. Empirical studies of the effects of structure in small groups. *Psychological Bulletin*, **58**, 1–27.

Gustafson, D. H., Shukla, R. K., Delbecq, A., and Walster, G. W. (1973) A comparative study of differences in subjective likelihood estimates made by individuals, groups, delphic groups and nominal groups. *Organizational Behavior and Human Performance*, **9**, 280–291.

Hackman, J. R., and Oldham, G. R. (1975) Development of the job diagnostic survey. *Journal of Applied Psychology*, **60**, 159–170.

Hackman, J. R., and Oldham, G. R. (1980) *Work Redesign*. Addison-Wesley, Reading, Massachusetts.

Hammond, K. R., Rohrbaugh, J., Mumpower, J., and Adelman, L. (1977) Social judgement theory: Applications in policy formation, in Kaplan, M. F., and Schwartz, S. (eds.), *Human Judgement and Decision Processes in Applied Settings*. Academic Press, New York.

Herbst, P. G. (1962) *Autonomus group functioning*. Tavistock, London.

Hewett, T. T., O'Brien, G. E., and Hornik, J. (1974) The effects of work organization, leadership style, and member compatibility upon the productivity of small groups working on a manipulative task. *Organizational Behavior and Human Performance*, **11**, 283–301.

Hill, G. W. (1982) Group versus individual performance: Are N = 1 heads better than one? *Psychological Bulletin*, **91**, 517–539.

Hoffmann, L. R. (1965) Group problem solving, in Berkowitz, L. (ed.) *Advances in experimental social psychology*. Academic Press, New York.

Ilgen, D., and O'Brien, G. E. (1974) Leader-member relations in small groups. *Organizational Behavior and Human Performance*, **12**, 335–350.

Janis, I. L. (1972) *Victims of Groupthink*. Houghton Mifflin, Boston.

Kabanoff, B., and O'Brien, G. E. (1979a) Co-operation structure and the relationship of leader and member ability to group performance. *Journal of Applied Psychology*, **64**, 526–532.

Kabanoff, B., and O'Brien, G. E. (1979b) The effects of task type and co-operation upon group products and performance. *Organizational Behavior and Human Performance*, **23**, 163–181.

Kelly, H. H., and Thibaut, J. W. (1969) Group problem solving, in Lindzey, G., and Aronson, E. (eds.), *The handbook of social psychology*. Volume 4. (2nd Edn.) Addison-Wesley, Reading, Massachusetts.

Kozan, K. (1982) Work group flexibility: Development and construct validation of a measure. *Human Relations*, **35**, 239–258.

Landsberger, H. A. (1958) *Hawthorne Revisited*. Cornell University Press, Ithaca.

Lawler, E. E. (1971) *Pay and Organizational Effectiveness: A Psychological View*. McGraw-Hill, New York.

Leavitt, H. J. (1951) Some effects of certain communication patterns on group performance. *Journal of Abnormal and Social Psychology*, **46**, 38–50.

Lewin, K. (1939) Field theory and experiments in social psychology: Concepts and methods. *American Journal of Sociology*, **44**, 868–897.

Lewin, K., Lippitt, R., and White, R. (1939) Patterns of aggressive behaviour in experimentally created social climates. *Journal of Social Psychology*, **10**, 271–299.

Linstone, H. A., and Turoff, M. (1975) *The Delphi Methods: Techniques and Applications.* Addison-Wesley, Reading, Massachusetts.

Locke, E. A., and Schweiger, D. M. (1979) Participation in decision making: One more look, in Straw, B. M. (ed.), *Research in Organizational Behavior.* JAI Press, Greenwich, Connecticut.

Locke, E. A., Feren, D. B., McCaleb, V. M., Shaw, K. N., and Denny, A. T. (1980) The relative effectiveness of four methods of motivating employee performance, in Duncan, K., Gruneberg, M., and Wallis, D. (eds.), *Changes in Working Life.* Wiley, Chichester.

Locke, E. A., Shaw, K. N., Saari, L. M., and Latham, G. P. (1981) Goal setting and task performance: 1969–1980. *Psychological Bulletin,* **90,** 125–152.

Lott, A. J., and Lott, B. E. (1965) Group cohesiveness and interpersonal attraction: A review of relationships with antecedent and consequent variables. *Psychological Bulletin,* **14,** 259–309.

Madsen, D. B., and Finger, J. R. (1978) Comparison of a written feedback procedure, group brainstorming, and individual brainstorming. *Journal of Applied Psychology,* **63,** 120–123.

Mayo, E. (1919) *Democracy and freedom.* MacMillan, Melbourne.

Mayo, E. (1933) *The human problems of an industrial civilization.* MacMillan, New York.

McGrath, J. E. (1976) Stress and behavior in organizations, in Dunnette, M. D. (ed.), *Handbook of industrial and organizational psychology.* Rand McNally, Chicago.

Meadow, A., Parnes, S. J., and Reese, H. (1959) Influencing of brainstorming instructions and problem sequence on a creative problem solving test. *Journal of Applied Psychology,* **43,** 413–416.

Mitchell, T. R. (1974) Expectancy models of job satisfaction, preference, and effort. *Psychological Bulletin,* **6,** 1053–1077.

Mitchell, T. R. (1982) Expectancy-value models in organizational psychology, in Feather, N. T. (ed.), *Expectations and actions: Expectancy models in psychology.* Lawrence Erlbaum Associates, New Jersey, Chapter 10.

Mulder, M. (1977) *The daily power game.* Martinus Nijhoff, Leiden.

Nadler, D. A. (1979) The effects of feedback on task group behavior: A review of experimental research. *Organizational Behavior and Human Performance,* **23,** 309–338.

O'Brien, G. E. (1968) The measurement of co-operation. *Organizational Behavior and Human Performance,* **3,** 427–439.

O'Brien, G. E. (1969) Group structure and the measurement of potential leader influence. *Australian Journal of Psychology,* **21,** 277–289.

O'Brien, G. E. (1982) Evaluation of job characteristics theory of work attitudes and performance. *Australian Journal of Psychology,* **34,** 384–401.

O'Brien, G. E. (1983) Locus of control, work, and retirement, in Lefcourt, H. (ed.), *Research in locus of control.* Academic Press, New York, Volume 3, (in press).

O'Brien, G. E., Biglan, A., and Penna, J. (1972) Measurement of the distribution of potential influence and participation in groups and organizations. *Journal of Applied Psychology,* **56,** 11–18.

O'Brien, G. E., and Gross, W. (1981) Structural indices for potential participation in groups. *Australian Journal of Psychology,* **33,** 135–148.

O'Brien, G. E., Hewett, T. T., and Hornik, J. (1972) The effects of co-operation, leadership style and member compatibility upon small group productivity. *Proceedings of the XXth International Congress of Psychology,* pp. 678.

O'Brien, G. E., and Ilgen, D. (1968) Effects of organizational structure, leadership style, and member compatibility upon small group creativity. *Proceedings, 76th Annual Convention American Psychological Association,* pp. 555–556.

O'Brien, G. E., and Kabanoff, B. (1981) The effects of leadership style and group structure upon small group productivity: A test of a discrepancy theory of leader effectiveness. *Australian Journal of Psychology*, **33**, 157–168.

O'Brien, G. E., and Owens, A. G. (1969) Effects of organizational structure on correlations between member abilities and group productivity. *Journal of Applied Psychology*, **53**, 525–530.

Odiorne, G. S. (1978) MBO: A backward glance. *Business Horizons*, **October 1978**, 14–24.

Oeser, O. A., and Harary, F. (1962) A mathematical model for structural role theory. I. *Human Relations*, **15**, 89–109.

Oeser, O. A., and Harary, F. (1964) A mathematical model for structural role theory. II. *Human Relations*, **17**, 3–17.

Oeser, O. A., and O'Brien, G. E. (1967) A mathematical model for structural role theory. III. The analysis of group tasks. *Human Relations*, **20**, 83–97.

Osborn, A. F. (1957) *Applied Imagination* (Revised edition). Scribness, New York.

Payne, R., and Cooper, C. L. (1981) Introduction, in Payne, R., and Cooper, C. L. (eds.) *Groups at Work*, Wiley, Chichester.

Pepitone, A. (1981) Lessons from the history of social psychology. *American Psychologist*, **36**, 972–985.

Rice, A. K. (1953) Productivity and social organizations in an Indian weaving shed. *Human Relations*, **6**, 297–329.

Rice, A. K. (1958) *Productivity and social organization*. Tavistock, London.

Roberts, K. H., and Glick, W. (1981) The job characteristics approach to task design: A critical review. *Journal of Applied Psychology*, **66**, 193–227.

Roethlisberger, F. J. (1941) *Management and morale*, Harvard University Press, Cambridge, Massachusetts.

Roethlisberger, F. J., and Dickson, W. J. (1939) *Management and the Worker*. Harvard University Press, Cambridge, Massachusetts.

Rohrbaugh, J. (1979) Improving the quality of group judgement: Social judgement analysis and the Delphi technique. *Organizational Behavior and Human Performance*, **24**, 73–92.

Rohrbaugh, J. (1981) Improving the quality of group judgement: Social judgement analysis and the nominal group technique. *Organizational Behavior and Human Performance*, **28**, 272–288.

Rose, M. (1978) *Industrial behavior*, Penguin, Middlesex.

Schutz, W. C. (1955) What makes groups productive? *Human Relations*, **8**, 429–465.

Schutz, W. C. (1958) *FIRO: A three-dimensional theory of interpersonal attraction*, Rinehart, New York.

Schutz, W. C. (1961) On group composition. *Journal of Abnormal and Social Psychology*, **62**, 275–281.

Shachter, S., Ellertson, N., McBride, E., and Gregory, D. (1951) An experimental study of cohesiveness and productivity. *Human Relations*, **4**, 229–238.

Shaw, M. E. (1964) Communication networks, in Berkowitz, L. (ed.), *Advances in experimental social psychology*, Academic Press, New York.

Shaw, M. E. (1976) *Group dynamics*, 2nd edition, McGraw-Hill, New York.

Shaw, M. E. (1978) Communication networks fourteen years later, in Berkowitz, L. (ed.), *Group processes*, Academic Press, New York.

Shiflett, S. C. (1972) Group performance as a function of task difficulty and organizational interdependence. *Organizational Behavior and Human Performance*, **7**, 442–456.

Spector, P. E. (1982) Behavior in organizations as a function of employee's locus of control. *Psychological Bulletin*, **91**, 482–497.

Stasser, G., and Davis, J. H. (1981) Group decision making and social influence: A social interaction sequence model. *Psychological Review*, **88**, 523–549.

Steiner, I. D. (1972) *Group processes and productivity*. Academic Press, New York.

Strube, M. J., and Garcia, J. E. (1981) A meta-analytic investigation of Fiedler's contingency model of leadership effectiveness. *Psychological Bulletin*, **90**, 307–321.

Tannenbaum, A. (1968) *Control in organizations*. McGraw-Hill, New York.

Triplett, N. (1898) The dynamogenic factors in pacemaking and competition. *American Journal of Psychology*, **9**, 507–533.

Trist, E., and Bamforth, K. W. (1951) Some social psychological consequences of the long-wall method of coal getting. *Human Relations*, **4**, 3–38.

Turner, A., and Lawrence, P. (1965) *Industrial jobs and the worker*. Harvard University Press, Cambridge, Massachusetts.

Vroom, V. H. (1964) *Work and motivation*. Wiley, New York.

Vroom, V. H., Grant, L. D., and Cotton, T. S. (1969) The consequences of social interaction in group problem solving. *Organizational Behavior and Human Performance*, **4**, 77–95.

Vroom, V. H., and Jago, A. G. (1978) On the validity of the Vroom–Yetton model. *Journal of Applied Psychology*, **63**, 151–162.

Vroom, V. H., and Yetton, P. W. (1973) *Leadership and decision making*. University of Pittsburgh, Pittsburgh.

Wall, T. D., and Lischeron, J. A. (1977) *Worker participation*. McGraw-Hill, London.

Weber, M. (1947) *The theory of social and economic organization*. Oxford University Press, Oxford.

Whitehead, T. N. (1938) *The industrial worker*. Volumes I and II. Harvard University Press, Cambridge, Massachusetts.

Williams, E. (1977) Experimental comparisons of face-to-face and mediated communication: A review. *Psychological Bulletin*, **84**, 963–976.

Witz, K., and O'Brien, G. E. (1971) Collaboration indices in structural role theory. *Journal of Mathematical Psychology*, **8**, 44–57.

Woodward, J. (1965) *Industrial Organization: Theory and Practice*, Oxford University Press, London.

Zajonc, R. B. (1966) *Social Psychology: An Experimental Approach*, Brooks-Cole, Belmont, California.

Zander, A. (1971) *Motives and Goals in Groups*, Academic Press, New York.

Social Psychology and Organizational Behaviour
Edited by M. Gruneberg and T. Wall
© 1984 John Wiley & Sons Ltd

Chapter 4

Decision-Making and Negotiation: Leadership and Social Skills

IAN E. MORLEY and D. M. HOSKING

INTRODUCTION

Organizations are systems of power and influence. Members respond to perceived threats and opportunities in the environment of work. They act to protect or pursue their own values and interests, and those of reference groups within the organization. Activity of this kind may be considered as a set of social skills. In this chapter we shall attempt to characterize some of the skills. We shall argue that the skills of the participants provide an important (and often neglected) source of political power.

ORGANIZATIONS AS SYSTEMS OF POWER AND INFLUENCE

Robbins (1979, p. 6) has described organizations as associations of people 'who accept co-ordinated direction to achieve certain goals'. This is a useful definition because it reminds us that industrial organizations have features in common with schools, shops, hospitals, police departments, military units, offices of local and central government, and the like. We propose to emphasize this similarity by considering examples in a variety of organizations, not just manufacturing and service firms. We shall also attempt to bring together some of the literature usually considered under headings such as cognitive psychology, social psychology, organizational behaviour, industrial relations, and political science.

When we say that people accept co-ordination direction to achieve goals we do not wish to imply that organizations are held together because goals are shared. This view is widely held. However, the work of Perrow (1961), Fox (1966), Weick (1978), and Tajfel (1981) shows it is mistaken. People in organizations belong to different groups. The organization consists of coalitions of groups with different attitudes, values, and goals. Further, there may be considerable diversity within the group (Hargreaves, 1967). The coalitions are held together because members perceive common means rather than common ends. Only by co-ordinating their activity will they acquire the means to obtain certain valued outcomes. However, different people may want very different things.

The term *group* requires further consideration, since different people define groups in different ways. Different definitions serve different purposes but, broadly speaking, there are two kinds of definition. First, a group may be defined as a set of people who share a social identity because they belong to the same social category. This is the position adopted by Tajfel and his associates (Tajfel, 1981; Turner and Giles, 1981). They argue that individuals strive to find an identity which is positive, distinctive, and secure. From this point of view organizations are characterized by *social competition* within and between groups. Competition between groups occurs when people seek to demonstrate the superiority of their own group, on dimensions valued by themselves and others. Competition within a group occurs when people seek to establish they, rather than others, are prototypical members of the group. Competition of this kind may lead to conflicts, tensions, prejudices, and even pathologies of one kind or another.

Second, a group may be defined as a social unit with a social order based on systems of power and systems of value. This is the position adopted by Sherif and Sherif (1969). Essentially, they say that groups build more or less stable relationships over time and that group members conform to certain more or less idiosyncratic norms. The relationships involve considerations of role and status. *Role* relationships are patterns of reciprocal behaviour characteristic of the give and take between two individuals. *Status* relationships are role relationships defined in terms of social power. To quote the Sherifs:

'Status is a member's position (rank) in a hierarchy of power relations in a social unit (group or system) as measured by the relative effectiveness of initiative (a) to control interaction, decision-making, and activities, and (b) to apply sanctions in cases of non-compliance' (Sherif and Sherif, 1969, p. 140).

Social norms are shared standards, defining what group members should and should not do.

There may still be elements of social competition. However, competition is more obviously political activity in which group members compete to control the interaction, decision-making, and activity of others. Typically, the competition takes the form of negotiation. That is, it has the object of negotiating rules defining the terms of a business relationship between the groups (Morley, 1981b). Competition within groups takes the form of competition to create social order within the group: broadly, it is competition about who leads the group (Kelvin, 1970). The object of the exercise is to 'secure another's advocacy of the option that one would . . . like to see become the consensus of the group' (Lerner, 1976, p. 26).

According to the Sherifs, groups are what they are because they develop more or less stable status hierarchies and because they develop sets of social norms. The *leader* of the group is the person with the top rank in the status hierarchy of the group. He or she has a special responsibility to create and maintain stability and order in the group. That is, the leader is the person expected to do this job and the person who does it most often and most effectively (Kelvin, 1970). This is one reason why *leaders are central to the dynamics of social behaviour in organizations* (Hosking and Morley, 1983).

Three aspects of the process of leadership deserve special treatment in the present context:

1. Leaders exercise influence by adopting a *symbolic* or an *executive* role (Kelvin, 1970).
2. Leaders *negotiate relationships* within and between groups (Hosking and Morley, 1983).
3. To be a leader an individual must do more than comply routinely with the directives of the institution in which he or she works (Katz and Kahn, 1978).

Leadership: Symbolic and Executive Roles

Leaders exercise influence in their symbolic role by providing information for others. They provide pictures which help others to interpret actions, to give meaning and perspective to events (Weick, 1978; Selznick, 1957; Hollander, 1980). They acquire power to the extent that people rely on them because (typically) they have provided better (more useful) pictures than other members of the group (Weick, 1978).

In some cases the pictures derive from *philosophical* beliefs defining threats and opportunities in the political environment of work. George (1974) and others have attempted to work out how political leaders, such as John Foster Dulles, would answer questions such as: What is the fundamental nature of conflict in this context? What are other groups (opponents?) really like? Is the political future predictable? In what sense? And to what extent? Which political values and aspirations are likely to be realized? And when? Answers are used to spell out an *operational code*, defining a 'fundamental orientation to the problem of leadership and action' (George, 1974, p. 188). Thus, leaders may interpret actions for others because they provide persuasive images of the nature of the political environment of work. They may also define reality for others because they have knowledge which others do not. The knowledge may come from position, expertise, or informal relationships (Bacharach and Lawler, 1980). But, whatever the source, control of information provides a base for power.

The executive role of the leader has been rather more closely studied than the symbolic role. This may be because psychologists have concentrated on contexts in which leadership is virtually confined to the executive role (Kelvin, 1970). In many cases executive power is given to a leader by his or her position within an organization. And it is tempting to say that such position power or authority gives the leader the ability to *direct* the behaviours of the led. However, leaders do not have unlimited power. *Influence has to be accepted.* As Burns (1978) has pointed out:

'. . . even the most despotic are continually frustrated by foot-dragging, quiet sabotage, communications failure, stupidity, even aside from moral resistance, and sheer physical circumstance' (Burns, 1978, p. 11).

From this point of view, one key element in the exercise of leadership is the ability of the leader to negotiate relationships within the group. To quote Burns once again, leadership involves negotiation precisely because its essence is:

'. . . the interaction of persons with different levels of motivations and of power potential, including skill, in pursuit of a common or at least a joint purpose' (Burns, 1978, p. 19).

If leaders use their executive power in ways not deemed legitimate by those they lead they will fail to generate the right kinds of purpose, commitment, and order within their groups.

Negotiation Within and Between Groups

Established groups have a structure. This means that the job of the leader cannot be understood apart from the jobs, status, and motivation of other members of the group. Further, groups exist in social systems which include other groups. Part of the leader's job is to define the attitudes of group members toward outsiders, members of other groups. That is to say, leadership *cannot be understood apart from relations between groups.* The social psychology of leadership has concentrated on relations within groups rather than relations between groups (Hosking and Hunt, 1980). This has been an unfortunate emphasis. In our view it is important to recognize that:

'Leadership involves the role relationships between the leader and other members and instrumentalities for co-ordinating interaction. The leadership process centres around (a) the initiation of policy decisions and activities within the group *and with outsiders*; (b) following their course as they are executed; and (c) applying sanctions for non-compliance' (Sherif and Sherif, 1969, p. 170: our emphasis).

It is unfortunate that more recent accounts of the leader's role (e.g. Mintzberg, 1973) have tended to obscure the fact that activities outside the group may function to create and maintain order within the group.

First, the leader monitors information from outside the group and disseminates it within the group. Frequently, he or she relies on networks of co-operative relationships which supply information, interpretation, and advice (Batstone, Boraston, and Frenkel, 1977; Kotter, 1982). Second, leaders negotiate relationships between groups. There may be a process of internal adjustment also, in which leaders influence, and respond to, the demands of their group. Walton and McKersie (1965) call this the process of intra-organizational bargaining.

One further point. Leaders are given esteem to the extent that they provide services valued by members of their group. On some occasions this requires the exercise of power within the group. On others it requires the exercise of power outside the group. But systems of power (and systems of value) vary within and between groups. So do the qualities required of a leader (Sherif and Sherif, 1969; Kelvin, 1970). It follows, we think, that *the skills appropriate in one context may be irrelevant or inappropriate in another* (Kelvin, 1970). The general managers in Kotter's sample thought that they had the ability to manage nearly anything well, presumably by relying on universal principles and skills. Kotter himself believed they were mistaken. In reality 'they had specialized sets of interests, skills, knowledge, and relationships' (Kotter, 1982, p. 8). They were good at their jobs because they had a detailed knowledge of the specific business involved, and because they developed close relationships with key people in that business.

Leadership as Influential Increment

Katz and Kahn (1978) have argued that leadership involves relationships which go beyond (or increment) those formally required by the organization. That is to say, leaders develop *strong* relationships within and between groups. We shall call relationships which are strong and co-operative *close* relationships. They are characterized by high trust and high exchange of information. They are most likely to occur when each participant profits from the exchange, and when each contributes equally to it.

It may be particularly important for leaders to develop close relationships when relations between groups are typified by conflict or struggle. The 'leader' shop stewards studied by Batstone, Boraston, and Frenkel (1977) were efficient negotiators because they were able to exploit a close relationship with someone on the other side. Mistakes were less serious because they were less likely to be exploited. Confidential information was exchanged off the record, much of it detailing the internal politics of the other side. This meant that bargaining developed on the basis of shared understandings. It also meant that agreements made were more likely to 'stick'.

Organizations, then, are systems of bargaining and influence, containing different social groups. Groups may be regarded as sets of people who share a social identity because they belong to the same social category. They may also consist of people organized into more or less stable relationships based on considerations of role and considerations of status. Leaders play a key role in establishing group norms and in regulating competition within and between groups. In many respects leaders act as *negotiators*. Much of their time is spent building close relationships, within and between groups. These help them to define problems and to generate commitment to solutions which are proposed.

DECISION MAKING IN ORGANIZATIONS

We have said that leaders initiate policies for the groups they lead. But the process of policy making has not yet been described. We shall now attempt that task. To begin with, let us suppose that policies are the output from a process of decision making. Further, let us suppose that decision making has four components.

1. Decision makers *collect and interpret information* which helps define a problem. They must work out what is going on, and plan an appropriate response.
2. Decision makers attempt to *influence* others. Some decisions are possible only when issues are recognized by others. When some people desire change and others do not it may take considerable time to generate acceptable ideas, 'ideas in good currency', so to speak (Schon, 1971).
3. Eventually a *choice* is made, to adopt this policy rather than that.
4. Decisions, once made, are *implemented* by other people. We have implied that leaders monitor the progress of decisions as they are executed, and apply sanctions for non-compliance (Sherif and Sherif, 1969). This is true only part of the time. In extreme cases decisions made by one group may be completely circumvented by members of other groups. Hall (1980) describes the decision to build a third London airport at Maplin as a case in point. In less extreme cases policies run into difficulties not expected by the decision maker. A fresh cycle of activity may then be required.

We shall now consider some of the more detailed models of decision making which are available, beginning with the paradigms identified by Allison (1971).

Explaining the Cuban Missile Crisis: Three Paradigms

Decision making is a complex process. To think about it at all we have to simplify what is going on. The object of the exercise is to produce models which are simple and powerful. Allison has argued that to understand decision making in organizations we require three kinds of model, each looking at a different aspect of the process as a whole. He has set out his thesis in a classic series of case studies of the Cuban missile crisis.

Models of the first kind belong to what Allison calls the *rational actor paradigm.* Allison uses the paradigm to describe the deliberations of a small group of presidential advisors, sometimes called the Executive Committee of the National Security Council. The process is simplified by assuming that the group can be treated as if it contained only one member. If we can focus upon ideas without having to say who has the idea we can utilize mathematical models such as those outlined by Peston and Coddington (1968). Broadly speaking, it is assumed that decision making begins when the actor identifies major threats in his environment. After careful consideration he establishes a set of priorities, ranked in order of importance. Possible options or policies are detailed. The consequences of each choice are worked out as fully as possible. It is recognized that a given policy may have several effects, some beneficial and some not. Computations of costs and benefits are weighted according to their likelihood (forming a product: probability times value). The environment is monitored and the calculations updated from time to time. Finally, the actor chooses that option with the highest net gain (computed by summing the products of probability and value). The assessment of alternatives need not be done with any precision. What is important is that the rational actor structures a decision problem roughly in this way. Excellent discussions of the rational actor paradigm are given in Steinbruner (1974), Hall (1980), and Pfeffer (1981). The reader may also like to consider Robert Kennedy's (1969) *Thirteen Days* which (not surprisingly) emphasizes considerations of rational choice.

The rational actor paradigm has its most obvious applications at levels in an organization dealing with what Katz and Kahn (1978) call the introduction of structural change. The actor strives to satisfy a number of goals, trading one consideration against another to provide the best result over all. The *organizational process paradigm* begins from the assumption that most decisions are not of this kind. Rather, organizations are designed so that problems can be solved one at a time, using standard operating procedures.

Two general conclusions follow, typically. First diagnostic routines help the actor to keep problems as *simple* as possible. To find a solution the actor need consider only one or two alternatives. He is not asked to find the best solution over all. Instead he is able to accept the first choice which satisfies his minimum goals. The process is often described as conservative. To quote Pfeffer (1981) it:

'. . . substitutes procedural rationality for substantive rationality . . . rather than having choices made to maximize values, choices are made according to rules and processes which have been adaptive and effective in the past' (Pfeffer, 1981, p. 22).

Second, problems may be broken down into components which are handled by different people. This may lead to conflicts between priorities which are never fully resolved. Organizations such as governments may find it extremely difficult to handle changes unless they are relatively small in magnitude and direction. In one sense complex decisions are never made. Rather,

'. . . they *evolve* from the policies, procedures, and rules which constitute the organization and its memory' (Pfeffer, 1981, p. 23, emphasis added)

and evolution takes time.

Differences between the rational actor and organizational process paradigms are often discussed with reference to decisions about the allocation of financial resources. In many organizations what happens this year is largely a function of what happened last year. Minor adjustments are made to deal with changes required by new laws or regulations, increases in work load, and the like. Two lines of argument seem to be used. One, what happened last year may have little to do with what should happen this year, particularly if the environment is turbulent (Pfeffer, 1981). Two, whereas rational actors engage in instrumental behaviour (primarily) members of budgeting committees engage in expressive behaviour (primarily). According to Olsen (1970) members of budgetary committees spend relatively little time making decisions. Instead, they spend a great deal of time interpreting decisions. The process helps participants to confirm their beliefs and provides them with arguments to support the allocations made.

Allison's third paradigm deals with *bureaucratic politics*. In one sense the key word is politics. That is to say, it is not just ideas that matter. It matters who has them. Detzer's (1980) book, *The Brink: The Cuban Missile Crisis of 1962*, is instructive in this regard. As he says:

'One wonders whether the President rejected bombing because of who supported it and who spoke against it, not because of the cogency of the arguments on either side' (Detzer, 1980, p. 137).

Apparently, those in favour of the blockade were all men the President liked and admired. It also matters who has ideas because people located at different points in a status hierarchy may have different preferences and different stakes in the issue. Each struggles to get a policy he (or she) favours adopted by other members of the group. The outcome of the struggle depends crucially on perceptions of mutual resolve. The group cannot be treated as if there were only one member because the political process involves negotiation within the group.

There is much to be learned from Allison's discussion of the Cuban missile crisis. Allison's work has been extremely influential, and deservedly so. We believe, however, that it is important to separate two questions. One concerns the strategies used by individuals to structure the decisions they have to make. The other concerns the nature of the decision unit; the individual or the group. We shall consider each in turn.

Strategies for Making Decisions

In one sense a decision making strategy describes an *attitude* to the processing of information. We shall assume that actors diagnose problems, develop solutions, and select policies in ways which are *more or less vigilant*. The former (more vigilant) are sometimes described as optimizing, maximizing, or analytic; the latter as sub-optimizing, satisficing, or cybernetic.

Vigilant information processing strategies strive toward the ideal of rational choice built into the rational actor paradigm. Thus, Janis and Mann (1977) assume that each individual:

1. Seriously considers more than one policy or course of action.
2. Carefully considers the full range of objectives to be met, and the values implicated by each choice.
3. Carefully works out the costs and benefits of each of the alternatives.
4. Intensively searches for new information which may change his or her opinion of what is important, and what is not.
5. Is sensitive to new information or expert judgement, even when the new information is unpalatable and does not support the option initially preferred.
6. Re-examines the consequences of all known alternatives (*including those initially discounted*) before making a final choice.
7. Makes detailed provisions for executing the policy chosen, paying special attention to contingency planning.

Implicit in Janis and Mann's account is the idea that the individual is seeking the best choice within the constraints of the task. Item 2, for example, implies some kind of integration of values. It is not clear whether the actors decribed by Janis and Mann compute probabilities, but there is certainly some attempt to work out a balance sheet, comparing the pros and cons of each possible choice.

Non-vigilant information processing strategies are like those described in the organizational process paradigm. They allow actors to avoid the uncertainty which comes from lack of task related information. According to Janis and Mann (1977) the actor avoids cognitive strain because he:

1. Considers a restricted number of alternatives, sometimes only one.
2. Considers a restricted number of consequences, sometimes only one.
3. Evaluates each alternative once only. Options are evaluated sequentially as they arise.
4. Each consequence is regarded as acceptable or unacceptable. The actor is looking for a decision which is acceptable (good enough) rather than optimal (the best over all).

The spirit of the analysis is captured by saying that the actors use simple decision rules such as 'consult an expert and do what he says'; 'select that alternative superior on the most important dimension'; and so on. Activity is highly focussed and highly programmed.

If Janis and Mann (1977) are correct vigilant and non-vigilant strategies are appropriate to different kinds of decision. In their view it is essential to adopt a vigilant strategy when fundamental decisions are being made. A non-vigilant strategy is much more sensible, however, when decisions have to be made quickly, but are easy to reverse.

The Nature of the Decision Unit

Decisions may be made by individuals or groups. As we move from the description of the individual to the description of the group two kinds of complexity arise. First, groups may be composed of individuals adopting different information processing strategies. We shall say that the *group* process is vigilant if individual activities *combine* collectively to follow the procedures (1 through 7, above) identified by Janis and Mann. The group process is non-vigilant if individual activities combine collectively to follow the procedures (1 through 4, above) identified by Janis and Mann. The attitude of the leader may be crucial in determining the process followed by the group.

Second, groups may be composed of individuals from different parts of the organization: with different interests, different values, different experience, different philosophies, and different kinds of skill. Thus, decision making becomes a political process. Diagnosis of a problem, for example, does not always precede the search for a solution. Perceptions of problems may be self-serving (or serve sectional interests). Actors are likely to search for explanations which allow them to avoid unacceptable options: reductions in staff, budget cuts, and the like.

Group Decision Making: Two Kinds of Task

McGrath (1966) has distinguished two kinds of task. First, there is what might be called the *standard* decision making task. Broadly, group members belong to the same social category and are given terms of reference by the larger group. Examples include budget committees, policy-making groups, advisory groups, juries, and meetings of members of staff. Second, there is the task of *formal negotiation*. Group members belong to different social categories (management, union, etc.). They represent parties. They confer, or exchange ideas, to define or redefine the terms under which the parties will do business (Morley, 1981a, b). The terms involve the distribution of money, status, or other scarce resources. The bargaining is almost always 'distributive bargaining' (Anthony, 1977; Morley, 1979). It allows sectional groups to reach accommodations, however temporary.

McGrath (1966) has argued that it is easy for standard groups to *turn into* negotiation groups. When members come from different parts of the organization they may see themselves as representatives of sectional groups. The responsibility to protect those interests may conflict with performance of the official task. Statements of this kind have to be made with care, however. For example, Morley (1982) prefers to say that the standard decision making group combines elements of 'pure bargaining' with elements of 'co-operative negotiation'. Members of the group engage in negotiation, but negotiation of a rather special kind.

In summary, Allison has argued that we require three kinds of model to understand decision making in organizations. The models identify different strategies for processing information: some vigilant, and some not. They also indicate some of the differences between decisions made by individuals and decisions made by groups. Groups reach decisions which may be regarded as the outcomes of negotiations. The negotiation may be competitive, as in formal negotiation, or co-operative, as in standard decision-making groups.

SOCIAL SKILLS AND DECISION MAKING IN ORGANIZATIONS

Decision-making is a complex social activity which requires diagnosis of problems, development of solutions, selection, and implementation of policies. Tasks of this kind may be performed well or badly. We propose that the skilful performer is someone who:

1. Understands the risks and opportunities associated with the environment of work (Morley, 1981a; Kotter, 1982).
2. Recognizes key dilemmas inherent in the structure of the decision making task (Walton and McKersie, 1965; Morley, 1981a; Kotter, 1982).
3. Is attracted to, and able to cope with, the demands of the task (Janis, 1972; Janis and Mann, 1977; Kotter, 1982).
4. Is able, therefore, to protect or pursue the values and interests of his or her group (Morley, 1981a).

Each of these elements will be considered in turn.

Risks and Opportunities in Environment of Work

Decision-making begins when actors identify an issue—when a discrepancy between what is observed and what is expected is sufficiently large to imply that they may have something to lose (a stake) or something to gain (a prize). Snyder and Diesing (1977) describe such discrepancies as 'violations of tolerance'. In other words we may say that decision making begins when actors begin to recognize significant *risks* and *opportunities* in the political environment of work.

The skilled performer is a skilled perceiver in many respects. He or she is able to recognize tasks and opportunities using constructs such as operational codes, images, attitudes, ideologies, or other kinds of *script* (Eiser, 1980; Morley,

1981a). That is, the skilled actor is able systematically to organize knowledge of the environment, and how to work in it. George (1974) refers to beliefs of this kind as 'philosophical' and 'instrumental', respectively. They are stabilized by past experience. They allow the actor to order the environment in terms of value (Kelvin, 1970).

Steinbruner (1974) has described some of the difficulties which follow when actors are unable to order the environment in this way. They may, for example, oscillate between one policy and another, quite unable to find a rational basis for choice.

However, it is also clear that actors may see too much order in the environment. Certain beliefs may be internally quite consistent but impervious to new evidence. The risk is that people see only what they expect to see. Consider, for example, John Foster Dulles' image of the Soviet Union. Apparently:

'If the Soviets made an active move, this proved they were aggressive; if they were conciliatory, this proved they were in internal economic difficulty due to the inherent unworkability of Communism; if they yielded on some issue, this proved they were bluffers' (Snyder and Diesing, 1977, p. 331)

In general, evidence to confirm an image is quickly found. Other evidence is often denied, distorted, or ignored. People see the world as more predictable and certain than it is (Steinbruner, 1974; Jervis, 1976; Kinder and Weiss, 1978; Nisbett and Ross, 1980; Morley, 1981a).

Neisser (1976) has argued that risks of this kind are endemic to all kinds of perception. In his view ordinary seeing is vertical simply because people *move around.* They are forced to recognize input to the perceptual system has changed. It can no longer be interpreted in the same kind of way. Social perceptions are less easily corrected. Nevertheless, *to be effective the decision-maker must move around his environment in some sense. He or she must be forced to recognize that input requires interpretation in a different kind of way.*

One way of moving round the environment is to talk to people. It is no accident that the general managers studied by Kotter (1982) spent most of their time with other people. They met people regularly and developed close relationships with them. Rather than develop formal plans they used the meetings to create rough agendas. They asked questions day after day, updating the agendas as and when required. The better managers:

'. . . tended to get information for agenda setting more aggressively and to use it to create more complete . . . and more strategic . . . agendas. They also approached network building more aggressively and built stronger networks (better people, better relationships)' (Kotter, 1982, p. 117)

Close relationships are also important in the context of formal negotiations, as shown by Batstone, Boraston and Frenkel (1977). Leader stewards developed close relationships with other union negotiators and with members of management. Participants learned what was going on within the organization and were given guidance how to act.

Dilemmas in the Decision-Making Task

We have not the space to provide a complete analysis of the dilemmas built into standard decision making and formal negotiation tasks. Instead, we shall attempt to show the kind of analyses which might be given. For more detail the reader is referred to McGrath (1966), Janis (1972), Steinbruner (1974), Janis and Mann (1977), and Morley (1981a, b; 1982).

Not to Disagree Means Not to Solve the Problem

It is quite clear that certain kinds of decision are made well only if there is a dialogue between different points of view (Drucker, 1970; Morley, 1981b). Such decisions ought to be made better by groups of people working on the problem than by individuals working alone. The superiority of group decision-making is hard to demonstrate, however (Davis, 1982). There are losses due to faulty process (Steiner, 1972). In particular, leaders fail to organize disagreement so that the appropriate dialogue can occur. Under certain circumstances this may lead to a form of defective decision making known as 'groupthink'.

Janis (1972) studied the behaviour of *cohesive* groups making fundamental decisions under *crisis* conditions. The groups worked with various Presidents of the United States and played an important part in determining American policy. They made decisions which led to military fiascos such as the decision by the Kennedy administration to invade Cuba, landing at the 'Bay of Pigs'.

According to Janis, decisions of this kind deserved to go wrong. The group process met *none* of the criteria for vigilant information processing (1 through 7) described above (see p. 79). Further, group members engaged in a form of thinking ('groupthink') in which they:

1. Showed excessive optimism, generated by an 'illusion of invulnerability'.
2. Pooled their resources collectively to rationalize warning signs, suggesting incorrect assumptions had been made.
3. Ignored the ethical and moral implications of policy choice.
4. Stereotyped members of outgroups as evil, weak, or stupid.
5. Defined as *disloyal* any person expressing severe doubts about the policy preferred by a majority of the group.
6. Exercised self-censorship; that is *kept silent about their own doubts and misgivings.*
7. Shared an 'illusion of unanimity' (partly generated by the false assumption that silence means consent).

Those who raised objections outside the context of the advisory group found that their objections had no effect. Memos sent to the President were blocked by high status members of the group. Janis describes such people as 'mindguards'. They shield others from information which may interrupt the process of decision-making, requiring the group to recycle to an earlier stage.

To understand how things can go so badly wrong it is important to consider three key variables: *crisis*, *leadership*, and *group cohesiveness*. These produce three kinds of effect.

1. Note, first, that one critical task of the leader is to shape and enforce *norms*. It is assumed that this task is easier in highly cohesive groups. Norms refers to shared expectations about acceptable standards of behaviour. They are of considerable interest in the present context because they regulate the intellectual life of the group. They also regulate the activity of forming and maintaining consensus within the group. When group norms facilitate critical enquiry groupthink is *less* likely in cohesive than non-cohesive groups. Otherwise, groupthink is more likely in cohesive than non-cohesive groups. (Janis' position is commonly misunderstood. Groupthink is *not* more likely in cohesive groups, without qualification).

2. The kind of leadership, directive versus non-directive is also important. According to Janis and Mann (1977) directive leadership

> '... increases the likelihood that the leader will use his power, subtly or blatantly, to reduce the members to conform to his issues' (Janis and Mann, 1977, p. 131).

From this point of view, groupthink occurs when members of a policy making group see their task as helping the leader to justify a policy choice which has, in effect, already been made. Conformity is induced through direct pressure making it clear that *dissent* is not expected from *loyal* members of the group (Janis and Mann, 1977; Raven, 1974; Golembiewski and Miller, 1981). The pressure is effective because the group is cohesive. Members seek approval from those they like and respect. Consequently, any doubts which are felt are not expressed *within* the group.

3. Janis and Mann (1977) have argued that groupthink may be seen as a collective response to the effects of stress. In their view, crisis decision-making is stressful because each of the obvious options carries serious risks (the situation is lose–lose). Further, the actors may see little hope of finding a better alternative in the given time. In such cases actors will try to delay making the decision. Failing that, they will try to shift responsibility to someone else, or some set of people within the group (the majority?). Finally, they will try to 'bolster' the decision in various ways. They will use mechanisms of selective attention and distorted information processing to minimize the risks associated with one of

the options. Groupthink occurs when group members shift responsibility by seeking out the policy alternative favoured by the leader (or a majority of people within the group). Then they pool their resources collectively to bolster (rationalize) the choice he (they) would like to make. It is as if being in a group amplifies the tendency of individuals defensively to avoid raising controversial issues or confronting difficulties head on (Morley, 1981b).

Janis (1972) studied groups in which cohesiveness was based on mutual liking and respect. There are other forms of cohesiveness, however. A cohesive group is simply one in which members identify with the group and want to belong to it. Raven's (1974) analysis of Nixon's 'Young Team' shows that group norms can be widely shared *without* mutual liking and respect. Members were united in the sense that they each accepted Nixon's operational code, the 'Nixon Way'. There was nevertheless bitter rivalry within the group (between Haldeman and Mitchell, for example). This took the form of (social) competition for Nixon's favours—doing things his way. Thus, each attempted to show he was a prototypical Nixon man—accepting 'hard driving methods and contempt for the President's enemies' (Golembiewski and Miller, 1981, p. 33). To be *good* group members—to *stand out* from others—individuals tried to conform more and more closely to the norms of the group. They became more and more willing to take risks and to suspend judgement about the values of the Nixon Way.

Janis does not believe that the way to counteract groupthink is to change the composition of the group. Those responsible for the Bay of Pigs fiasco were quite capable of critical evaluation once Kennedy changed the *mode of operation* of the group. To help combat groupthink Janis suggests that leaders organize disagreement by:

1. Not stating their own initial preferences and expectations.
2. Ask group members to act as critical evaluators, ready to raise objections and doubts.
3. Assign one of the members to the role of devil's advocate, and divide members into subgroups from time to time.
4. Allocate a sizeable block of time to consider the *possible* intentions of other groups, surveying all warning signs that incorrect assumptions have been made.
5. Reach *preliminary* consensus about the selection of a policy but hold a 'second chance' meeting at which members are encouraged to work through residual doubts.

Procedures of this kind can be a help, although they are not easily performed with sufficient integrity to have the desired effects (George, 1974). It is also important that skills in bargaining and persuasion are equally distributed among members of the group.

Dilemmas in the Formal Negotiation Task

Broadly speaking the outcomes of negotiation reflect the costs each actor incurs in rejecting rather than accepting a given demand (Morley, 1981a). Initially these costs are not precisely known. The actors are thus uncertain—possibly mistaken—about their relative bargaining power. Negotiators are unable to estimate how firm the others ultimately will be. Estimates of cost are sharpened in the process of negotiation allowing actors to generate more accurate perceptions of mutual resolve (Snyder and Diesing, 1977). Typically negotiators are not looking for optimal agreements: just agreements that are good enough.

At any point a negotiator can ask: Shall I make a concession? Shall I stand firm but signal flexibility? Shall I commit myself further to the position I am now advocating? According to Pruitt (1971) negotiators incur costs whichever option they take. If they stand firm they may commit themselves to a position they cannot defend. They may also give the impression they are not trying to reach an agreement at all. But to move too early may give the other the impression that more is to follow. The other may now believe that he or she is the more resolved. (Morley (1981b) has argued that the concession dilemma may induce decisional conflicts of the kind described by Janis and Mann (1977)).

There is evidence that successful negotiations go through stages in which negotiators begin by establishing a reputation for resolve (Snyder and Diesing, 1977). At the same time negotiators separate in time the *interparty* and *interpersonal* demands of their task. (Douglas, 1962; Morley and Stephenson, 1977). The former derive from negotiators' role obligations to represent sectional groups. The latter derive from relationships between individuals at the bargaining table. The party relationship is the superordinate or dominant one. It is the main struggle. The personal relationship is the subordinate or diplomatic one. It tidies up the battle, so to speak.

Once again, not to disagree means not to solve the problem, in some sense. Apparently, good and stable settlements come from negotiations in which participants begin by emphasizing their representative role (stage 1). Participants formally state their own position. They show a prodigious zeal for discrediting the position of the other side. What is achieved is an initial assessment of strength of position which rules out certain possibilities and may force negotiators to look beyond the easy, obvious solutions.

Subsequently (stage 2) negotiators engage in unofficial behaviours designed to give a more precise idea of how settlements might be obtained. Party and opposition roles are still salient but the style of the negotiation is now affected by the personal relationship between the negotiators. The second stage allows the argument to get truly under way but the content of the argument depends on the closeness of the relationship between the individuals (Batstone, Boraston, and Frenkel, 1977). The closer the bargaining relationship the more sympathetic one negotiator will be to the problems of his opponent. Negotiators with close relationships will also pay a good deal of attention to problems which may arise when agreements are put into effect.

Finally (stage 3), negotiators return to their representative roles as a decision-making crisis is reached.

To sum up, negotiators structure disagreement so that they begin by establishing a convincing image of firmness before concessions are made. The personal relationship between the negotiators is allowed to come to the fore only when they have done full justice to the formal statement of the party case. Four aspects of this process deserve further comment, however.

1. The stages in Douglas' account are almost certainly notional. Stephenson (1981) has suggested that negotiators learn rapidly to switch roles from intergroup antagonist to group problem solver. For this to occur it is essential that disagreement between the negotiators as representatives is not interpreted as dislike or antagonism between the negotiators as persons. There is anecdotal evidence that those unable to maintain the distinction are not highly regarded as negotiators (Hyman, 1972).
2. A close relationship between the negotiators helps each to get what he wants on issues that are really important. In the long term there is a balance of advantage. In the short term, however, the skills of the negotiator are the skills of the leader. To quote Dubin (1979):

   'What is most important . . . is that the losing party be willing to return to the battle the very next time with the same vigour in pursuing its functional objectives' (Dubin, 1979, p. 229).

3. The positions adopted by the negotiators are often a result of intra-organizational bargaining. Those remote from the negotiation frequently generate much too optimistic expectations of what can be achieved. There is some evidence that successful negotiators give much more adequate information to their principals, particularly in the final stages of negotiation (when the decision-making crisis is reached) (Winham and Bovis, 1978).
4. Effective negotiators use fewer reasons to back up each position than uneffective negotiators. They state the same reason repeatedly, only giving another when the main reason is clearly losing ground. (Rackham and Carlisle, 1978). This may help opponents to understand the case. It means, however, that the process of formal negotiation is very different from the processes expected to occur in standard decision-making groups.

Negotiators have many other skills. For example, they structure negotiation so that the capacities of the performers are efficiently linked to the demands of the task (Morley, 1981a, b; Welford, 1980). The object of the exercise is to ensure that negotiation is no harder than it needs to be. Recent research has shown some of the ways in which this is achieved. For details the reader is referred to Morley

(1981a, b). Essentially, effective negotiators help other—colleagues and opponents—to deal with problems of information processing, influence, and choice.

Coping with the Demands of the Task

We have said that the effective decision-maker moves around his environment. It may be important to note that some people are more ready to move around than others. Dixon (1976) has argued that some people make irrational decisions because they strive to maintain an image of themselves as bold and daring or as careful and judicious. In some cases, apparently, they are sufficiently neurotic that:

> '. . . the urge to sustain their particular conceit will take precedence over the need to behave realistically' (Dixon, 1976, p. 167).

This kind of thesis has a wide application (George, 1974). Dixon advances it in a study on the psychology of military incompetence.

Dixon's (1976) book contains two kinds of data. First, he analyses a number of military fiascos: the Siege of Kut, the fall of Singapore, etc. He argues a certain pattern of errors is found in case after case. Further, the errors seem to go with certain attitudes of mind. Taken together these points suggest to Dixon that less than adequate generals are likely to have authoritarian personalities. Second, Dixon looks for evidence to establish the generals concerned were authoritarian in the technical sense. He is forced to rely on biographical data which is by no means extensive. However, the source material is readily available and the reader is recommended to study some of it himself or herself.

If Dixon is correct military incompetence cannot always be attributed to ignorance or stupidity. (The 'bloody fool' theory is wrong.) Rather those with authoritarian personalities will:

1. Be less likely than others to understand enemy intentions.
2. Tend to reject evidence which does not fit their own beliefs.
3. Not accept technical innovations.
4. Tend to underestimate the ability and capability of the enemy. They will overestimate the ability and capability of their own side ('particularly when the enemy are coloured or considered racially inferior').
5. Emphasize blind obedience and loyalty.
6. Punish those who appear to be critical of their superiors.
7. Blame others rather than accept blame themselves.
8. Exhibit certain dysfunctional obsessive tracts.
9. Lack empathy with other human beings.

Dixon also suggests that personalities of this kind will be susceptible to groupthink as described by Janis (1972).

Protection of Values and Interests

We take the view that to understand social skills we have to understand the nature of the problems, challenges, and dilemmas built into jobs. *The skilful performer is someone whose behaviour follows naturally from the key characteristics of the tasks he or she is asked to undertake.* The term *naturally* is used to imply the job holder understands what kinds of performance the job demands. His or her behaviour follows logically from the nature of those demands. In addition, he or she is probably 'a specialist of sorts', as Kotter (1982) says (p. 92).

We take the view that the skills of the participants are an important determinant of outcomes in both standard decision-making and formal negotiation groups. The first proposal is not contentious. The second is.

Writers on industrial relations have tended to neglect the importance of negotiators' skills. There is, no doubt, a feeling that effectiveness depends so much on the perspective of the judge that any kind of generalization is impossible. Psychologists have concentrated upon cases in which (1) parties agree negotiation is the appropriate method of conflict management and (2) are trying to reach agreements. They have looked at stages in successful and unsuccessful negotiations. They have also looked at the behaviour of negotiators with and without a track record of success. The results of this kind of research have been summarized by Morley (1981a).

Many people feel that the outcomes of negotiation are, in some sense, determined in advance. There is no room, therefore, for negotiators to exercise their skills. We believe that this view is a mistake. Morley (1979) has argued that there is an irreducibly psychological component in the process of negotiation. Further, that component is important. The skill of the negotiators is itself a form of negotiation power. Indeed, Karrass (1970) has gone so far as to say that:

'There is probably no other activity in which improved skill can be so quickly converted to profit' (Karrass, 1970, p. 225).

Similar comments have been made by Rackham and Carlisle (1979).

Negotiation is frequently just one element in a many sided job. In this respect the negotiator is no worse off than the members of many standard decision-making groups. Somehow effective decision-makers find the time to do their homework and prepare well. Let us repeat the resources actors bring to bear are an important determinant of outcomes in standard decision-making and formal negotiation groups.

REFERENCES

Allison, G. T. (1971) *Essence of Decision: Explaining the Cuban Missile Crisis*, Little, Brown, Boston.

Anthony, P. D. (1977) *The Conduct of Industrial Relations*, Institute of Personnel Management, London.

Bacharach, S., and Lawler, E. (1980) *Power and Politics in Organizations*, Jossey Bass, New York.

Batstone, E., Boraston, I., and Frenkel, S. (1977) *Shop Stewards in Action*, Blackwell, Oxford.

Burns, J. M. (1978) *Leadership*, Harper and Row, New York.

Davis, J. H. (1982) Social interaction as a combinatorial process, in Brandstatter, H., Davis, J. H., Stocker-Kreichgauer, G. (eds.) *Group Decision-Making*, Academic Press, London.

Detzer, D. (1980) *The Brink: The Cuban Missile Crisis of 1962*, Dent, London.

Dixon, N. (1976) *On the Psychology of Military Incompetence*, Jonathan Cape, London.

Douglas, A. (1962) *Industrial Peacemaking*, Columbia University Press, New York.

Drucker, P. (1970) *The Effective Executive*, Pan Books, London.

Dubin, R. (1979) Metaphors of leadership: an overview, in Hunt, J. G., and Larson, L. L. (eds.) *Crosscurrents in Leadership*, Southern Illinois University Press, Carbondale and Edwardsville.

Eiser, J. R. (1980) *Cognitive Social Psychology*, McGraw-Hill, London.

Fox, A. (1966) *Industrial Sociology and Industrial Relations. Research Paper 3, Royal Commission on Trade Unions and Employers Associations*, HMSO, London.

George, A. (1974) Adaptation to stress in political decision-making: the individual, small group, and organizational contexts, in Coeltho, G. V., Hamburg, D. A., and Adams, J. E. (eds.) *Coping and Adaptation*, Basic Books, New York.

Golembiewski, R. T., and Miller, G. J. (1981) Small groups in political science, in Long, S. L. (ed.) *The Handbook of Political Behaviour*, Volume 2. Plenum Press, London.

Hall, P. (1980) *Great Planning Disasters*, Weidenfeld and Nicholson, London.

Hargreaves, D. H. (1957) *Social Relations in a Secondary School*, Routledge and Kegan Paul, London.

Hollander, E. (1980) Leadership and exchange processes, in Gergen, K., Greenberg, M., and Willis, R. (eds.) *Social Exchange: Advances in Theory and Research*, Free Press, New York.

Hosking, D. M., and Hunt, J. G. (1980) *Social psychological contributions to the study of leadership*, paper presented to the International Workshop on Social Psychology and Social Policy, University of Kent, at Canterbury, England.

Hosking, D. M., and Morley, I. E. (1983) Leadership and organization: the negotiation of order. *The University of Aston Management Centre Working Paper Series, Number 29.*

Hyman, R. (1972) *Disputes Procedure in Action*, Blackwell, Oxford.

Janis, I. L. (1972) *Victims of Groupthink*, Houghton Mifflin, Boston.

Janis, I. L., and Mann, L. (1977) *Decision Making: A Psychological Analysis of Conflict, Choice and Commitment*, Collier-Macmillan, London.

Jervis, R. (1976) *Perception and Misperception in International Politics*, Princeton University Press, Princeton, N.J.

Karrass, C. L. (1970) *The Negotiating Game*, World Publishing, New York and Cleveland.

Katz, D., and Kahn, R. (1978) *The Social Psychology of Organizations*, Wiley, New York.

Kelvin, P. (1970) *The Basis of Social Behaviour*, Holt, Rinehart and Winston, London.

Kennedy, R. F. (1969) *Thirteen Days*, Norton, New York.
Kinder, D. A., and Weiss, J. A. (1978) In lieu of rationality. Psychological perspectives on foreign policy decision-making. *J. Conflict Resolution*, **22**, 707–35.
Kotter, J. (1982) *The General Managers*, The Free Press, New York.
Lerner, A. W. (1976) *The Politics of Decision-Making: Strategy, Cooperation and Conflict*, Sage, Beverly Hills.
McGrath, J. E. (1966) A social psychological approach to the study of organizations, in Bowers, R. (ed.) *Studies on Behaviour in Organizations: A Research Symposium*, Athens, Georgia: University of Georgia Press.
Mintzberg, H. (1973) *The Nature of Managerial Work*, Harper and Row, New York.
Morley, I. E. (1979) Behavioural studies of industrial bargaining, in Stephenson, G. M., and Brotherton, C. J. (eds.) *Industrial Relations: a Social Psychological Approach*, Wiley, London.
Morley, I. E. (1981a) Negotiation and bargaining, in Argyle, M. (ed.) *Social Skills and Work*, Methuen, London.
Morley, I. E. (1981b) Bargaining and negotiation, in Cooper, C. L. (ed.) *Psychology and Management: A Text For Managers and Trade Unionists*, Macmillan/The British Psychological Society, London.
Morley, I. E. (1982) Preparation for negotiation, in Brandstätter, H., Davis, J. H., and Stocker-Kreichgauer, G. (eds.) *Group Decision Making*, Academic Press, London.
Morley, I. E., and Stephenson, G. M. (1977) *The Social Psychology of Bargaining*, Allen and Unwin, London.
Neisser, U. (1976) *Cognition and Reality*, Freeman, San Francisco.
Nisbett, R., and Ross, L. (1980) *Human Inference: Strategies and Shortcomings of Social Judgment*, Prentice Hall, Englewood Cliffs, N.J.
Olsen, J. P. (1970) Local budgeting: decision-making or a ritual act. *Scandinavian Political Studies*, **5**, 85–115.
Perrow, C. (1961) the analysis of goals in complex organizations. *American Sociological Review*, **26**, 854–866.
Peston, M., and Coddington, A. (1968) *Statistical Decision Theory*, HMSO CAS Occasional Paper/number 7, London.
Pfeffer, J. (1981) *Power in Organizations*, Pitman, Boston.
Pruitt, D. G. (1971) Indirect communication and the search for agreement in negotiation. *J. Appl. Soc. Psychol.*, **1**, 205–239.
Rackham, N., and Carlisle, J. (1978) The effective negotiator—part 1. *J. Eur. Industr. Training*, **2**, 6–10.
Rackham, N., and Carlisle, J. (1979) The effective negotiator—part 2. *J. Eur. Industr. Training*, **2**, 2–5.
Raven, B. H. (1974) The Nixon Group. *Journal of Social Issues*, **29**, 297–320.
Robbins, S. P. (1979) *Organizational Behaviour: Concepts and controversies*, Prentice Hall, Englewood Cliffs, N.J.
Schon, D. A. (1971) *Beyond the Stable State: Public and Private Learning in a Changing Society*, Temple Smith, London.
Selznick, P. (1957) *Leadership in Administration*, Row, Paterson, Evanston, Illinois.
Sherif, M., and Sherif, C. W. (1969) *Social Psychology*, Harper and Row, New York.
Snyder, G. H., and Diesing, P. (1977) *Conflict Among Nations: Bargaining, Decision-Making and System Structure in International Crises*, Princeton University Press, Princeton, N.J.
Steinbruner, J. D. (1974) *The Cybernetic Theory of Decision*, Princeton University Press, Princeton, N.J.

Steiner, I. (1972) *Group Process and Productivity*, Academic Press, New York.
Stephenson, G. M. (1981) Intergroup bargaining and negotiation, in Turner, J. C., and Giles, H. (eds.) *Intergroup Behaviour*, Blackwell, Oxford.
Tajfel, H. (1981) *Human Groups and Social Categories*, Cambridge University Press, Cambridge.
Turner, J. C., and Giles, H. (eds.) (1981) *Intergroup Behaviour*, Basil Blackwell, Oxford.
Walton, R. E., and McKersie, R. B. (1965) *A Behavioural Theory of Labor Negotiations: an Analysis of a Social Interaction System*, McGraw-Hill, New York.
Weick, K. (1978) *The Social Psychology of Organizing*, (2nd Edn.) Addison-Wesley, Reading, Mass.
Welford, A. T. (1980) The concept of social skill and its application to social performance, in Singleton, W. T., Spurgeon, P., and Stammers, R. B. (eds.) *The Analysis of Social Skill*, Plenum Press, New York and London.
Winham, G. R., and Bovis, H. E. (1978) Agreement and breakdown in negotiation: report on a State Department Training Simulation. *J. Peace Res.*, **15**, 285–303.

Social Psychology and Organizational Behaviour
Edited by M. Gruneberg and T. Wall
© 1984 John Wiley & Sons Ltd

Chapter 5

Job Satisfaction

E. A. LOCKE

Job satisfaction has been one of the most intensively studied subjects in the field of industrial and organizational psychology. Literally thousands of books and articles have been written on it. This attention reflects the importance of the subject both to researchers and to people in general.

Clearly one reason that job satisfaction is important is that for most employees it is an end in itself (or a means to the end of personal happiness). Job satisfaction and dissatisfaction are also associated with a number of organizational consequences. However, the number of possible consequences or reactions is quite varied and complex. Job satisfaction and dissatisfaction are, after all, simply emotional responses. There are a wide range of alternative actions that one can take in response to emotions. The major categories of response are shown in Table 1. Observe that some of these responses are psychological (e.g., toleration, defence mechanisms) and others are behavioural.

All emotions contain built-in action tendencies, i.e., felt desires to act (Arnold, 1960), although these tendencies may or may not be acted on. Characteristically a person feels like approaching or retaining objects which are appraised positively, and feels like avoiding (or harming) objects which are appraised negatively.

Thus one common category of responses to job dissatisfaction is *behavioural withdrawal* from the job situation. Behavioural withdrawal can be achieved basically in three ways: lateness, absenteeism, and/or labour turnover. There is considerable evidence for a relationship between dissatisfaction and behavioural withdrawal (Beehr and Gupta, 1978; Mobley, Griffeth, Hand, and Meglino, 1979), although the relationships are now always consistent (Nicholson, Brown, and Chadwick-Jones, 1976). The reason, as noted earlier, is that dissatisfaction, while entailing an action tendency, does not compel action.

Before leaving a job, for example, an employee first may have thoughts of resigning, consider what alternative jobs have to offer compared to the present one, plan to look for another job, and actually form an intention to leave (Mobley, Griffeth, Hand, and Meglino, 1979). Typically, when the intention to leave is statistically controlled, satisfaction is unrelated to turnover.

Table 1.   Classification of action alternatives following positive and negative emotions. Based on Locke, 1976; reproduced by permission of Dr. Marvin D. Dunnette

---

Positive appraisals (emotions):
1.   Approach object; retain object; protect object; repeat act.
2.   If satiated or if anticipate future boredom (or failure): switch activities; set new goal; choose new task; pursue new endeavour.

Negative appraisals (emotions):
1.   Take no action; gather more information.
2.   Avoid object; leave situation; think about leaving situation; make plans to leave; spend less time in situation.
3.   Change or attack object.
    a.   Physical attack; destroy, damage, injure, punish object or person (threaten attack).
    b.   Persuasion; complain; argue; convince agent to modify actions; bargain; criticize; harass; strike.
    c.   Change own actions or performance (if they are the disvalued object).
4.   Change or blunt reaction to object.
    a.   Modify content or hierarchy of own values (self-persuasion; counselling; therapy).
    b.   Modify estimate of relationship between situation or object and one's values.
    c.   Use ego-defence mechanisms: psychological withdrawal; drugs; repression; fantasy; displacement, etc., to distort perception or appraisal of situation.
5.   Tolerate situation (focus on valued aspects of situation).
6.   Repeat previous action (rigidity, compulsion, fear of change).

The individual may not translate dissatisfaction into an actual intention to leave, because there are no viable alternatives (e.g., in a tight job market there may be no other jobs available), or because there is a fear of the uncertainty involved in a job change, or because there is too great an investment in the present job (e.g., pension plan).

Generally job dissatisfaction is more reliably associated with labour turnover than with absenteeism. Absenteeism may be controlled, regardless of job attitudes, by organizational constraints such as loss of pay, suspension, criticism, etc. Similarly, lateness may invite penalties such as poor performance appraisals which the employee desires to avoid, despite disliking the job. In addition, lateness and absenteeism are only short-term or temporary solutions to the problem of job dissatisfaction whereas resigning is a permanent solution (at least for that job).

There are possible responses to dissatisfactions other than behavioural withdrawal. For example, the employee may simply *withdraw psychologically* and become passive and disinterested in the job. Dissatisfied employees may also retreat into alcohol or drugs (Cook, Walizer, and Mace, 1976). Drugs do not solve the problem of dissatisfaction but make the individual temporarily less aware of it. Like all defence mechanisms, they involve evasion of reality, and may cause more problems than they solve in the long run.

A third class of alternative responses to job dissatisfaction consists of assertive/aggressive responses which attempt to change the conditions producing dissatisfaction, Brett (1980), for example found that interest in joining trade unions is fostered by two key factors: dissatisfaction with present organizational conditions, and the belief that support for the trade unions will lead to improvements in these conditions. Once a union is recognized, aggressive actions may be taken, e.g., strikes. In extreme cases employees may attempt to harm the employing organization or its property through stealing, sabotage or other forms of unlawful activity (Mangione and Quinn, 1975).

Note that nothing has been said about a direct effect of dissatisfaction on the productivity of individual employees. This is because there is no consistent evidence for any such association (Locke, 1976b). Lower output or poorer work quality are possible responses to dissatisfaction, but they do not seem to occur reliably in all employees.

Generally the determinants of productivity are considerably more varied and complex than the determinants of satisfaction. Productivity depends upon, for example: the employees' knowledge and abilities; the work load (White and Locke, 1981); supervisory competence; technology; the work environment; team co-ordination; the reward system; and other factors. Dissatisfied employees may be prevented from lowering ouput through various control mechanisms (e.g., goals or standards, work measurement, punishments, supervisory pressures, etc.). Thus many combinations of satisfaction and productivity are possible; an employee can be high on both, low on both, or high on one and low on the other.

It should be noted, however, that there can be *indirect* effects of dissatisfaction on productivity. To take the most obvious case, if widespread dissatisfaction leads to a strike, productivity is reduced to zero. Again if a substantial number of the more competent employees resign it may be some time before unit output is restored to normal; and if a disgruntled employee fails to inform his boss of some important piece of information about the work (e.g., a design flaw, faulty production, a complaining customer, etc.), this may affect performance in the long run.

From the point of view of labour turnover, it is especially important that the most competent employees be reasonably satisfied, since these are the ones whom the organization can least afford to lose. Dissatisfaction on the part of the least competent employees may actually be functional in that their leaving rids the organization of malcontents and allows it to replace them with more able employees. It also may benefit the employees who leave by encouraging them to find an organization where they can be more successful.

Dissatisfaction also can have effects other than on productivity. Absenteeism, labour turnover, militancy, etc. can be detrimental to the organization, for example, because they increase costs.

Let us now consider the 'psychological architecture' that underlies the phenomenon of job satisfaction.

THE PSYCHOLOGICAL BASIS FOR JOB SATISFACTION

Motivation is concerned with the factors that direct, energize, and prolong action. Motivation starts with the concept of *needs*. The existence of every living organism is conditional. If it does not take the actions its survival requires, it perishes. Needs are the conditions required for an organism's survival and well being. Needs are of two types: physical and psychological.

Physical needs are the conditions required for a healthy, properly functioning body (e.g., food, water, temperature, air, etc.). Psychological needs are the requirements of a healthy, properly functioning mind or consciousness (e.g., pleasure, love, efficacy, growth, self-esteem, etc.). Need fulfilment leads to a condition of health (physical and psychological or mental) while prolonged, substantial need frustration leads ultimately to illness or death.

Physical and psychological needs are not independent. A healthy properly functioning body facilitates and makes possible a sense of psychological well-being and pleasure, while a healthy mind facilitates and makes possible the care and feeding of a healthy body.

The form in which need frustration initially is experienced is that of (physical or psychological) discomfort or pain. Such information, however, does not in itself enable the individual to identify the cause of the discomfort nor does it provide the knowledge of how to correct the problem or how to avoid it in the future. The link between needs and action is therefore learned (Locke, 1980).

Clearly, cognitive factors play a crucial role. The cognitive link between needs and action is that of *knowledge*. The motivational link between needs and action is that of *values*.

Values are 'that which one acts to gain and/or keep' (Rand, 1964, p. 15). They are what one considers to be good or beneficial. While needs are inborn, values (and knowledge) are acquired. Warmth, for example, is a need. But one's values will determine for example what type, colour, and style of clothes one will buy in order to keep warm. The issue of warmth illustrates another aspect of the relationship between values and needs. A given value can serve more than one need. Thus one's choices in clothing involve not only the physical need for protection from the elements but are indirectly related to the psychological needs for self-esteem, efficacy, growth, and love.

Since values are acquired, and since people are not omniscient, the values they choose or acquire may or may not be consistent with or conducive to the fulfilment of their needs. For example, individuals may value: smoking cigarettes, drinking large quantities of alcohol, taking mind-destroying drugs, speeding, making decisions by 'gut feel', and the use of elaborate psychological defence mechanisms. We may describe such values as irrational in that they serve to undermine one's health and well being. This is not to deny that such values yield some degree of short-term pleasure or the temporary removal of pain. If they did not, no one would seek them. But that does not stop them from being ultimately self-destructive.

It should be noted that when talking about an individual's values, this does not refer solely to his professed values. What a person says he values and what he actually values may not coincide. A person may claim to value certain things because such claims (or self-deceptions) temporarily boost his (illusion of) self-esteem. A person's actual values must be inferred by integrating all available information about that person, i.e., words, emotional responses, choices, and actions—especially actions.

Related to this is the fact that all of an individual's values are not necessarily conscious. Values, like knowledge and beliefs, can be subconscious. A given individual may or may not be able to pull the relevant material out of his subconscious, identify his values, or rate their relative importance.

(It should be noted that the concept of values provides the underlying explanation for the effects of what the behaviourists call 'reinforcement'. A reinforcement is an event which follows an action, which makes subsequent actions of the same type more likely in similar, future situations. Reinforcers only reinforce if the individual values the events which follow the action and expects similar actions to produce such values in the future; Locke, 1977.)

Goals are similar in meaning to the term values, only they are more specific. Thus we say that an individual values growth, but his specific goal may be to gain new responsibility through a specific promotion or to take courses to improve his knowledge and skills. Just as value attainment is a means to need satisfaction, goal attainment is a means to value satisfaction.

Emotions can be viewed as the form in which one experiences the attainment or frustration of one's values (Locke, 1976b). Emotions are the result of value appraisals, but involve, as part of the total psychological sequence, the individual's knowledge and beliefs. Let us consider this sequence in some detail.

The basic causal sequence leading to an emotion is:

$$\text{Object} \rightarrow \text{Cognition} \rightarrow \text{Value Appraisal} \rightarrow \text{Emotion}.$$

Each of these elements will be considered in turn.

Object

Every emotion is about something. The thing may be an object, an action, an attribute, a situation, an idea, a person, or even a prior emotion. Anything that can be perceived or conceived can be the object of an emotion. This is not to say that an individual can always identify the actual object of an emotion. The individual may not be skilled at introspection. Sometimes there is more than one object involved (e.g., a sequence of actions or consequences) or the situation or object is highly complex (e.g., another person), making the identification of the object difficult.

Cognition

This stage actually involves two processes (although they are not experienced as separate): sensory perception and conceptual identification. For example, if during a hike in the wilderness one meets a large bear on the trail, one automatically perceives the bear and this perception is automatically associated with one's conceptual knowledge about bears (e.g., 'this is a grizzly bear; grizzly bears are very strong and can kill you; they have been known to attack human beings') as well as one's knowledge of the context in which the object is perceived (e.g., 'the bear is quite close to me; I have no weapons; there is no place to hide; maybe there are cubs nearby which will make her especially dangerous; somebody was attacked last week in this park').

No claim is made that one must be *fully* aware of an object to have an emotion about it. There are *degrees* of awareness. One can have an emotion about something that is in *focal* awareness or about something which is in *peripheral* awareness.

Enduring emotional states, called *moods*, can remain even when one has forgotten (or never was able to identify) what started them, although one had to be aware of something in order for them to have started.

Value Appraisal

The third stage involves an automatic, subconscious estimate of the relation between what was perceived and one's value standards. If the situation is perceived as furthering or facilitating the attainment of one's values, then a positive emotion is experienced. If the situation is perceived as threatening, blocking, or destroying one's values, then a negative emotion is experienced. For example, if one gets a letter in the mail announcing that one has won the state lottery, one immediately experiences joy (and perhaps relief, if one has a mountain of debts). In contrast, if the letter announces that your neighbour is suing you for $100,000 because he slipped on your path you may experience anything from anxiety to depression to anger (and perhaps all three).

The intensity of an emotion will depend upon the place in one's *value hierarchy* of the values implicated in the emotion. If the values involved are not important, then attaining or not attaining the values will produce less intense emotion than in the case where the values are important.

This relationship is shown in Figure 1 below:

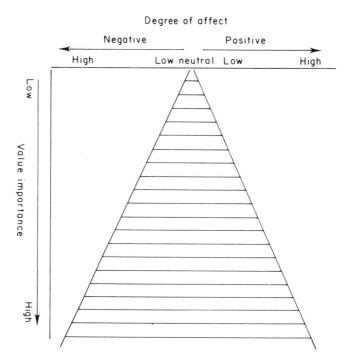

Figure 1.   The relation of value importance to affect. Adapted from Locke (1976b) and reproduced with permission of Dr Marvin D. Dunnette

The more important the value, the wider the possible range of affect; the actual amount of affect will depend both on value importance and on the degree of value attainment or loss (for further details see Mobley and Locke, 1970; Locke, 1976b).

The above relationships are illustrated by the data in Table 2. These data were obtained by asking individuals to rate the importance of various job characteristics (e.g., chance to use skills, location of water fountains) and to describe the degree to which a specific previous job possessed these characteristics. These latter estimates were correlated with a rating of over-all job satisfaction after the characteristics were grouped according to their rated importance. The results show that obtaining important characteristics is associated with high satisfaction; obtaining unimportant characteristics is unrelated to satisfaction; while the presence of disvalued characteristics is associated with job dissatisfaction. The over-all rank order correlation between mean characteristic desirability (importance) and the Pearson correlation between the rated presence of the characteristic and job satisfaction was + 0.93.

A well known theory developed by Herzberg (1966) argues that certain aspects of the job function to satisfy but not to dissatisfy employees (e.g., the work itself)

Table 2.   Relation of presence and importance of job characteristics to job satisfaction

Item group*	Mean desirability rating (value importance)†	Correlation between degree of presence of job characteristics and over-all job satisfaction	
5 Desirable job characteristics	+ 0.996	+ 0.65§	
			$t = 3.04$‡§
5 Irrelevant job characteristics	+ 0.10	+ 0.25	
			$t = 3.28$‡§
5 Undesirable job characteristics	− 0.88	− 0.39§	

* The desirable job characteristics were: chance to use skills and abilities; chance for advancement; consideration by supervisor; fair pay; facilitative working conditions.
The neutral characteristics were: water fountains near work place; bright walls; work within ten minutes of home; can eat on job; uses paper clips. The undesirable characteristics were: exposure to physical hazards; close supervision; not getting paid on time or correct amount; getting falsely blamed; no variety.
† Desirability scale ranged from + 1 ('should have') to 0 ('does not matter') to − 1 ('should not have').
‡ t-test for non-independent r's (d.f. = 46).
§ $p < 0.01$ (d.f. = 47).

while other aspects function to dissatisfy but not to satisfy (e.g., company policies, pay). Herzberg's theory of work motivation is based on a parallel theory of needs. So-called 'motivators' such as the work itself are claimed to only satisfy growth needs, while 'hygiene' factors such as company policies and pay are alleged only to eliminate deficits in animal (physical) needs. According to Herzberg frustrated growth needs lead to no satisfaction rather than dissatisfaction, while fulfilled animal needs lead to no dissatisfaction rather than to satisfaction.

Actually it seems safer to assume that this theory is incorrect, and all needs and values work on both directions. If they are attained, they bring (some degree of) satisfaction or some positive emotional response, and if they are frustrated, threatened, lost or destroyed, they bring dissatisfaction or some negative emotional response. Research which has eliminated the conceptual and methodological flaws in Herzberg's procedures has clearly confirmed this (see Locke, 1976b, for a detailed critique of Herzberg's theory; see also Wall, Stephenson, and Skidmore, 1971, not cited in that review). The bi-directional functioning of values is also consistent with the evidence of introspection. For example, when we have to do work that we hate, we do not feel lack of satisfaction but dissatisfaction.

Herzberg's view of certain hygiene factors is made superficially plausible by the existence of values which when maintained without action are usually taken for granted. For example, an employee who has always worked in a physically attractive workplace may not take special notice of it on a day-to-day basis. But if he learns that his organization is planning to move out of the present quarters into an ugly, delapidated structure, he may become quite upset. The employee was not focusing on the work environment before the move, because *maintaining that value did not require his attention or action*. Thus it got swept into the background. The proof that the work environment can be a positive value is the fact that, when changes are made for the better (especially as a result of the employee's own efforts), there is a feeling of pleasure in the outcome.

Emotion

Emotions are the result of value appraisals. They are the form in which one experiences the attainment or negation of one's values. Emotions involve both psychological and physiological reactions. For example, the feeling of anxiety involves the experience of being threatened, out of control, helpless and/or worried and may be accompanied by such physical symptoms as: muscle tension, sweating of the palms, digestive upset, increased respiration and heart rate, trembling, dizziness, dryness of the mouth, restlessness, decreased (or increased) appetite, and other reactions.

In daily life there are few 'pure' emotions, i.e., emotions which involve only one object and one simple value appraisal. Most emotions are more complex. For example, consider an individual who has just been fired from his job. He might feel: *anger* at his boss or the company for treating him unjustly; *fear* and *anxiety* because he does not know whether he will have enough money to live on or whether he will find another job; *despair* because years of work seem to have gone down the drain; *self doubt* or *self condemnation*, because maybe it was, in some respects his fault; and *guilt* because he should have seen it coming and done something about it and/or because he is letting his family down.

How a given individual actually would experience being fired would depend upon numerous factors such as his particular values, his knowledge, his self-concept, etc. For example, an individual who has low self-esteem is more easily threatened than one who has high self-esteem. A person who has numerous psychological defences will handle threats differently than one who is not defensive. Thus sorting out and analysing complex emotions can be a very difficult task, especially because when having an emotion one does *not* consciously experience the full sequence described above. For example, if one meets a grizzly bear in the wilderness, one does *not* consciously make an assessment of the entire situation and then reach a conscious conclusion which then produces an emotion. What one would actually experience in this situation would be: bear→fear.

The intervening steps occur automatically and subsconsciously. We discover their existence through inference, such as by working backwards from the emotion and looking for the values and premises behind it. The individual's stored knowledge and values are automatically 'activated' as soon as the object is perceived.

The value estimate that takes place is fast—usually too fast to observe as it occurs. The survival value of the automaticity of emotions is obvious; in emergencies one needs an immediate estimate of the fact that there is danger and an immediate impetus to take some action in regard to it. The emotion provides both.

As Arnold has observed (Arnold, 1960), and as noted earlier, every emotion contains, as part of the emotional experience, a felt impetus to action. If an object is appraised as beneficial the action tendency is to approach, keep or protect the object. If an object is appraised as harmful, there is a felt tendency to avoid, remove or destroy the object.

Emotions, of course, also *result* from actions and their outcomes. If an action is successful one experiences satisfaction or joy; if it is unsuccessful one experiences dissatisfaction or suffering. Thus emotions are at the same time a payment or penalty for past actions and, since man can anticipate the future based on past experience and reason, an incentive (positive or negative) for future actions.

Emotions provide not just the impetus but the psychological fuel for action. If man experienced no emotions (for example, if he experienced his values only as abstract principles, or cognitive abstractions), he would have no motivation to act. His values would not be experienced as personally real, significant or important. A creature like Mr Spock in the TV and movie series *Star Trek* is a psychological impossibility.

It should be stressed once more that, while emotions provide an impetus and incentive to action, *they do not force or compel one to act*. One has numerous choices or action alternatives following an emotion (see Table 1).

However, the fact that emotions do contain action tendencies or felt urges to action, suggests the possibility (see Locke, 1976b) of an approach to the measurement of job satisfaction through the measurement of such action tendencies. Skaggs and Lissitz (1981), for example, developed the action tendency items shown in Table 3. They found that these items were highly correlated with more traditional measures of job satisfaction (e.g., 'Is your job interesting?').

Table 3. Action tendency items indicative of job satisfaction. Reproduced by permission from Skaggs and Lissitz, 1981

1.	I feel like calling in sick when I am not really physically ill.
2.	I do not feel like waking up on mornings I have to work.
3.	I feel energetic during the work day.
4.	I feel like leaving work immediately after the final required minute of the day.
5.	I feel like checking the unemployment ads in the newspaper.
6.	When I tell my friends about my work, I feel like talking about good things.
7.	I think about what other type of work I could be doing.

JOB SATISFACTION: WHAT DO PEOPLE WANT?

Job satisfaction is a positive emotional response to the job resulting from an appraisal of the job as fulfilling or allowing the fulfilment of the individual's job values. Job dissatisfaction is a negative emotional response resulting from the appraisal of the job as ignoring, frustrating, or negating one's job values (Locke, 1976b).

While there are important individual differences in what employees want in a job, extensive job satisfaction research has also indicated that there are also broad similarities among employees in what they want. These broad similarities are presumably the result of people having the same underlying needs.

Below is a summary of what has been found (based mainly on Hackman and Oldham, 1980; Gruneberg, 1979; Locke, 1976b; Vroom, 1964; additional references are provided where relevant).

Work Content

In the realm of the work itself, employees value work which corresponds to their *personal interests*. Research generally has been unsuccessful in discovering the roots of interests. A number of factors may be involved, e.g., early experience, the influence of parents and teachers, initial success (early competence), thinking style, etc. People differ widely, of course, in what they find interesting, but interesting work is axiomatically valued. An interesting activity is one which the individual enjoys for its own sake—rather than, for example, for the values to which it leads such as money, promotion etc. The narrowest definition of *intrinsic motivation* would refer to activities that one enjoys because of their interest. Intrinsic motivation would not necessarily lead to a faster rate of work than low intrinsic motivation but it might lead to greater persistence, i.e., the individual might spend more time on interesting, discretionary activitites than on uninteresting activities.

Employees also like to feel that the work they are doing is *important*. Again people differ in what they consider to be important and in the frame of reference they use to judge it (e.g., important within the company, important in the culture, in the family, etc.). Hackman and Oldham (1980) call this task significance.

Employees want the *chance to use their (valued) skills and abilities* (O'Brien, 1980), especially the skills and abilities which they acquired in their pre- or post-job training. Many employees (especially those in higher level professional and managerial jobs) want a chance to *grow*. This is facilitated by *varied* task assignments and by giving the employee personal *responsibility* for the work and *autonomy* in making decisions. The integrating principle tying together the use of one's abilities, growth, variety, responsibility, and autonomy is *mental challenge*. The desire for mental challenge, for the constant stimulation of acquiring new knowledge and developing new skill is what distinguishes a person pursuing a career from a mere job holder (Rand, 1974).

Employees value completing a *whole* piece of work with a definite, visible end or outcome; this fosters *task identity*.

Virtually all employees want to feel a sense of *achievement* by succeeding at the tasks they undertake. Success does not have to be final, so long as there is a sense of *purpose* (Organ and Greene, 1974) or of *progress* towards a goal (Locke, Cartledge, and Knerr, 1970). Gaining a sense of achievement or accomplishment requires measuring one's progress or competence against a standard. This is facilitated by the well known management practice of setting specific, challenging *goals* (Locke and Latham, 1983) for employees to reach. Successful achievement gives the individual a sense of competence and efficacy (Bandura, 1982; White, 1959).

The desire to achieve in reference to a standard is called *achievement motivation*. It differs from intrinsic motivation or interest in that the pleasure is derived from task mastery rather than from the task activity as such.

To know they have succeeded, employees need *feedback* regarding how well they are performing. (Obviously employees like positive feedback, meaning that they succeeded, better than negative feedback, meaning that they failed.) Feedback can come from a variety of sources. For example, the employee can measure the quantity and quality of his own work. In job enrichment studies, employees often are given the responsibility of inspecting their own output. Feedback can also be provided through direct client contact, through computer information systems, through colleagues and through supervisors. For feedback to be meaningful it must be accurate, believable, and informative (Ilgen, Fisher, and Taylor, 1979).

Employees want *clarity* in their assigned jobs so that they know what is expected of them and how they will be evaluated (the opposite of this is called role ambiguity). They also prefer *harmony or integration* of expectations among the different individuals and factions they deal with as opposed to its opposite: role conflict. There is some evidence that role clarity and harmony are fostered by allowing the employee to *participate* in work decisions (Schuler, 1980).

Pressure or strain (due to high work load and limited time) is usually thought of as a negative factor in job satisfaction, but the context in which it occurs seems to be crucial in determining how it is appraised. When combined with high autonomy, skill level, and responsibility, it is associated with job satisfaction; whereas when it is combined with low autonomy, skill level, and responsibility, it is associated with job dissatisfaction (Karasek, 1979). *Physical fatigue* is generally disvalued in repetitive manual work. Such work is gradually being replaced in technologically advanced countries by automatized machines, including robots.

Pay

Working for money is the paradigm case of *extrinsic motivation*; the individual performs the task in order to get some other value. The value of money derives from its role as a medium of exchange; it is used to buy other values. In addition money has symbolic value, e.g., as a measure of competence within the market system or of the success of the organization as a whole. All employment involves entrinsic motiviation, in that if people were not paid (and did not expect to be paid in the future) they would not show up for work at all.

It should be stressed that most jobs entail a combination of extrinsic achievement and intrinsic motivation. Achievement motivation can be built into any job by the use of goal setting. Intrinsic motivation can be facilitated through appropriate selection and placement procedures and through job design. While some theorists have argued that extrinsic motivation can undermine intrinsic motivation, this writer takes the position that the more types of motivation the better. Thus the ideal case would involve the promotion of all three types.

Employees want, above all, a payment system which is *fair or equitable* (Lawler, 1971). The wider value at stake is that of *justice*. Again, employees differ among themselves as to what they consider to be fair, but typically this includes: fairness in the relative pay of different jobs within the same company; fairness in granting pay or merit raises (Dittrich and Carrell, 1979); and fairness in relation to the market price (employees paid below the market price for their location will feel underpaid). In organizations which have incentive systems, the same principle applies: the rates should be set fairly and changed only for an objectively defensible reason.

Even when the pay system is perceived as fair, employees will not necessarily be satisfied unless the pay is enough to *meet their expenses* (in the context of their preferred life style).

The principle of equity also applies to *benefits* which are an indirect form of payment. What employees feel is equitable depends on what is typically available in the job market. The typical benefit package in the U.S. now includes: pension, medical insurance, paid holidays and annual leave, unemployment insurance, and perquisites which amount to between 30% and 66% of base salary (Strauss and Sayles, 1980).

Employees also value *job security* which really means pay security. Organizational changes (such as incentive systems, automatization) are often resisted because employees fear that they will result in lay-offs. It is important to note that complete job security can never be guaranteed. In times of economic crisis when a particular company is failing, there may be no alternative to lay-offs. Even government workers can be laid off. However, through careful manpower planning and product mix, lay-offs can often be minimized, especially in large companies.

Promotion

Not every worker wants to be promoted. Promotion means increased responsibility, sometimes less pay (e.g., for a foreman as compared to a skilled worker on incentive pay), and always more headaches (especially role conflict due to the conflicting demands of the workers below and the managers above).

A recent study has shown that, despite their managerial status, the job satisfaction of middle managers in the U.S. has been declining rapidly in recent years (Opinion Research Corporation, 1980). They feel less secure in their jobs, more sceptical of the fairness of the promotion systems, more frustrated by communication blocks between themselves and higher management, and less confident in the ability of those above them. They feel that they have too little authority to deal with the problems below them and too little knowledge of what is going on above.

But promotion still appeals to those who want a chance to grow and achieve. As in the case of pay, employees want promotions to be given *fairly*. In unionized firms fairness is often defined in terms of seniority rather than merit. Fairness properly means: promotion for the most qualified. Individuals who are technically competent may not make good managers unless they also have (or are given training in) good managerial skills, including the ability to manage other people.

Recognition

Virtually every employee wants to be recognized. Tangibly this can come in the form of pay rises and promotions, but employees want verbal recognition as well. The wider values involved are those of *justice* and *visibility*. An employee wants to *know* that his employer or boss personally appreciates his work.

Recognition can be provided in many forms: giving credit for an accomplishment, praise, a letter (with a copy put in the personnel file), a public announcement at a company function or in the company paper, or an informal pat on the back with a 'Thanks, Joe; I really appreciate it'.

Many managers make the mistake of taking good work for granted and recognizing, in a negative way, only bad work. The implication of such a practice is that *bad work is more important than good work*. The result may be: more bad work.

Even the average employee can and should receive recognition, although in this case the managers must be very careful not to mislead the employee into thinking he is a top performer. For example, if the employee is very reliable but an average producer, he should be praised for his reliability, not for his productivity.

Working Conditions and the Work Environment

There are many different elements involved here. Employees want sufficient *resources* (time, money, equipment, help, etc.) to be able to do their jobs effectively. Resources, of course, are always limited; thus decisions must be made as to how to distribute them fairly, although the ultimate standard must be the needs and goals of the organization.

Employees prefer *work hours* which are maximally *compatible with their valued activities outside of work*—thus the great popularity of flexitime (Golembiewski and Proehl, 1978) and part-time work. Such schedules allow employees maximum freedom to integrate their jobs with the rest of their lives.

Shift work (other than regular day shift) is typically disliked (Frost and Jamal, 1979). It usually interferes with the employees' usual off-the-job routine and may be associated with physical and emotional problems, e.g., sleep and digestive disorders. Many innovative techniques have been developed to deal with this problem, including alternating periods of concentrated work (e.g., twelve-hour days) and concentrated time off (e.g., four to seven days). This does not eliminate the problem so much as compensate for it by providing other values not usually found in non-shift jobs.

As a mimimum the physical conditions of work (noise, air, hazards, etc.) should not threaten the *physical well being* of employees. This requires the elimination of unsafe conditions, the enforcement of safety rules and safety monitoring.

Some recent research indicates that many or most employees prefer closed to open offices (Oldham and Brass, 1978; Sundstrom, Burt, and Kamp, 1980). There are at least two major reasons for this: open offices inhibit *concentration* due to the higher noise level and continual interruptions, and they reduce *privacy*.

Most employees prefer work locations close to home, clean, spacious work areas, and aesthetically attractive surroundings.

Coworkers and Subordinates

Employees prefer coworkers who *share their values* to those who do not, but close personal friendships are not essential for smooth organizational functioning. Coworkers who are polite and friendly, as a minimum, and who share the same work goals and standards may be enough to ensure that they will *co-operate* in getting the job done. From the point of view of managers or supervisors, *reliability and competence* on the part of subordinates is essential to getting their (the manager's) job done.

Management and Supervision

One recent study found that attitudes toward management had a greater effect on employee morale than any other aspect of the job (Ruch, 1979). This finding is not surprising if one considers that management is not a separate element of the job, but is the agent or agents which are (or at least are held to be) responsible for all of the foregoing job elements (Locke and Whiting, 1974). It is management which does recruiting and selects the employees (within the constraints set by law). It is management which designs training programmes. It is management which directly or indirectly designs the work and provides the rewards. It is management which chooses or designs the work environment. In short, it is their actions and policies (within the context of their power) which determine what values are available to employees and how they are to be attained.

Fundamentally, employees will have a positive attitude toward management to the degree that they believe management is *considerate*, (which means *facilitates the achievement of their values*); and will dislike management to the degree that it blocks or negates value attainment or gives them things they do not want (such as dangerous working conditions). From the point of view of management, being aware of and willing to act on the workers' values and knowledge is the essence of *showing respect* for the employees as human beings. Respect, among other things, implies *honesty*.

From the point of view of the employees, management honesty results in *trust* (Muchinsky, 1977). Trust is the expectation that one will be dealt with honestly and fairly. It can only be earned through action, e.g., through fairness in administering rewards and promotions, through keeping promises, through telling the truth, (e.g., giving the real reasons for decisions), through making rational decisions, through ensuring that words and actions are consistent, through giving the same information to all parties, etc.

Trust is greatly facilitated by good *communications* with employees. The quality of communications between management and employees have been found to have a major impact on job satisfaction (Downs, 1979; Muchinsky, 1977). Most employees are especially anxious to know: how their work fits into the total activity of the organization; the reasons behind important company decisions; the plans and objectives of their organization; how they can improve their work performance; and how the pay system works (Opinion Research Corporation, 1980). About two-thirds of employees in the U.S. feel that their organizations do not do a good job of giving them such information. Most employees would prefer to get such information from their immediate supervisors but typically get it, when they can, through the grapevine.

Ideally communications should be two-way rather than one-way (up and down rather than just down; or better yet, up, down, lateral and diagonal). The reason for this is that a one-way procedure implies omniscience on the part of management. Managers cannot possibly know everything that goes on among the people below them, thus decisions which are made without this knowledge (where such knowledge is relevant) may be poor ones. When downward communication occurs, it should be truthful and sufficiently frequent so that employees know what is going on.

Participation in decision-making has frequently been mentioned as a determinant of job satisfaction and there is some evidence for this view, with about 60% of the studies showing a positive association (Locke and Schweiger,

1979; it should be noted that these authors, in a lengthy review of the literature, found relatively weak evidence for the effects of participation on productivity). Participation, when used to describe organizational functioning, refers to joint decision-making, typically between supervisor and subordinate.

Note that the concept of participation does not specify what the participation is about. The content could be anything from work methods to performance appraisal to the pay system. The effects of participative decision-making on job satisfaction should be a function of: (a) the importance of the issues or values involved; and (b) the degree to which the subordinate is able to influence the supervisor to give the subordinate the desired values. If the values involved are trivial or if the subordinate is not articulate or persuasive enough to convince the supervisor of his or her views (of if the supervisor is not open-minded enough to listen), then participation may have no effect, or even a negative effect (if it is seen as a phoney gesture).

It is reasonable to assume that employees who are perceived as more competent by their bosses are more likely to be given the opportunity to participate in decision-making than those perceived as less competent. This is not surprising since the more competent employees will generally be liked better and have better ideas than the less competent ones. In line with this hypothesis, Schilit and Locke (1982) found, in a study of upward influence attempts, that supervisors who were influenced successfully by their subordinates were more likely to describe them as competent than those who were not successfully influenced.

Unions

Relatively few studies have examined the relationship between union membership and job satisfaction. Probably the most thorough and theoretically sophisticated study to date is that by Berger, Olson, and Boudreau (1981) using data from a national probability sample. They found that union members valued pay more, received higher wages, and more fringe benefits, and had greater pay satisfaction than non-union members. Union members saw supervisors as less supportive and facilitative and were therefore less satisfied with them than were non-union members. Those in unions also saw their work as less interesting and were therefore less satisfied with it than were non-members. Finally, union members placed less value on promotion and were less satisfied with promotions than were employees who were not union members. These findings are consistent with the view that unions affect satisfaction in the same manner (though not necessarily in the same direction) as employers: by affecting the employee's values or their opportunity to gain values from the organization.

The foregoing points are summarized in Table 4 along with a brief statement of the wider value or need on which each particular value is based and some suggested means of implementing these values.

Table 4. Major job values and ways to implement them

Job aspect	Job value	Wider value or need	Ways to implement
Work	Personal interest	Pleasure	Recruiting, selection, placement, job enrichment, goal setting, participation in decision making
	Importance		
	Chance to use skills	Growth	
	Responsibility		
	Autonomy		
	Variety		
	Achievement, progress	Self esteem	
	Feedback	Efficacy	
	Clarity		
	Harmony		
	Participation		
	Pressure		
	Fatigue avoidance	Physical well being	Design of workplace
Pay and benefits	Fairness	Justice, need satisfaction	Job analysis; wage surveys; objective work measurement or performance ratings; high pay and benefits; incentive plans
	Job security		Manpower planning

Promotions	Fairness	Justice, visibility, growth	Promotion on merit
Recognition	Recognition	Justice, visibility	Praise and credit for work and effort
Working conditions	Resources Hours Shift work($-$) Safe physical conditions Privacy	Helps to get work done Helps get off-the-job values Interferes with home life, health Health, well being Facilitates concentration; privacy	Provide resources Flexitime, four-day week Compensation (through pay, time off) Remove hazards, safety programmes Closed office design
Coworkers/subordinates	Similarity Competence, co-operation	Friendship Helps get work done	Recruiting, selection, placement Same as above, plus training
Management/supervision	Respect Trust Two-way communication Provide above values	Self-esteem See above	Being honest with employees; concerned with their wants Consistent honesty Listening to employees Participation, influence
Unions	Pay	See above	Higher pay, benefits

JOB SATISFACTION: WHOSE RESPONSIBILITY?

An increasingly popular view today is that job satisfaction is the employee's 'right' which the organization that he works for is duty-bound to provide. Some people have even urged that legislation be passed which would penalize organizations which do not provide sufficient job satisfaction for their work force (see Locke, 1976a, for a further discussion of this issue).

The present writer opposes this view because of its coercive implications. Job satisfaction is viewed here as the responsibility of both employer and employee; by responsibility is meant that it is worth pursuing from the viewpoint of the rational self-interest of both parties.

It is important to note, in this regard, that while there is no fundamental conflict of interest between employer and employee (Rand, 1962), their priorities are not identical. From the standpoint of the employee, his own job satisfaction is an end in itself, while the satisfaction of his employer is a partial means to that end. For the employer, his own satisfaction is an end in itself, while employee satisfaction is a partial means to that end.

Consider the employee first. His goal is to achieve his own happiness. One of the ways he achieves it is through his job. To get satisfaction from his job, he must get the things he wants out of it. But to get these things he has to do what his employer wants; for example, to get raises and promotions, he has to do competent work. Thus, at least, in a well-integrated organization, the employee achieves some of his own goals by helping his employer to achieve the employer's goals.

Observe that the employer's goals could not be the employee's primary goals; if they were, the employee would be willing to work endless hours on tasks he disliked for below market wages—a course of action which would negate the employee's happiness.

The employer also wants to achieve his own happiness. One of the ways he achieves it is by getting the organization to succeed in achieving its goals. In the private sector, the ultimate goal is profitability, whereas in the public sector it is the fulfilment of the organization's function (e.g., the function of the police is to protect people from criminals). Employee morale is a means to these ends. Without a reasonable degree of employee satisfaction an organization would not be able to recruit, retain or gain the co-operation and involvement of a competent work force (Likert, 1967). In cases of extreme employee dissatisfaction, it might be faced with union militancy and strikes or worse.

The morale of his employees could not be an employer's primary goal, however. Imagine the consequences if an organization's major focus were to provide every employee with everything he 'wanted', without regard to context, e.g., in the areas of pay, promotions, hours of work, benefits, equipment, coworkers, etc. Conflict and chaos would be the result—not to mention low productivity, high costs, and ultimate bankruptcy.

Both the employee and the employer want to achieve their own satisfaction with the help of the other; but each must give the other something in return in order to get it. The employee–employer relationship is a form of trade with each party offering a value (e.g., time and effort) in return for a value (e.g., money). Each attempts to influence the terms in order to protect his own interests.

This difference in priorities, while not a fundamental conflict of interest, implies the possibility of disagreement over particulars. A given individual may not always want to help an organization attain its goals, while an organization may not always want or be able to concern itself with employee job satisfaction. On the other hand, each has a means of protecting its own ultimate interests in the matter. A dissatisfied employee may quit the organization, while an organization may fire an employee with whom it is not satisfied.

The respective responsibilities of employee and employer are summarized in Table 5.

Table 5.   Joint responsibility for job satisfaction

The individual's responsibility
1. A rational code of values: including wants which do not contradict needs or reality or the individual's abilities.
2. Rational expectations: e.g., that value attainment cannot be guaranteed, that rewards are not always automatic or immediate.
3. Proper choice of job and willingness to change jobs when previous choices do not work out.
4. Conscientious efforts to obtain values on the job through sustained, competent performance, and rational persuasion.

The organization's responsibility
1. Realistic job previews given to job applicants; pre-employment promises kept.
2. Proper selection and placement and willingness to make changes when selection and placement errors occur.
3. Reasonable provision of job values through:
    (a) identifying what employees want, and
    (b) providing these values as a condition of employment, or
    (c) providing these values in return for competent performance.
4. Giving honest and justifiable reasons for inability to provide certain job values.

Let us consider the individual first. To attain satisfaction the individual must have rational values, that is values that do not contradict his needs or reality. For example, an employee cannot rationally advocate contradictions, such as a merit system for others and favouritism for himself. Nor can he rationally expect a promotion, if he lacks the ability to perform the job in question, or a higher salary than either the market price or that which the organization can afford to pay.

Second, the individual must have rational expectations regarding the attainment of his values. For example, rewards cannot always be guaranteed or be given immediately after a goal is attained. Nor does every effort always pay off. An individual may work very hard on a product for a year only to find that, when marketed, it does not sell. Despite the hard work, a reward is not mandated in such circumstances. And even if the product did sell and a promotion were deserved, a position might not open up in the immediate future.

Third, the individual is responsible for choosing carefully the career and job that he selects. The employee–organizational match is as much the employee's task as the organization's. Successful career and job choice requires good decision-making techniques (e.g., see Wheeler and Janis, 1980). In addition, the individual must be willing to change careers and/or jobs or to adapt to change if previous choices do not work out as expected. There can be no guarantee, after a person makes a career choice, that one, five, or 25 years later conditions will not change in ways that no one could have predicted.

Fourth, in whatever career or job a person chooses, he must make conscientious efforts to obtain the desired values through appropriate action, especially sustained competent performance, and rational persuasion. Values go to those who work for them. However, it should be recorded that lower levels of the blue collar and white collar ranks contain many individuals who, despite the possession of ability or potential, are not willing to take the actions which their professed values require, or who do not have ambitious values at all. They may suffer not just from material impoverishment but also from *value impoverishment*. They do not want much, and/or are not willing to work for much and, as a result, do not get much. On the basis of his studies of the mental health of the industrial worker, Kornhauser concludes:

'... the unsatisfactory mental health of working people consists in no small measure of their dwarfed desires and deadened initiative, reduction of their goals and restriction of their efforts to a point where life is relatively empty and only half meaningful' (Kornhauser, 1965, p. 270).

Now consider the organization's responsibilities. First, it is in its own interest to give realistic pre-employment job previews to prospective employees (Wanous, 1980). Such previews allow employees to better match themselves with the job and to be aware of what they can realistically expect once hired. In addition, it is important that pre-employment (as well as post-employment) promises be kept. If such promises are made contingently, the contingencies should be spelled out (e.g., 'We should be able to promote you within two years, *assuming* that we continue our present rate of growth').

Second, the organization will benefit from proper selection of employees. It should insure that the employees it hires have the skills needed to perform effectively (or are given these skills through training); that they have the motivation to use these skills; and that their long-term goals are compatible with organizational opportunities (Hannan, 1980).

Third, the organization will foster satisfaction most effectively if it first identifies what it is that its employees want and then attempts, within reason and the limitations of cost, to provide the employees with what they want (e.g., a safe work environment, fair pay) or with the opportunity to earn what they want.

Fourth, an organization will benefit greatly from being honest and truthful with its employees with respect to the values it can and will offer and with respect to the reasons for its inability to provide the values it cannot offer. In practice, no organization could possibly satisfy all of the job values of all of its employees. All employees do not want the same things, thus satisfying one employee can sometimes dissatisfy another (e.g., overtime work). Further, an organization cannot use all of its resources to make employees happy when it has to compete in the market place to make a product or provide a service. In addition not all of the values of all employees are necessarily rational (e.g., one employee might want a large pay rise despite being incompetent and unreliable), so that trying to satisfy them would be self-destructive for the organization. And, employee values can change over time; keeping up with such changes (which occur to different degrees and at different rates in different employees) can be very difficult.

The best an organization can do is to choose employees who like what the organization offers and to offer what is reasonable in the context of their knowledge, time, and financial position. If a given organization does significantly less well at the job of satisfying employees than most other organizations, the market will force it to conform eventually, since (except in times of high unemployment) it will lose many of its best employees. Most organizations can compensate to a considerable degree for value deficits in one area by providing more in another area. For example, small organizations often cannot afford to pay as much as large ones, but they can offer other values that are harder for large, bureaucratized companies to provide: such as a personal relationship with the owner and job variety and flexibility (Ingham, 1970). Government organizations often compensate for dull work and 'politics' with generous fringe benefits and job security. While these may not make the employees work harder, it keeps them in the organization.

REFERENCES

Arnold, M. B. (1960) *Emotion and personality: psychological aspects*, Columbia U. Press, New York, Volume 1.
Bandura, A. (1982) Self efficacy mechanism in human agency. *American Psychologist*, **37**, 122–147.
Beehr, T. A., and Gupta, N. (1978) A note on the structure of employee withdrawal. *Organizational Behavior and Human Performance*, **21**, 73–79.
Berger, C. J., Olson, C. A., and Boudreau, J. W. (1981) *Effects of unions on job satisfaction: The role of work related values and perceived rewards*. Graduate School of Management, Purdue University.
Brett, J. M. (1980) Why employees want unions. *Organizational Dynamics*, **8(4)**, 47–59.
Cook, R., Walizer, D., and Mace, D. (1976) Illicit drug use in the Army: a social-organizational analysis. *Journal of Applied Psychology*, **61**, 262–272.

Dittrich, J. E., and Carrell, M. R. (1979) Organizational equity perceptions, employee job satisfaction, and departmental absence and turnover rates. *Organizational Behavior and Human Performance*, **24**, 29–40.

Downs, C. W. (1979) The relationship between communication and job satisfaction, in Husemen, R. C., Loque, C. M., and Frashley, D. L. (eds.) *Readings in Interpersonal and Organizational Communication*, Allyn & Bacon, Boston.

Frost, P. J., and Jamal, M. (1979) Shift work, attitudes, and reported behavior: some associations between individual characteristics and hours of work and leisure. *Journal of Applied Psychology*, **64**, 77–81.

Golembiewski, R. T., and Proehl, C. W. (1978) A survey of the empirical literature on flexible workhours: character and consequences of a major innovation. *Academy of Management Review*, **3**, 837–853.

Gruneberg, M. M. (1979) *Understanding Job Satisfaction*, Wiley, New York.

Hackman, J. R., and Oldham, G. R. (1980) *Work Redesign*, Addison-Wesley, Reading, MA.

Hannan, R. L. (1980) Measures of expected work motivation as an alternative to written ability tests for federal personnel selection. *Personnel Research Report 80–24*, U.S. Office of Personnel Management, Washington DC.

Herzberg, F. (1966) *Work and the Nature of Man*, World Pub. Co., Cleveland.

Ilgen, D. R., Fisher, C. D., and Taylor, M. S. (1979) Consequences of individual feedback on behavior in organizations. *Journal of Applied Psychology*, **64**, 349–371.

Ingham, G. K. (1970) *Size of Industrial Organization and Worker Behaviour*, Cambridge University Press, Cambridge.

Karasek, R. A. (1979) Job demands, job decision latitude, and mental strain: implications for job redesign. *Administrative Science Quarterly*, **24**, 285–308.

Kornhauser, A. (1965) *Mental Health of the Industrial Worker*, Wiley, New York.

Lawler, E. E. (1971) *Pay and Organizational Effectiveness: a Psychological View*, McGraw-Hill, New York.

Likert, R. (1967) *The Human Organization*, McGraw-Hill, New York.

Locke, E. A. (1976a) The case against legislating the quality of work life. *The Personnel Administrator*, **21(4)**, 19–21(a).

Locke, E. A. (1976b) The nature and causes of job satisfaction, in Dunnette, M. D. (ed.) *Handbook of industrial and organizational psychology*, Rand McNally, Chicago.

Locke, E. A. (1977) The myths of behavior mod in organizations. *Academy of Management Review*, **2**, 543–553.

Locke, E. A. (1980) Behaviorism and psychoanalysis: two sides of the same coin. *The Objectivist Forum*, **1(1)**, 10–15.

Locke, E. A. (1983) A new look at work motivation: theory V, in Franke, R. (ed). *The Science of Productivity*, Jossey-Bass, San Francisco (in press).

Locke, E. A., and Latham, G. P. (1983) *Goal setting: A Key to Employee Productivity*, Prentice Hall, Englewood Cliffs, N.J.

Locke, E. A., and Schweiger, D. M. (1979) Participation in decision-making: one more look, in Staw, B. M. (ed.) *Research in Organizational Behavior*, JAI Press, Greenwich CT, Volume 1.

Locke, E. A., and Whiting, R. J. (1974) Sources of satisfaction and dissatisfaction among solid waste management employees. *Journal of Applied Psychology*, **59**, 145–156.

Locke, E. A., Cartledge, N., and Knerr, C. S. (1970) Studies of the relationship between satisfaction, goal setting, and performance. *Organizational Behavior and Human Performance*, **5**, 135–158.

Mangione, T. W., and Quinn, R. P. (1975) Job satisfaction, counterproductive behavior, and drug use at work. *Journal of Applied Psychology*, **60**, 114–116.

Mobley, W. H., and Locke, E. A. (1970) The relationship of value importance to satisfaction. *Organizational Behavior and Human Performance*, **5**, 463–483.

Mobley, W. H., Griffeth, R. W., Hand, H. H., and Meglino, B. M. (1979) Review and conceptual analysis of the employee turnover process. *Psychological Bulletin*, **86**, 493–522.

Muchinsky, P. M. (1977) Organizational communication: relationships to organizational climate and job satisfaction. *Academy of Management Journal*, **20**, 592–607.

Nicholson, N., Brown, C., and Chadwick-Jones, J. (1976) Absence from work and job satisfaction. Journal of Applied Psychology, **61**, 728–737.

O'Brien, G. E. (1980) The centrality of skill utilization for job design, in Duncan, K., Gruneberg, M., and Wallis, D. (eds.) *Changes in Working Life*, Wiley, Chichester, England.

Oldham, G. R., and Brass, D. J. (1979) Employee reactions to an open-plan office: a naturally occurring quasi-experiment. *Administrative Science Quarterly*, **24**, 267–284.

Opinion Research Corporation (1980) *Strategic Planning for Human Resources: 1981 and Beyond*, Princeton, N.J.

Organ, D. W., and Greene, C. N. (1974) The perceived purposefulness of job behavior: antecedents and consequences. *Academy of Management Journal*, **17**, 69–78.

Rand, A. (1962) The 'conflicts' of men's interests. *The Objectivist Newsletter*, **1(8)**, 31ff.

Rand, A. (1964) *The Virtue of Selfishness*, Signet, New York.

Rand, A. (1974) From my 'future' file. *The Ayn Rand Letter*, **3 (No. 26)**, 3–4.

Ruch, R. S. (1979) A path analytic study of the structure of employee job satisfaction: the critical role of top management. *Journal of Vocational Behavior*, **15**, 277–293.

Schilit, W. K., and Locke, E. A. (1982) A study of upward influence in organizations. *Administrative Science Quarterly*,**27**, 304–316.

Schuler, R. S. (1980) A role and expectancy perception model of participation in decision making. *Academy of Management Journal*, **23**, 331–340.

Skaggs, G., and Lissitz, R. W. (1981) *Discriminant and convergent validation of behavioral tendencies approach to determining job satisfaction.* Department of Measurement, Statistics, and Evaluation. University of Maryland.

Strauss, G., and Sayles, L. R. (1980) *Personnel* (4th edn.), Prentice Hall, Englewood Cliffs, N.J.

Sundstrom, E., Burt, R. E., and Kamp, D. (1980) Privacy at work: architectural correlates of job satisfaction and job performance. *Academy of Management Journal*, **23**, 101–117.

Vroom, V. (1964) *Work and Motivation*, Wiley, New York.

Wall, T. D., Stephenson, G. M., and Skidmore, C. (1971) Ego-involvement and Herzberg's two-factor theory of job satisfaction: an experimental field study. *British Journal of Social and Clinical Psychology*, **10**, 123–131.

Wanous, J. P. (1980) *Organizational Entry*, Addison-Wesley, Reading, MA.

Wheeler, D. D., and Janis, I. K. (1980) *A Practical Guide for Making Decisions.* Macmillan (Free Press), New York.

White, R. W. (1959) Motivation reconsidered: the concept of competence. *Psychological Review*, **66**, 297–333.

White, F. M., and Locke, E. A. (1981) Perceived determinants of high and low productivity in three occupational groups: a critical incident study. *Journal of Management Studies*, **18**, 375–387.

Social Psychology and Organizational Behaviour
Edited by M. Gruneberg and T. Wall
© 1984 John Wiley & Sons Ltd

Chapter 6

Formal and Informal Structure

R. MANSFIELD

There can be little doubt that the basic structure of organizations has a pervasive and significant effect on most aspects of organizational processes, and on the behaviour and attitudes of individual organizational members. In the present context the view taken of structure is a broad one encompassing not just the basic shape of the organization, as shown on an organization chart, but also the institutionalized procedures by which it is governed. Although all social systems have structures, organizations tend to be unique in as much as their structures, to a very considerable extent, can be said to be deliberately designed by those with authority in the system.

It is also clear that organizations differ very considerably in the structural arrangements adopted within them. Examination of a variety of organizations typically reveals marked differences in such factors as the number of levels in the hierarchy, the number of workers reporting to first line supervisors, the extent of specialization, the degree of bureaucracy, and the distribution of decision-making authority. The fact that organizational structures vary in this way raises two very important questions. First, what forces and constraints operate to create particular structural patterns in any given case? Second, what are the implications of the arrangements adopted. The purpose of the present chapter is to try to answer these two questions. However, before attempting to suggest the nature of the answers it is useful to consider the nature of organizations themselves, and also to outline in greater detail what is meant by the idea of structure in the organizational setting.

Examination of the very extensive literature on organizations reveals a large number of definitions. However, within the variety offered there would seem to be considerable commonalities. It is therefore possible to suggest that organizations generally are conceptualized as relatively enduring social systems which are purposive and hierarchical. As the characteristics of purposiveness and hierarchy are vital to the discussion that follows it is worthwhile to consider these concepts further before moving on.

It must first be noted that organizations are not people, nor are they like them in having motives and ambitions. Clearly then, organizational goals are not conceptually the same or even similar to individual goals. Perhaps the most convenient and useful way of defining organizational goals is in terms of those objectives that an organization is ostensibly designed to achieve. As such they need not be identical with the goals of senior management, or indeed of anyone else in the organization. However, in the majority of cases the goals of the organization as defined above will be exceedingly similar to the goals for the organization of the senior management group, particularly when there is a large measure of agreement among such senior managers on what the organization should be designed to achieve. However, it should not be forgotten, as Hall has argued, that:

> '. . . even in an organization in which there is high participation in decision-making and strong membership commitment, it is unlikely that there will be a totally unanimous consensus on what the organization should attempt to do' (Hall, 1972, p. 80).

It should also be noted that the goals that senior managers have for their organization will be different from their personal goals, although it is clear that these will influence one another. In particular it is likely that the personal goals of senior managers will greatly affect the ways in which they try to move the organization or modify its objectives.

Organizational goals may be analysed in two categories (Perrow, 1961). First there are the official or charter goals which are usually stated formally in written documents such as the royal charter of a university or the articles of association of a public company. Examination of such documents shows that in the vast majority of cases charter goals tend to be stated in very general and vague terms. The effect of this in most cases is that charter goals serve only the limited purpose of defining the broad type of activity which is legitimate in a particular organizational context. What they do not typically provide is any clear indication of what strategies should be developed or guidelines for choosing between alternative strategies.

The second type are referred to by Perrow as operational goals. These are in essence the goals the organization, or more accurately its members, appear to be trying to achieve. As such the assessment of operational goals may be useful for the observer as a way of understanding the nature of organizational processes. On the other hand it should be noted that operational goals seen in this light are not the basis for strategic decision-making, rather they are inferred from the results of such decision-making.

Turning now to the question of hierarchy it must be noted that what is implied is that organizations are differentiated into levels in terms of authority. That is to say those at the top of the hierarchy have authority over those at lower levels. It must be realized that in most if not all organizations there are many sources of power (Pettigrew, 1973), and that it is not necessarily the case that those at higher levels have more power than their subordinates, as is sometimes demonstrated in industrial disputes. In the case of authority, however, the situation is somewhat different and it is in the nature of organizations that they have a monolithic authority structure. Typically this authority system is legitimized in terms of the rules of the organization, that is it is a system of rational-legal authority (Weber, 1947). It should be noted that in joining an organization whether as an employee or as some other sort of member (e.g., as a member of a trade union) an individual typically agrees to accept the rules of the organization and the authority relationships that such rules define. However, the fact that the hierarchy usually has such a contractual basis does not make the acceptance of directives or instructions non-problematic.

The conclusion then is that rational-legal authority is the cement which holds together the human building blocks of formal organizations even though such authority may be challenged from time to time. It is convenient for simplicity to refer to those holding positions of authority in organizations of all types as managers whether that term is commonly employed in a particular type of organization or not. Thus trade union officials, senior civil servants and hospital administrators can all be seen to exercise a managerial function and hence carry out similar duties *vis-à-vis* their organization as do those described as managers in industrial companies.

THE NATURE OF ORGANIZATIONAL STRUCTURES

As we have already noted all organizations are structured, and such structures stem in large measure from deliberate design processes. That is to say that the structural blueprint for any organization emanates from managerial decision-making processes. This being the case the particular structural arrangements arrived at may be viewed in terms of attempted answers to the problems which management confronts. Although these problems will vary in detail both between organizations and over time in a single organization, they can be seen to be variants of three generic issues which one way or another have to be confronted in any organization. First there is the basic problem of getting things done or achieving organizational objectives. For example, in a car company a system must be devised to ensure that cars are actually designed, manufactured, and sold. This inevitably means that a large number and variety of sub-tasks must be carried out. The second problem is that of control. Obviously the first and second problems are substantially interlocked in that control will be necessary to achieve task accomplishment. The third problem is that of cost. To be effective, indeed to survive, organizations must operate within cost limits even if these are not clearly defined. It must be noted that structural arrangements not only provide mechanisms for the monitoring and control of operating costs they also have direct implications for cost. Indeed it can be said that one of the penalties of co-ordinated or organized activity is that the very process of organizing incurs costs if only in the time and effort spent in its achievement. In large organizations, of course, the cost of administration can be very considerable both in absolute money terms and also as a percentage of the total operating cost.

These three problems influence organizations in different ways and constrain decision-making to varying extents, depending on the market forces and social, political, and economic processes to which the organization is subject. With these problems in mind we can now turn our attention to examining different aspects of structure. Clearly organization structures are complex phenomena which can be examined from a variety of different standpoints and analytically broken down in different ways. The literature reveals a number of approaches to the general problem of analysing structural arrangements and a plethora of different concepts of the underlying dimensions of structure. At the present time it is not possible to say that any particular approach is necessarily better than any other, although some seem to have been very much more influential in shaping the development of empirical research and theoretical ideas than others.

Following Weber's (1946) essay on bureaucracy, which has dominated much of the thinking in this area, many of the early approaches tended to try to characterize whole organizational structures to form typologies very often in terms of variants of bureaucracy or modifications to the bureaucratic type. Thus Gouldner (1954) identified three categories of structure which he referred to as mock bureaucracy, representative bureaucracy, and punishment-centred bureaucracy; and later Burns and Stalker (1961) classified organizational structures as mechanistic (similar to bureaucratic) and organismic. Such an approach focussed attention on some of the key features of structural arrangements but did not form a suitable basis for large scale research or for the examination of the full complexities of the phenomenon in question.

Subsequently attention was turned in a different direction and attempts were made to determine the component aspects or dimensions of structure such that these could be empirically examined and compared across large samples of organizations. This latter approach has tended to dominate more recent work in the field and is the basis for most of our present knowledge concerning organizational structure. Inevitably, different commentators have suggested different approaches to the isolation of such dimensions based either on the factor analysis of large amounts of data or on theoretical ideas, or some combination of the two (e.g., Pugh, Hickson, Hinings, and Turner, 1968).

The study of the dimensions of structure has been complicated not merely by the variety of approaches and concepts that have been employed but also by a certain amount of terminological confusion in that writers have not only used different labels for similar concepts but also the same names for different concepts. There have also been a number of different approaches to the problem of measurement which have added further complexity to the field. Rather than proceed by examining a number of these approaches it is perhaps most useful to consider the basic logic of organizations in order to gain an overview of how these different suggested dimensions interrelate.

The Division of Labour

One of the basic reasons for the existence of organizations would seem to be that they allow a co-ordinated division of labour between functions and between persons carrying out those functions. Indeed this seems so fundamental that some writers (e.g., Porter, Lawler, and Hackman, 1975) have incorporated the idea within their definition of organizations. The nature of the division of labour within organizations both between individuals and between departments (or sections) is clearly of importance both for task accomplishment and for the maintenance of organizational control. One critical aspect of this is the basic logic by which such a division of labour proceeds. Perhaps the most common basis is in terms of task or function, such that persons each perform a limited and specified task. A clear example of this is the motor car assembly line where the over-all task is split up into a large number of sub-tasks such as putting on wheels, bumpers, etc., each of which is carried out by an individual worker. A second relatively common form of division of labour is based on the product being manufactured or service provided, thus one might have a cost clerk for one type of car and another one for a different type. In this case the clerks would essentially be carrying out the same task or function but on different products. Alternatively the split in duties may be based on geography so that one has a salesman for London and another for Birmingham say, each carrying out the same task relating to the same product or service. The fourth relatively common reason behind a division of labour is based on the type of customer to be supplied. Thus one might have an accounts clerk for industrial customers and a different one carrying out the same task, relating to the same product in the same place for retail customers. Undoubtedly most organizations of any size employ more than one basis for sub-dividing the variety of work to be performed. Indeed in some of the largest companies all the methods mentioned are employed simultaneously in a complex mixture.

The logic implied in the division of labour is quite simply that, by sub-dividing tasks, those tasks can be carried out more effectively by being done better or faster or cheaper. This can occur for a variety of reasons such as those associated with the ability for individuals to learn one task more effectively than several, save time by not having to change from one activity or place to another, build up closer relationships with particular customers, or using machinery full time rather than part time. In theory at least increased specialization can aid task accomplishment and cut costs. However, in practice such benefits may not always be achieved due to a variety of factors, particularly where the division of labour results in very limited, boring jobs (see Chapter 8). Also of course the division of labour creates the need for communication and co-ordination which may cause difficulties and will certainly occasion some extra costs (see Chapter 5).

The division of labour in organizations is not just between different parts of the basic productive tasks which need to be carried out. In addition there is a division of labour between the carrying out of tasks and the control of those tasks. This further aspect of the division of labour takes two rather different forms. Most obviously in any organization there is some division between operatives and supervisors and managers, that is between those that basically carry out the directly productive work of the organization and those who are their hierarchical superiors who plan, co-ordinate, and control these directly productive activities. However, in many organizations, and in virtually all large ones, there is also a lateral division of labour between those functions such as production and sales which contribute directly to the task accomplishment of the organization and those functions such as inspection and accounting which together with management help to co-ordinate and control these former activities. This distribution which has been described frequently in the management literature is often referred to simply as the division between line and staff (e.g., Allen, 1956).

The various forms of the division of labour in organizations between individuals as well as between sections, departments and divisions has been conceptualized in a number of different ways and given rise to a wide variety of nomenclature. Among the many terms which have been used to describe aspects of the division of labour or its organizational manifestations are functional and role specialization (e.g., Pugh, Hickson, Hinings, and Turner, 1968), professionalization (e.g., Hage and Aiken, 1969), differentiation (e.g., Lawrence and Lorsch, 1967), departmentalization (Wheeler, Mansfield, and Todd, 1980), divisionalization (Chandler, 1962), and number of hierarchical levels or vertical span (e.g., Pugh, Hickson, Hinings, and Turner, 1968). In most instances there have been a variety of different ideas and different measures used to assess each of these terms. This proliferation of terminology, concepts, and measures is evidence no doubt of a certain amount of confusion as mentioned above, but also of the complexity of the division of labour phenomenon and its importance for organizational functioning. Why organizations or their managers opt for one form and extent of division of labour rather than another, and what implications such design decisions have on organizational effectiveness and the attitudes of participants, will clearly depend on a large number of factors both organizational and environmental. These issues will be considered further below.

Co-ordination

In the preceding section attention was focussed on different aspects of the division of labour, some elements of which at least are inherent in the very concept of organization and which must be essential if organizations are to be in any sense more effective in purposeful social action than collections of independent individuals. At this point it is necessary to switch attention to the structural mechanisms of co-ordination in organizations. Clearly some such mechanisms must be designed into organizations if they are in any real sense to be organized and hence survive as social systems. Broadly, in social systems generally, two types of mechanism have been identified. One depends on exchange relationships regulated by some sort of market forces, and the other depends on some kind of authority system (Williamson, 1975). Both are obviously ways in which different forms of power may under certain circumstances be channelled in reasonably stable ways. In the organizational setting both are relevant and both would seem to be employed by all organizations. However, it is often considered that market transactions characterize the dealings of organizations with their environments, while authority relationships characterize the internal workings of organizations. Such a division frequently stems from the way the concepts are defined. For example, Williamson (1975, p. xi), in the preface to his book on the subject, suggests that '... market transactions involve exchanges between autonomous economic entities' whereas authority relations which he refers to as 'hierarchical transactions' are ones for which '... a single administrative entity spans both sides of the transaction, some form of subordination prevails, and, typically, consolidated ownership obtains'. While such analytically pure distinctions may serve some theory building purposes they seem not to reflect the full complexity of reality. With increased state intervention and a plethora of regulatory agencies, few if any actors can really be said to be autonomous and few if any transactions are free of some sort of overarching legal or administrative constraints. On the other hand, probably no administrative systems are so all-encompassing as to render market forces irrelevant to internal transactions. The contention that will be followed here is that both authority relations and market forces are relevant to both internal organizational co-ordination and relationships between organizations and their environments. Indeed within the open system perspective (e.g., Katz and Kahn, 1966) it is not clear that it is possible to make clear-cut distinctions between internal and external transactions.

In the present context it is suggested that the internal co-ordination processes of most if not all organizations are based on an interactive combination of the dual forces of market exchange relationships and authority systems. As we have already pointed out, from the point of view of the typical organizational employee, the decision to join a particular organization involves as part of the deal the acceptance of the organizational authority system. In this respect there is a difference between the employment relationship and most other contractual transactions relating organizations to outside individuals and agencies. Rather than contracting to carry out specific tasks for a particular amount of money, the employee agrees to allow the employer the power to define the task in accordance with organizational needs as these develop in return for some regular form of income (Simon, 1957; Williamson, 1975). This is most clearly illustrated in the pure type of bureaucracy where the individual accepts a clearly defined authority structure according to set rules and procedures in exchange for a given salary.

In a sense then, one can see the logic of Williamson's contention that authority relations rather than market forces are the co-ordinating pressures within organizations, and indeed it fits with the argument advanced at the beginning of this chapter. However, that distinction does not take full account of the fact that the acceptance of authority is conditional on the rewarding of compliance. Further it must follow that the system for allocating rewards in the form of salaries, wages, bonuses, etc. is an important aspect of the structural arrangements for ensuring co-ordination. Of course, if it is wished to consider the full variety of organizational situations it must be acknowledged that the compliance of participants is not always ensured on the basis of an instrumental exchange relationship. As Etzioni (1961) pointed out, the compliance of inmates in prisons and other custodial institutions is ensured by coercive means and of acolytes in some religious organizations by moral forces. Although in some individual employment situations there may be a partial reliance on coercion and moral pressures it nonetheless remains that financial remuneration is at the heart of the employment relationship as it has evolved in modern society. However, it must be noted that the characteristics of reward systems are rarely considered in studies of organizational structure and hence our knowledge in this area is severely limited.

The authority system is essentially bureaucratic in form in any organization and depends on the rules and procedures of the organization. This is most clearly institutionalized in the hierarchical arrangement of organizational positions or offices into levels of subordination or superordination. The characteristics of the system of co-ordination stemming from bureaucratic authority have been assessed by organizational researchers using a range of concepts and terminology. It would seem that the most critical elements can be subsumed under three broad headings, namely bureaucracy, centralization, and integration.

In the Weberian description of the ideal type bureaucracy the two prime characteristics are impersonal standardized rules and procedures covering most contingencies, and a system of record keeping and files to act as a sort of collective memory of organizational actions. These two structural dimensions are referred to as standardization and formalization by the Aston group (Pugh, Hickson, Hinings, and Turner, 1968). However, as the term formalization has regularly been used in other senses (e.g., Hage and Aiken, 1969) the more everyday term of paperwork (Blau and Schoenherr, 1971) will be used in its place, even though in the modern electronic age records may be kept on magnetic tape or discs rather than on paper. Virtually all studies which have examined the relationship between standardization and the extent of paperwork have found that they are very strongly positively linked (e.g., Pugh, Hickson, Hinings, and

Turner, (1968), and Child (1971), report correlations of greater than 0.80). Indeed this relationship is so stable and so closely linked to the central conception of bureaucracy as described by Weber that it may be more convenient to refer to the two dimensions collectively as the extent of bureaucratization.

The second broad basis which has been used by social scientists in assessing aspects of the operation of the organizational authority system has tended to revolve around a consideration of the style and locus of decision-making. Again a variety of concepts, terms, and measures have been employed but the commonest would seem to refer to the extent of centralization of decision-making (although this is frequently termed in the opposite sense, i.e., decentralization of decision-making). The extent to which centralization was part of the original bureaucratic concept is a matter of considerable dispute. Many writers have stated or clearly implied that the Weberian notion of bureaucracy incorporates the idea of centralized decision-making (e.g., Hage and Aiken, 1967; Blau and Schoenherr, 1971; Pugh, Hickson, Hinings, and Turner, 1968). On the other hand Child (1971), interpreted Weber's analysis quite differently and suggested that it implied a negative relationship between centralization of decision-making and the amounts of rules, procedures, and paperwork. Although it does not seem fruitful to continue the argument about what Weber wrote or implied, the substantive point of debate is critical to our understanding of organizations.

Child (1971) has suggested that bureaucratization and centralization are evidence of different strategies of control in organizations and as such should be regarded if not as opposites at least as negatively related phenomena. Mansfield to some extent agrees with this when he suggests that:

'. . . it can be argued, paradoxically, that the only method by which the directorate in large organizations can retail over-all control of the organization's functioning is by decentralizing much of the decision-making within the framework of bureaucratic rules' (Mansfield, 1973, p. 478).

However, he goes on to suggest that the relationship is highly contingent on size (and possibly by implication other variables). This being the case the issue will be left until a later section in which the determinants of structures are considered.

In terms of the three basic problems for administration suggested above (i.e., task accomplishment, control and cost) then it is clear that decisions regarding the extent of bureaucratization and centralization in any given organization are made particularly in order to solve the second problem of control. Obviously such decisions may routinely start from consideration of the problems of achieving task accomplishment but the solutions involve using greater or different forms of control. Clearly the design decisions made with regard to these particular parameters of structure will also have cost implications. Most obviously bureaucratic mechanisms of control are expensive in an obvious and direct way due to the cost of paperwork itself and, usually more significantly, the salary costs of bureaucratic officials and their clerical assistants.

Before leaving the examination of structural dimensions designed to achieve co-ordination in organizations it is necessary to consider the range of structural integrative devices available to organizational designers in order to co-ordinate the work of different departments. Lawrence and Lorsch (1967), in their major study of differentiation and integration, suggested that increasing differentiation between functional departments created the need for enhanced integrative effort. They suggested that reliance on bureaucratic procedures alone was relatively minimal in and of itself as a form of integration. In some rudimentary ordering of structural mechanisms in terms of integrative effort they suggested *ad hoc* meetings, formal committees, liaison officers, and whole co-ordinating departments formed a sequence of higher levels of integration than pure reliance on hierarchy and procedure.

Clearly integrative effort must also be seen as operating primarily as a solution to the problem of control and hence assisting in task accomplishment via that route. Clearly significant integrative mechanisms such as whole departments created with the objective of linking the work of other departments will have very significant cost implications. Therefore such design characteristics will have to contribute significantly to the solution of the first two problems of organization in order to be justified given the extent to which they are likely to aggravate the third.

It can not be argued that the discussion of structural dimensions under the two general headings of division of labour and co-ordination is in any way exhaustive. However, it is hopefully adequate to illustrate the main ideas and issues.

Formal and Informal Structures

Historically a distinction was made between formal and informal organizational structures largely in terms of their origins. Formal structure encompassed those arrangements designed by management for the sound running of the organization whereas informal structure referred to those more or less regularized procedures which 'people in the organization have informally added' (Litterer, 1963, p. 138). There can be little doubt that the basis of such a distinction is real in that the structural arrangements laid down by those with organizational authority to do so are routinely modified, elaborated and even subverted by others in the organization. However, the attempt to clearly distinguish between the formal and informal would seem to be based on a very mechanistic approach to the study of organizations. In reality they are, of course, live social systems where organizational designs stem not exclusively from a completely rational managerial decision-making process but rather are the product of very complicated processes in which social, economic, political, and psychological factors all interact.

Up to the present the discussion in this chapter has tended to emphasize the more rational aspects of the organizational design process and probably over-emphasized the ability of senior managers to impose their will on the organizations they administer. However, this is an area where it is difficult to achieve a suitable balance. The very concept of organization in modern industrial society would appear to imply a determined attempt at rationality among those responsible for organizational management. At the same time there can be no doubting that a wide variety of political forces, social relationships, and psychological commitments as well as historical accidents limit the extent to which organizational decision-making and organizational activities generally can ever be truly rational. Rather such decision-making is best characterized in terms of 'bounded rationality' (Simon, 1957) or as part of 'the science of muddling through' (Lindblom, 1959).

The exaggerated emphasis on the role of senior management up to the present has largely reflected the powerful position that senior managers typically have to propose structural arrangements. The power of other parties tends to be of a more negative nature and will be likely to show itself in difficulties that senior managers may have in getting their ideas accepted and implemented. Even allowing the point made above it is clear that the arrangements adopted will often depend on ideas from many sources both inside and outside the organization.

It must be noted in addition that in many cases the structures designed and laid down by management are incomplete in as much as they do not attempt to define all the procedures, relationships, etc. which form the on-going patterns of behaviour in the organization. In such cases individuals and groups do informally add to the designed structure. However, managers are usually aware of this and by accepting such additions effectively adopt them willingly or unwillingly.

Of course, structural arrangements are not always implemented appropriately according to the rules and procedures laid down. Where such modifications or even negations are routinized it must be accepted that elements of structure have been *de facto* changed. It can be seen then that the formal or management designed structure is only part of the over-all picture, but given the very considerable interactions between formal and informal processes it is difficult to sustain any clear and meaningful distinction between formal and informal structures.

THE DETERMINANTS OF ORGANIZATIONAL STRUCTURES

Having considered the nature of organizational structures and their component dimensions it is now possible to move on to examine the forces and constraints that lead to particular structural arrangements being adopted in any given case.

As structures are largely designed by senior managers, albeit as a consequence of processes to which others make inputs, it is necessary to couch the question in terms of the factors which operate to influence their decisions. Generally we can suggest that a large variety of non-structural organizational parameters together with characteristics of the organizational environment will be relevant to the decision-making process. The danger is that the list of such factors can be virtually endless and hence of dubious utility for understanding the choice of structures. However, examination of the literature suggests a limited number of such factors which would seem to be most important in the process. It must be noted at the outset that these will operate in different ways and to differing extents in different cases. Also in as much as structures stem from decision-making processes, then those factors which are relevant are important to the extent and only to the extent that they impinge directly or indirectly upon the consciousness of those involved in those processes.

Strategy

We have already suggested that structures are adopted in an attempt to deal with the problems of task accomplishment, control, and cost. This being the case it would seem inevitable that one of the most critical factors which will influence the choice of structure will be the definition of the organizational task, that is the strategy which the organization adopts towards the accomplishment of its goals. Despite this apparently obvious contention, strategy has often been very much neglected by organizational researchers. Indeed the main impetus for research on the relationship between strategy and structure has come from the work of business historians rather than students of organizational behaviour. Chandler (1962), in his seminal work on the subject, concluded from his studies of the development of American business firms that strategy was the key variable in understanding the forces which created particular structures in the organizations he studied. Not merely did he see strategy as the major variable which influenced choices of structures but he clearly argued that it also acted as an intervening variable in the processes by which other factors such as environmental conditions would come to have an effect on the design of organizations. This view is endorsed by Ansoff (1965) from the different perspective involved in formulating a theory of business strategy.

One of the difficulties that organizational researchers have encountered in their efforts to examine the implications of strategy for structure has been the problem of finding appropriate ways of characterizing strategy in ways which are specific to a single organizational context. The sorts of elements of strategy which have been considered are stress on innovation (Burns and Stalker, 1961) extent of diversification or territorial expansion (Mansfield, Todd, and Wheeler, 1978) and merger inclination (Pfeffer, 1972), all of which have been shown to have some relationship with structure in particular studies. However, no very clear general pattern has yet emerged.

Size

Clearly organizational size, however measured, will be closely related to structure. Indeed some writers (e.g., Porter, Lawler and Hackman, 1975) have gone so far as to suggest that size should be considered as an aspect of structure itself. Certainly many studies have shown large and consistent correlations between size and a number of dimensions of structure. For example, the Aston studies and their replications (e.g., Pugh, Hickson, Hinings, and Turner, 1969; Child and Mansfield, 1972; Child, 1973) found that size was strongly positively related to the extent of standardization, formalization, and functional and role specialization in the organizations they studied. Also not surprisingly larger organizations tend to have more hierarchical levels. Such relationships are scarcely surprising when the nature of the problems confronted by management in different sized organizations are considered. In small organizations personal forms of control are possible and likely to be relatively cheap and efficient. In addition the possibility of employing specialists other than in production and sales is usually precluded on grounds of costs. In large organizations on the other hand some form of impersonal control, communication, and record keeping is essential in order to cope with the problems of size. At the same time the increased complexity tends to make the employment of specialists in many areas desirable and their cost can be spread over a greater volume of output.

In addition there is also a tendency for the centralization of decision-making to decrease in larger organizations (Pugh, Hickson, Hinings, and Turner, 1969; Child and Mansfield, 1972) although this finding is not consistently replicated in all other studies. This lends weight to Child's (1971) argument regarding strategies of control. Basically it seems organizational managements tend to choose between bureaucratic, decentralized, impersonal control aided by the employment of staff specialists on the one hand, and personal, centralized, non-bureaucratic control on the other. The latter method is likely to have enormous benefits in terms of low administration costs but is unlikely to provide effective co-ordination in larger organizations. This general theory is supported by Chandler's (1962) finding that as firms grow they tend to move from an initial stage based on a single product or at least a limited range, when administration is generally entrepreneurial in character, to a second stage characterized by increased bureaucracy and more decentralized decision-making.

Technology

Perhaps the most contentious potential influence on structure is operating technology. Woodward (1965) and Zwerman (1970) among others have reported findings suggesting that technology has a very strong influence upon structure, particularly relating to variables depicting features of the 'shape' of the organization such as spans of control and the number of levels in the hierarchy. The theoretical writings of Thompson (1967) and Perrow (1970) also suggest that technology is likely to have a significant effect on structure. However, the Aston studies (Pugh, Hickson, Hinings, and Turner, 1969; Child and Mansfield, 1972) revealed only a limited relationship between technology and structure, and this tended to be pronounced only in the case of structural parameters associated with activities close to the workflow. However, Child and Mansfield's study did show that the effect of technology was greater in small companies. In a later study carried out by Dewar and Hage (1978) a longitudinal approach was adopted and tended to confirm both that technology does influence structure but also that the size of this influence was limited.

Over-all then it must be concluded that technology is clearly one of the factors that will be relevant to managerial decisions regarding organizational design but that operating technology will generally only have great relevance to decisions regarding aspects of structure closely linked to the work to which the technology is applied. However, the notion of technology embodied in the idea of task scope (Dewar and Hage, 1978), a concept which relates to organizational strategy, is likely to have more pervasive effects.

Environmental Uncertainty

Clearly the environment in which an organization operates is of critical importance for all aspects of organizational functioning. A large number of different concepts have been employed by organizational researchers in an attempt to come to terms with relevant aspects of an organization's environment. Generally writers have tended to attempt to characterize environments in terms of two or three characteristics. For example, Thompson (1967) described environments in terms of the extent of homogeneity and stability, Child (1972) in terms of stability, complexity, and liberality, and Duncan (1972) in terms of diversity and dynamism. However, Aldrich (1972) attempts a substantially more complex approach and identifies seven dimensions of environmental characteristics, namely stability, concentration, capacity, domain consensus, homogeneity, placidness, and mutability. The problem regarding satisfactory conceptualization and description of the environment is clear and stems from the enormous complexity of organizational environments.

Two main approaches have been adopted as a basis for the study of organization–environment interaction. Although it can not be said that these encompass all the complexity or even all the dimensions of environment already mentioned, they do provide a suitable starting point for a consideration of the ways in which structures are influenced. As Aldrich and Mindlin (1976) have suggested these two approaches view the environment in terms of resource availability of information flows.

When the environment is considered in terms of information flows then the main concept employed has been that of environmental uncertainty, although as Aldrich and Pfeffer (1976) have argued theorists have generally assumed that competition, complexity, and instability are all relevant in that they generate uncertainty. Confronted with uncertainty organizational managers may attempt a strategic solution and attempt to act on the environment in order to reduce that uncertainty by such means as vertical integration, diversification, or advertising. However, in all cases some level of uncertainty will remain and structures must be designed in such a way as to make it possible for an organization to operate under such circumstances. Generally it would seem that to deal effectively with uncertainty organizations need to operate in such a way that decision-making is close to the source of uncertainty. This will typically mean some element of decentralization coupled with a reduction in bureaucracy and the employment of suitable specialists.

Lawrence and Lorsch (1967) in their major study of the implications of uncertainty for structure found that different organizational functions faced differing amounts of uncertainty. Thus in their study of companies in three industries, they found that research and development faced greater uncertainty than sales and marketing which in turn faced more uncertainty than production. Under conditions when environmental uncertainty was greatest organizations which were most effective had created large measures of differentiation between the different functional areas allowing each the greatest freedom to adapt their structures and processes to the particular circumstances they faced. This in turn led to a problem of co-ordination requiring great efforts to be made to ensure integration in the organization. Hence they found that under conditions of greatest uncertainty the most effective organizations had created whole liaison departments to deal with the problems of co-ordination created both by the uncertainty itself and the large measure of differentiation adopted to deal with the different problems of different environmental sectors.

Dependence

Aldrich and Pfeffer (1976) have suggested that where organization–environment interactions are seen in terms of resource flows then the main concept employed is that of dependence conceptualized in terms of the relative power of an organization *vis-à-vis* the other organizations and agencies with which it deals. Such an approach has been adopted by Jacobs (1974), Mindlin and Aldrich (1975), and Wheeler, Mansfield, and Todd (1980). However. there are also a number of writers who have tended to examine the resource availability aspect of the environment in terms of the competitiveness of the markets in which an organization operates (e.g., Pfeffer and Leblebici, 1973; Azma and Mansfield, 1981).

The theoretical work of writers such as Jacobs (1974) suggests that dependence is positively related to the need for the resources in question, and negatively related to the ease with which an alternative supplier can be found. As with uncertainty organizational managements may attempt a strategic solution, but where this fails to remove the dependency, structural arrangements must be adopted to allow effective operation.

The Aston group (Pugh, Hickson, Hinings, and Turner, 1969) found that dependence was positively related to the centralization of decision-making, but they found very little relationship with other aspects of structure. A number of other studies replicated this finding although Child (1973) using the same methodology as the Aston group found no relationships between dependence and structure. Further Neghandi and Reimann (1973) found the opposite relationship between dependence and centralization in their study of organizations in India. Mindlin and Aldrich (1975) suggested that these inconsistencies might be a consequence of the failure to discriminate between different types of dependence in different environmental sectors. This was supported by the findings of Wheeler, Mansfield, and Todd (1980) who showed different relationships between structure and dependence upon owners and dependence upon customers. Taken together these findings show a picture of considerable complexity. However, in the main it seems that organizations centralize decision-making relevant to critical dependencies but that this relationship has to be seen as just one aspect of the over-all response to a potential problem for managers in organizations.

Structural Contingency Theory

In this brief review a number of non-structural system parameters and environmental characteristics have been shown to relate in complex ways to dimensions of organizational structure. The main theoretical approach adopted for explaining this variety of relationships has been a contingency one based upon the conceptualization of organizations as open systems.

If there was a dominant perspective in organization theory in the 1970s it was without doubt the general framework of ideas generally subsumed under the title of structural contingency theory. It is not easy to state fairly the main tenets of this theory as it has been used in a variety of different ways. In its simplest form it suggests little more than the idea that structural arrangements will be contingent upon other parameters of the organizational system such as size and technology as well as characteristics of the environment and the organization's relationship with the environment. In a more complex form it suggests that the performance of an organization depends on the fit between structure and the environment in which it operates and the non-structural system parameters.

Despite the widespread acceptance of such a theory in the 1970s the evidence for it would seem to be rather limited as Pennings (1975), Child (1972), and Azma and Mansfield (1981) have all pointed out. Indeed the more exactly the theory has been formulated the less convincing has been the evidence in its support. Azma and Mansfield (1981, p. 167) suggested that the theory 'gained relatively widespread acceptance largely because of the inherent plausibility of the framework' rather than because of the convincing nature of the evidence. In any case, as Child (1972) argued, there can be little doubt that the constraints imposed by the contingencies considered in the literature can not be so severe as to preclude considerable scope for managers to exercise a large measure of strategic choice in the design of organizational structures. However, Aldrich (1979) taking a wider historical view has argued that the long term survival of organizations does depend on finding 'niches' where the structural arrangements are appropriate for (or fit) the particular situation.

Over-all, although there are clearly valid arguments on both sides, it is hard to accept the versions of contingency theory which have so far been formulated. This leaves the major question to be answered concerning what theoretical approach should be adopted to modify or replace structural contingency theory. However, it is not possible to answer this question purely in terms of the ideas and issues which have been considered up to now. We will therefore return to this point and attempt the beginnings of an answer when we have considered the implications of structural arrangements.

IMPLICATIONS OF ORGANIZATIONAL STRUCTURE

As we noted at the outset organizational structures have a very substantial effect on virtually all aspects of the processes and behaviour associated with organizations. Indeed this very pervasiveness creates problems when one tries to delineate the implications of any particular structural arrangement. It is important to note at the beginning that structure will rarely if ever be the sole determinant of outcomes in the organizational setting. All the factors mentioned in preceding sections will have a direct effect on many processes in addition to the influence they may have through structure.

When considering the implications of structure it is useful if somewhat artificial to distinguish different sets of implications and to consider these in relative isolation. Clearly structure is likely to be a significant factor in shaping the psychological environment or climate in which organizational participants act. It will also affect the behaviour and attitudes of such participants whether acting alone or in groups. As well as these micro-level implications structure will be likely to affect both the strategy making process and also the strategies which result. Finally the structure of organizations will be one factor which will influence their effectiveness whether in terms of goal accomplishment or operating efficiency. In the following sections each of these sets of implications will be considered in turn before an attempt is made to draw together the various threads in the concluding section.

Structure and Climate

Clearly, as has already been suggested, the structure of an organization is likely to be one of the major factors which help shape the psychological environment of participants. The idea of organizational climate has been widely used to characterize this latter concept. Payne and Pheysey (1971) have described climate as:

'. . . a molar concept reflecting the content and strength of the prevalent values, norms, attitudes, behaviour and feelings of the members of a social system' (Payne and Pheysey, 1971, p. 77).

As such it has been seen as:

'. . . a possible conceptual linkage between analysis at the organizational level and analysis at the individual level' (Payne and Mansfield, 1973, p. 515).

Climate itself is a multidimensional concept (Campbell, Dunnette, Lawler, and Weick, 1970) and incorporates ideas concerning the structure and rules of the organization, about interpersonal processes and relationships, and about how the tasks of the organization are achieved. A number of studies have shown relationships between a number of dimensions of structure and aspects of climate as Payne and Pugh (1976) illustrate in their substantial review of the subject. However, it is clear that there are many inconsistencies in the findings reported by different researchers and it is hard to see any clear pattern emerging.

Further examination of the results suggests two explanations of the apparent irregularities. First, although climate is generally seen to be a property of the organizational system, it is clear that considerable heterogeneity of perceptions of climate exist within any organization (Schneider, 1972; Payne and Mansfield, 1973). Some of these differences are relatively predictable such as the repeated finding that hierarchically senior people tend to see their organization's climate more favourably than do junior personnel. Indeed the distribution of views on climate within an organization may itself be partly a consequence of structural arrangements (Mansfield and Payne, 1977). Clearly until theoretical or methodological advances are made in the mapping of climate perceptions in organizations only the most robust relationships between climate variables and structural dimensions will be found with any degree of consistency.

The second explanation of the apparent variability of research findings in this area is suggested by Mansfield (1980). He reported empirical evidence that the relationship between the extent of decentralization of decision-making and certain climate scales (particularly those assessing leaders' psychological distance and management concern for employee involvement) was different under conditions of high market competition from the relationships appertaining under conditions of low market competition. From these results he concluded that the relationship between climate and structure was itself contingent upon other factors, particularly environmental conditions.

Structure and Individual Attitudes and Behaviour

The idea that the behaviour and attitudes of organizational participants would be significantly influenced by the structure of the organizations in which they participated has a long history in the literature. Indeed the whole purpose of designing structures is to exercise an influence on individual behaviour in order to solve the problems of task achievement, control and cost. The fact that structures are designed in order to influence behaviour in particular ways has tended to lead researchers to focus attention on the negative or unintended consequences of structural arrangements.

Many of the early writers (e.g., Merton, 1940; Argyris, 1957) stressed the negative effects of bureaucracy, task specialization, and hierarchy for individuals. They suggested that such organizational properties could create a pathological bureaucratic personality, frustration, and the blocking of psychological growth. Such effects they argued would be particularly pronounced among those working in hierarchically junior positions. It was also argued by writers of this school (e.g., Merton, 1940; Gouldner, 1954) that many structural arrangements, particularly those associated with bureaucracy, could under certain circumstances bring about organizationally dysfunctional consequences. For example, Merton argued that bureaucratic systems with their all-encompassing rules and procedures were likely to lead to lower level participants being socialized into rule following behaviour to such an extent that they would continue to follow the rules even when they were no longer appropriate.

March and Simon (1958) suggested that many of the difficulties encountered in the relationship between organizational systems and their individual participants stemmed from the potential conflict between values which was confronted when organization structures were designed. They suggested that the belief that individuals should be treated as individuals with their own unique personalities, attitudes, etc. was a deeply rooted value in most Western industrial societies which ran counter, at least in the organizational millieu, to another deeply rooted belief that all individuals should be treated fairly or equally. They argued that in making design decisions in organizations one of these values would be sacrificed to the other or some compromise reached. In any case there was likely to be a conflict between individual beliefs and organizational structures. In the case of highly bureaucratic organizations, for example, stress is placed very heavily on the institutionalization of the second value in that under bureaucratic administrations all individuals are treated according to universalistic criteria. This inevitably creates conflict with the first value that individuals should be treated in accordance with their particular unique characteristics, and this causes many of the difficulties encountered by bureaucracies.

Generally the literature suggests that two structural characteristics of organizations are particularly likely to influence individual attitudes and behaviour. The first is the extent of bureaucratization already mentioned and the second is the extent to which decision-making is centralized. As has already been noted early writers stressed the negative effects of bureaucratic structure on individual attitudes and there is some empirical support for such contentions (e.g., Aiken and Hage, 1966). However, many recent studies do not find evidence for such effects and some appeared to show that by reducing role ambiguity and conflict, increased bureaucracy might actually ameliorate individuals' perceptions of their positions (e.g., Organ and Greene, 1981; Morris, Steers, and Koch, 1980).

The evidence with regard to the effect of centralization of decision-making would also seem to be somewhat ambiguous and may suggest that the style of management has a strong interactive effect. Relatively centralized decision-making after consultation may have less alienating effects than authoritarian styled decentralized decision-making.

Over all it is clear that the relationships between dimensions of structure and individual attitudes and behaviour are highly complex and are influenced by a large number of non-structural variables. It would also seem likely, as a recent study of Oldham and Hackman (1981) showed, that while general structural parameters may have a significant effect much larger influences are likely to stem from the detailed structural arrangements incorporated in the design of individual jobs.

Structure and Strategy

In an earlier section it was noted that organizational strategy is one of the major factors which influences the choice of structural arrangements. As we noted, there is an appealing logic to the idea that management should first decide what the organization should be trying to achieve (i.e., its strategy) and then go on to design an appropriate structure to accomplish this. In reality, of course, strategic choices are made in ongoing situations where one of the factors influencing both the strategy making process and the actual strategy developed will be the existing structure. Indeed one of the major effects of structural arrangements will be on the extent to which managers perceive environmental changes and hence the need for strategic change. As Merton (1940) and Burns and Stalker (1961) have pointed out, one of the problems associated with bureaucratic structures is an inability to sense change in the organizational environment.

Structure and Performance

To many, particularly those with a managerial orientation, the crunch question relating to organizational structure has to do with its relationship with organizational performance. There can be little doubt that the overwhelming majority of researchers and commentators who have taken an interest in organizations have believed that one way or another organizational structure was one of the factors which would exercise influence on levels of organizational effectiveness or efficiency—no matter how these were conceived or measured. Historically it was believed by such writers as Weber (1946), Fayol (1949), and Mooney (1947) that there were universally applicable laws which suggested that particular structural and administrative arrangements would lead to high levels of performance in all situations. As was suggested earlier in this chapter, more recently such ideas have given way to contingency theories suggesting that organizational performance would depend on the fit between structural arrangements and the situation in which an organization operates (e.g., Lawrence and Lorsch, 1967; Woodward, 1965).

When the evidence of the very large numbers of studies reported in the literature is considered in an unbiased way, one is forced to the conclusion that the evidence for either universalistic or contingency relationships between structure and performance is distinctly limited and inconclusive. On the one hand there are a large number of studies which appear to link structure to performance although the percentage of variance explained is rarely large. On the other hand very few results seem capable of repeated replication. There are a variety of conclusions that could be drawn from these somewhat contradictory findings, but it is perhaps worth listing some of the more obvious ones (even though it is difficult to substantiate any of them convincingly). However, with many reservations, one could suggest that the evidence indicates:

1. Structure is only one among many factors which influence organizational performance.
2. There are a large number of possible indicators of performance which often relate differently to structural variables (Azma and Mansfield, 1981; Child, 1972).
3. There are probably no genuinely universal propositions relating structure to performance although there may be some rather limited variants with moderately wide applicability.
4. Probably no simple statement of structural contingency theory will adequately predict organizational performance except in limited ranges of organizations.
5. Very much more complex models or theories will be required if any generally applicable predictions are to be made regarding the relationship of organizational structure and organizational performance.

TOWARDS A THEORY OF STRUCTURE

In this chapter we have considered the nature of organizational structures, the forces that create, shape, and maintain them, and some of their implications. It will have been noted that at many points in the discussion it has been necessary to point out the inconclusive and even contradictory nature of much of the evidence. Examination of the literature in historical sequence suggests that many of the early writers seemed to believe in universalistic propositions. These were unable to stand empirical examination and were to a large extent replaced by various contingency propositions. However, further research has cast doubt on these in turn. This may in part be due to inadequate research methods but probably mainly reflects the complexity of the organizational phenomenon. Before considering the implications of this complexity for our knowledge of structure it is worth briefly considering the methodological issues and the way the field of study has developed.

It must first be noted that although organizational structure has been an object of study for many years it has all too often been considered in relative isolation from other organizational processes. It must also be admitted that much of the research that has been reviewed here has tended to be atheoretical, relying heavily on purely empirical approaches. Further, much of the empiricism has been based on cross-sectional studies, depending mainly on the statistical techniques of correlation and regression for the assessment of the relationship between structural variables themselves and between structure and other types of phenomena. There has been little in the way of theoretical attempts at model building, and a strong tendency to neglect processes of change and development. The end result of all this has tended to be a very large number of empirical research findings many of which seem incapable of replication.

One should not, however, take too negative a view of the end product of the very considerable quantity of research that has been carried out in this area. Much has been achieved and if our knowledge is still very limited it must be noted that it is greatly advanced compared to 25 years ago when the move towards systematic comparative research in the area first gathered momentum. During that time research data has accumulated which allow us to narrow down the possible arguments which may be proferred to explain the nature of structures and the relationships obtaining between structural parameters and other variables. More recently there has been a move towards cross-national studies of structures (e.g., Lammers and Hickson, 1979) which enable us to begin to understand organizations not just as isolated phenomenon but in the broader context of the societies of which they are a part.

Clearly organizations are particular sorts of social systems operating in interaction with other social systems such as families, communities, and societies. Within organizations there are other smaller social systems such as divisions, departments, and work groups. All of these systems are changing in a complex interactive way over time. The structure of all of these systems can be seen both as the product of human endeavour and interaction, and in turn to affect such. In any particular social system, as we have seen in the case of organizations, structures are partly the product of internal processes and partly of external forces, although as the open systems concept makes clear it is difficult to maintain any clear distinction between the two.

In order to make further progress towards a theory of organizational structure it will be necessary both to consider many sets of interacting variables at the same time and also to broaden our consideration of the relationship between organizations and their situation in time and space. Up to the present, in looking at many research reports one can not help being aware of a sense of placelessness and timelessness. Indeed there are many articles published in major journals which do not even report when and where the data were collected. This would seem to be partly a reflection of an implicit belief that the organizational phenomenon is to an extent 'culture free', and partly a consequence of the difficulty of measuring such amorphous concepts as culture.

Mansfield (1981) has suggested a number of societal level sets of variables are all likely to be relevant to the nature and functioning of organizations and have implications for the structures adopted and the effects of such structures. These sets of variables encompass:

1. Culture.
2. The nature of the political economy.
3. Stage of economic development.
4. Ideology.
5. Social institutions.
6. Political stability and national security.
7. History.

Although all of these variables have been mentioned as relevant in various studies of structure they have rarely been explicitly measured and have mainly been introduced into *post hoc* explanations of unexpected results. Such variables would potentially explain both the differences found in the types of structures likely to be adopted in different countries and also the implications of such structures.

The question which must now be addressed is how might it be possible to build a more elaborate theory which could provide both a better understanding of the causes and consequences of organizational structures in any single national context but also allow an understanding of the differences which are found between organizations operating in different countries. Perhaps surprisingly, considering the recent heightening of interest in cross-national studies and a broad agreement that some degree of increased theoretical sophistication is required to explain the results, there are very few serious attempts to provide the needed framework. Much too much effort seems to have been expended in debating issues such as whether one should seek for a culture-free or a culture-bound theory of organizations rather than getting on with the job or finding a theory of any type which actually fits the evidence. Among the relatively few attempts that have been made two warrant particular attention. Child (1979) has suggested a model in which different aspects of organizational structures are influenced by contingency variables and the capitalist or socialist nature of the economic system in which the organization is operating. In the model such influences are moderated by the culture of the society. Child suggests that his model:

'... reiterates the view that cultural effects will be most powerful in the processes of organization relating to authority, style, conduct, participation, and attitudes and less powerful in formal structuring and over-all strategy' (Child, 1979, p. 77).

He goes on to conclude his consideration of his model by pointing out the need for further development when he suggests:

'... we still require a more adequate theory of organizations which specifies the points at which contingency, culture and the system of economic relationships have their main effects' (Child, 1979).

A quite different approach to the general problem is adopted by Lammers and Hickson (1979) in the concluding chapter to their book on international and inter-institutional comparisons of organizations where they suggest that:

'... there is a pattern in the characteristics of organizations as seen by the researchers who have made contributions to this book' (Lammers and Hickson, p. 420).

The pattern they discern suggests an interaction between the cultural characteristics of a society and the types of organizations that are most likely to occur in that country. As an example of the types that can be found they suggest a Latin type found in countries such as France characterized by centralization, rigid stratification, bureaucratic control, conflicts, and lack of adaptiveness (Clark, 1979). The approach they suggest is presented in a largely classificatory way but suggests a rather different structure of relationships between variables than that suggested either by contingency theory or by Child's model of the effects of contingency, culture and capitalism.

Clearly both the work of Child and that of Lammers and Hickson raise as many questions as they answer, but they are important in suggesting possible ways in which the subject may move forward, and they also provide significant guidance for future research. There is, however, a third complementary approach. This is based on the basic assertion that structures stem from decision-making processes and on the approach which has been adopted in this chapter. In order to explain the main points it is necessary to somewhat oversimplify the model in terms of the organizational politics that will typically be involved, but it is hoped the exposition will provide a way of understanding the general nature of interaction between different classes of variables.

As we have noted earlier, decisions about structural arrangements will generally be made by managers who will be seeking ways in which organizational goals can be achieved and organizational strategies carried out. Clearly any choice must be within the range of what the managers in question deem to be possible or plausible in the situation. This range will depend on their appreciation of existing structural arrangements as well as of possible alternatives. A number of influences will bear directly on the choices between the alternative structures which are perceived as ways of achieving organizational goals.

One set of factors which will effect the outcome will be the economic interests, cultural values, and ideological views of the decision-makers themselves. In addition their ideas will be affected by the management theories they have been taught or acquired by experience. The critical element of these theories might be described as organizational path–goal expectancies; that is ideas about which structural forms will lead to organizational goal achievement in the situation. A third set of influences on the decision making process will be the managers' perceptions of the circumstances with which the structural arrangements must deal and which might affect the efficacy of any particular structural solution. The aspects of the situation which are likely to be seen as relevant are likely in the main to be those which are generally referred to as contingency variables; that is, organizational size, operating technology, dependence upon outside agencies, and environmental uncertainty. In addition to these conventional contingency variables a number of somewhat less frequently considered factors may be routinely considered, such as legal constraints, market conditions, and relationships with unions and other occupational interest groups.

Of course the managers' views on what might broadly be described as the logic of the situation will not necessarily define the structural solution adopted in any one to one way. Many other interested parties both inside and outside the organization, such as employees, unions, customers, suppliers, owners, and governments may also have views on what structural arrangements should be instituted, and they may be prepared and able to put pressure on decision-making managers. Such interested parties will of course also be influenced by their own interests, cultural values, ideologies, views on organizational goals and strategies, organizational path–goal expectancies and assessment of the organization's situation. Where those managers making decisions tend to share ideas or perceptions with the other interested parties then clearer relationships are likely to be found between the relevant variables and structural parameters than where little consensus exists. For example if all actors share a cultural norm emphasizing participative values then it is to be expected that centralization is likely to be limited to a greater extent than where conflict exists concerning such beliefs.

In addition to the relatively direct effects outlined above it is anticipated that a variety of aspects of the macro-environment will operate on the decision-making process indirectly through the contingency variables. Thus it is anticipated that the national political system, the extent of industrialization and economic development, the state of the national economy, considerations of national security, etc. will combine to influence such factors as organizational size, technology adopted, dependence, environmental uncertainty, market conditions and legal constraints as well as interacting with cultural values and ideology.

It might be objected that the model presented so far is overly rational, although as we have noted any such rationality will be limited by the political nature of the decision-making process. However, introduction of the notion of rationality must alert one to other possible complications of the model. First it is assumed in the foregoing argument that structural arrangements are to be seen as means to the ends of achieving organizational goals and carrying out organizational strategies. This view is clearly compatible with, but does not imply, Aldrich's (1979) natural selection model of the perpetuation of organizational structures. However, these assumptions may not always hold. There may be circumstances when structures are adopted not as a means to the end of strategy accomplishment but rather as ends in themselves. Thus, for example, it may be that participative structures are adopted not as ways of achieving organizational goals, but because they are, in a particular culture, seen as desirable in and of themselves.

In conclusion, then, it must be restated that organizational structures tend to be consciously designed although they will be informally modified and elaborated. They will have significant and pervasive effects on all forms of organizational behaviour. However, such influences may not always be consistent or readily discernible due to the effects of many other sets of variables.

REFERENCES

Aiken, M., and Hage, J. (1966) Organizational alienation: A comparative analysis, *American Sociological Review*, **31,** 497–507.

Aldrich, H. E. (1972) An organization-environment perspective on cooperation and conflict between organizations and the Manpower Training System, in Neghandi, A. R. (ed.) *Conflict and Power in Complex Organizations*, Kent State University, Kent, Ohio.

Aldrich, H. E. (1979) *Organizations and Environments*, Prentice Hall, New York.

Aldrich, H. E., and Mindlin, S. (1976) Uncertainty and dependence: two conceptions of the environment, in Karpik, L. (ed.) *Organization and Environment*, Sage, New York.

Aldrich, H. E., and Pfeffer, J. (1976) 'Environments of organizations' in *The Annual Review of Sociology*, Annual Reviews, Palo Alto, California. Volume II.

Allen, L. A. (1956) Improving line and staff relationships, *Studies in Personnel Policy No. 153*, National Industrial Conference Board.

Ansoff, I. (1965) *Corporate Strategy*, Penguin, Harmondsworth.
Argyris, C. J. (1957) The individual and organization: some problems of mutual adjustment, *Administrative Science Quarterly*, **2**, 1–24.
Azma, M., and Mansfield, R. (1981) Market conditions, centralization, and organizational effectiveness: contingency theory reconsidered, *Human Relations*, **34**, 157–168.
Blau, P. M., and Schoenherr, R. A. (1971) *The Structure of Organizations*, Basic Books, New York.
Burns, T., and Stalker, G. M. (1961) *The Management of Innovation*, Tavistock, London.
Campbell, J., Dunnette, M. D., Lawler, E. E., and Weick, K. E. (1970) *Managerial Behaviour, Performance and Effectiveness*, McGraw Hill, New York.
Chandler, A. (1962) *Strategy and Structure*, M.I.T. Press, Cambridge, Mass.
Child, J. (1971) Organization structure and strategies of control, *Administrative Science Quarterly*, **17**, 163–177.
Child, J. (1972) Organization structure and performance: the role of strategic choice, *Sociology*, **6**, 1–22.
Child, J. (1973) Predicting and understanding organization structure, *Administrative Science Quarterly*, **18**, 168–185.
Child, J. (1979) Culture, contingency and capitalism in the cross-national study of organizations, Mimeo, Aston University Management Centre, to appear in Star, B. M., and Cummings, L. L. (eds.) *Research in Organizational Behaviour*, J.A.I. Press, Volume III, New York.
Child, J., and Mansfield, R. (1972) 'Technology, size and organization structure', *Sociology*, **6**, 369–393.
Clark, R. (1979) *The Japanese Company*, Yale University Press, New Haven.
Dewar, R., and Hage, J. (1978) Size, technology, complexity, and structural differentiation: towards a theoretical synthesis, *Administrative Science Quarterly*, **23**, 111–136.
Duncan, R. B. (1972) Characteristics of organizational environments and perceived environmental uncertainty, *Administrative Science Quarterly*, **17**, 313–327.
Etzioni, A. (1961) *A Comparative Analysis of Complex Organizations*, Free Press, New York.
Fayol, H. (1949) *General and Industrial Management*, Pitman, London.
Gouldner, A. (1954) *Patterns of Industrial Bureaucracy*, Free Press, New York.
Hage, J., and Aiken, M. (1967) Relationship of centralization to other structural properties, *Administrative Science Quarterly*, **12**, 72–92.
Hage, J., and Aiken, M. (1969) Routine technology, social structure and organizational tools, *Administrative Science Quarterly*, **14**, 366–376.
Hall, R. H. (1972) *Organizations: Structure and process*, Prentice Hall, Englewood Cliffs, N.J.
Jacobs, D. (1974) Dependence and vulnerability: an exchange approach to the control of organizations, *Administrative Science Quarterly*, **19**, 45–59.
Katz, D., and Kahn, R. L. (1966) *The Social Psychology of Organizations*, Wiley, New York.
Lammers, C. J., and Hickson, D. J. (1979) *Organizations Alike and Unlike*, Routledge and Kegan Paul, London.
Lawrence, P. R., and Lorsch, J. (1967) *Organization and Environment*, Harvard Business School, Boston.
Lindblom, C. E. (1959) The science of 'muddling through', *Public Administrative Review*, **19**, 79–88.
Litterer, J. A. (1963) *Organizations: Structure and Behaviour*, Wiley, New York.

Mansfield, R. (1973) Bureaucracy and centralization, *Administrative Science Quarterly*, **18**, 477–488.

Mansfield, R. (1980) Organization climate: can it be controlled, in Duncan, K. D., Grunenberg, M., and Wallis, D. (eds.), *Changes in Working Life*, Wiley, New York.

Mansfield, R. (1981) Developing a cross national perspective, in Mansfield, R., and Poole, M. J. F. (eds.), *International Perspectives on Management and Organization*, Gower, Aldershot.

Mansfield, R., and Payne, R. L. (1977) Correlates of variance in perceptions of organizational climate, in Pugh, D. S., and Payne, R. L. (eds.), *Organizational Behaviour in Its Context*, Saxon House, London.

Mansfield, R., Todd, D., and Wheeler, J. (1978) Structural implications of the company–customer interface, *Journal of Management Studies*, **17**, 19–33.

March, J. G., and Simon, H. (1958) *Organizations*, Wiley, New York.

Merton, R. K. (1940) Bureaucratic structure and personality, *Social Forces*, **18**, 560–568.

Mindlin, S., and Aldrich, H. E. (1975) Interorganizational dependence: a review of the concept and a re-examination of the findings of the Aston Group, *Administrative Science Quarterly*, **20**, 382–392.

Mooney, J. (1947) *Principles of Organizations*, Harper, New York.

Morris, J. H., Steers, R. M., and Koch, J. L. (1980) The influence of organization structure on role conflict and ambiguity for three occupational groupings, *Academy of Management Journal*, **22**, 58–71.

Neghandhi, A. R., and Reimann, B. (1973) Correlates of decentralization: closed and open system perspectives, *Academy of Management Journal*, **16**, 570–582.

Oldham, G. R., and Hackman, J. R. (1981) Relationships between organizational structure and employee reactions: comparing alternative frameworks, *Administrative Science Quarterly*, **26**, 66–83.

Organ, D. W., and Greene, C. N. (1981) The effects of formalization on professional involvement: A compensatory process approach, *Administrative Science Quarterly*, **26**, 237–252.

Payne, R. L., and Mansfield, R. (1973) Relationships of perceptions of organizational climate to organizational structure, context and hierarchical position, *Administrative Science Quarterly*, **18**, 515–526.

Payne, R. L., and Mansfield, R. (1978) Correlates of individual perceptions of organizational climate, *Journal of Occupational Psychology*, **51**, 209–218.

Payne, R. L., and Pheysey, D. C. (1971) G. G. Stern's Organizational Climate Index: A reconceptualization and application to business organizations, *Organizational Behavior and Human Performance*, **6**, 77–98.

Payne, R. L., and Pugh, D. S. (1976) Organizational structure and climate, in Dunnette, M. D. (ed.), *Handbook of Industrial and Organizational Psychology*, Rand McNally, Chicago.

Pennings, J. M. (1975) The relevance of the structural contingency model of organizational effectiveness, *Administrative Science Quarterly*, **20**, 393–410.

Perrow, C. (1961) The analysis of goals in complex organizations, *American Sociological Review*, **26**, 854–865.

Perrow, C. (1970) *Organizational Analysis*, Wadsworth, Belmont, California.

Pettigrew, A. (1973) *The Politics of Organizational Decision-Making*, Tavistock, London.

Pfeffer, J. (1972) Merger as a response to organizational interdependence, *Administrative Science Quarterly*, **17**, 382–394.

Pfeffer, J., and Leblebici, H. (1973) The effect of competition on some dimensions of organizational structure, *Social Forces*, **52**, 268–279.

Porter, L. W., Lawler, E. E., and Hackman, J. R. (1975) *Behavior in Organizations*, McGraw Hill, New York.

Pugh, D. S., Hickson, D. J., Hinings, C. R., and Turner, C. (1968) Dimensions of organization structure, *Administrative Science Quarterly*, **13**, 65–105.

Pugh, D. S., Hickson, D. J., Hinings, C. R., and Turner, C. (1969) The context of organization structure, *Administrative Science Quarterly*, **14**, 91–114.

Schneider, B. (1972) Organizational climate: individual preferences and organizational realities, *Journal of Applied Psychology*, **56**, 211–227.

Simon, H. (1957) *Models of Man*, Wiley, New York.

Thompson, J. D. (1967) *Organizations in Action*, McGraw Hill, New York.

Weber, M. (1946) Bureaucracy, in Gerth, H. H., and Wright Mills, C. (trans.), *From Max Weber*, Routledge and Kegan Paul, London.

Weber, M. (1947) *Economy and Society*, Bedminster Press, New York.

Wheeler, J., Mansfield, R., and Todd, D. (1980) Structural implications of organizational dependence upon customers and owners: similarities and differences, *Organization Studies*, **1**, 327–348.

Williamson, O. (1975) *Markets and Hierarchies*, Free Press, New York.

Woodward, J. (1965) *Industrial Organization: Theory and Practice*, Oxford University Press, London.

Zwerman, W. L. (1970) *New Perspectives on Organization Theory*, Greenwood, Westport, Conn.

Social Psychology and Organizational Behaviour
Edited by M. Gruneberg and T. Wall
© 1984 John Wiley & Sons Ltd

Chapter 7

Industrial Relations Psychology

JEAN HARTLEY

The aim of this chapter is to introduce the reader to the psychology of industrial relations. This is approached in two ways. First, there is a brief outline of the field of industrial relations and some of the main contributions made to it by psychologists. Second, an analysis is offered of psychological approaches to a central element of industrial relations, that of conflict. This illustrates in greater detail both the nature of psychological research and how it complements other disciplinary contributions to industrial relations.

OVERVIEW OF INDUSTRIAL RELATIONS PSYCHOLOGY

Before surveying the substantive areas where psychology has contributed to industrial relations, it is important to describe the field as a whole.

The Field of Industrial Relations

Definitions of the field of industrial relations abound, but a broadly acceptable one is offered by Walker (1979). He suggests that industrial relations includes:

'The whole range of relations between workers, managers and government which determine the conditions under which work is done' (Walker, 1979, p. 11).

Other writers provide different emphases (contrast for example, Clegg (1979) with Hyman (1975)). *Conflict* is often highlighted as a central element (e.g. Margerison, 1969; Williams and Guest, 1969).

Industrial relations as a major field of inquiry has developed rapidly in the post-war period. An indication of its subject matter can be gained by considering the contents of textbooks such as those by Clegg (1979), Bain (1983) and Jackson (1977), in the U.K. context, and by Kochan (1980b) for the U.S.A. Typically these include coverage of the following topics: collective bargaining; conflict; the nature, structure and practices of trade unions; management and employers

149

associations; and third party intervention including that of the state. A second aspect of industrial relations to emerge from a scrutiny of textbooks is that it draws upon a variety of disciplines. Economics, sociology, law, political science, history, and psychology all contribute. A point to note is that these are not necessarily competing for the best explanation of events. Rather, each may be seen as a useful contribution emphasizing complementary levels of analysis or perspectives.

Dunlop's (1958) conceptualization of industrial relations, as a social system having as its output a *set of rules* governing relationships between parties has been particularly influential. Indeed this early view emphasizes an orientation which until recently dominated the area. This focusses on formal rules, procedures and institutions, and involves detailed descriptive investigations of, for example, the growth and development of trade unions, variations in the types and scope of collective bargaining agreements across industries, or the extent of legal regulation of industrial relations. Clegg's (1979) textbook exemplifies this approach. Indeed, many industrial relations specialists (e.g., Flanders, 1965) became so concerned with documenting the nature and extent of rules and structures that informal behaviours, such as individual and group processes, attitudes, leadership style, and bargaining skills, were excluded from consideration. Yet, as Hyman (1975), Bain and Clegg (1974), and Williams and Guest (1969) point out, informal behaviours play an important part. Increasingly, the need for a behavioural input into the subject has been argued for (e.g., Thomson and Warner, 1981).

Psychology in Industrial Relations: An Historical Outline

It is clear from the above discussion that many areas of industrial relations have an irreducibly psychological component. For example, concepts such as trust, industrial relations climate, ideology, motivation and commitment are all important aspects of industrial relations potentially amenable to psychological analysis. This was recognized in the early days of psychology by the eminent U.K. psychologist C. S. Myers, who placed industrial relations high on the list of issues which psychologists were well-equipped to tackle (Myers, 1933). In the United States Stagner (1956) and Stagner and Rosen (1965) wrote extensively about union–management relations, as did Kornhauser, Dubin and Ross (1954) in their book entitled *Industrial Conflict*. Yet these initiatives did not give rise to a strong and committed field of research. Rather, during the late 1960s and early 1970s, psychological interest in industrial relations declined.

This recent lack of interest by psychologists is exemplified by the contents of the *Handbook of Industrial and Organizational Psychology* (Dunnette, 1976), described by Dubin (1976) as '. . . the most thorough single compendium of knowledge in the area of industrial psychology' (Dubin, 1976, p. vii). As Gordon and Burt (1981) note, this volume lacks an interest in trade unions or union–management relations. It has no reference to trade unions in its index and there is only one reference to strikes. Similarly, most industrial psychology textbooks, even today, make little mention of trade unions, shop stewards, strikes, wage negotiations, or other aspects central to industrial relations.

This neglect is not because psychology lacks the analytical tools to address industrial relations issues. It is because, for a variety of reasons, psychology has adopted a managerial perspective, where industrial relations issues are mainly seen as tangential or 'abnormal' elements in the study of work organizations. Thus, we see considerable research on leadership but this is applied to managers and supervisors, not to shop stewards. We see a concern with motivation to work but not motivation to join or participate in a union. We see a concern to measure organizational climate where that refers to a workplace or company but not where it refers to a trade union. The potential, then, exists, but its application to industrial relations has been lacking. Nevertheless, some studies with a clear industrial relations focus have been reported. At present interest is reviving and a number of authors have documented the potential contributions of psychology to industrial relations (e.g., Nicholson, 1981; Stephenson and Brotherton, 1979; Strauss, 1979). In the following pages some of this work is outlined. It has been mainly concerned with levels of pay, bargaining and negotiation, union participation and industrial democracy. Industrial conflict is another area of contribution and this is discussed at greater length in the second part of the chapter.

Perceptions of Pay

An important feature of industrial relations is collective bargaining, especially over wage rates. What determines the pay increases workers ask for and negotiate over? Traditionally, interest in wage rates has been the domain of economists, but social psychological factors may be significant. Brown (1979) notes that pay structures (that is, the relative differences in pay for various occupations or pay differentials within a firm) tend to be stable over time, despite labour shortages and surpluses. This suggests that social comparisons are playing a part. Workers are not always trying to maximize their rewards, which would be predicted by economic theory, but rather they also adjust their claims to some notion of fairness of 'felt fair pay'. In other words, in deciding if your wage is fair, you compare it to the wages of some other people or groups.

But how is fairness assessed? Three closely-related psychological approaches have been influential in this area, namely reference group theory (Runciman, 1966), social exchange theory (Homans, 1961), and equity theory (Adams, 1965). In all three cases the general proposition has two aspects. First, that the determination of equity is a comparative process wherein one individual (or group) compares his or her pay with that of another. The second element is that the aim is not to achieve equality of pay as such, but equivalence in terms of the others' costs. This holds that it is the *ratio* of costs to rewards which is the real basis for comparison. Costs are defined as that contributed to the job in terms of such factors as effort, levels of training undertaken, responsibility, experience, or seniority. If the individual perceives that his or her cost–reward ratio is commensurate with that of chosen others, then it is predicted satisfaction will ensue. If, however, there is a disadvantageous discrepancy two outcomes will occur. The individual will feel dissatisfied, and he or she may attempt to restore equity. This might be achieved by a number of means, such as reducing costs (e.g., making less effort), putting pressure on to increase rewards (e.g., pay level or fringe benefits), cognitive distortion or by changing the reference or comparison group.

Most research based on these propositions has been conducted in laboratory settings. This has shown that for underpayment conditions the predictions hold up quite well. Thus the approach points both to comparison groups and cost–reward ratios as central elements in felt fair pay and show these to be of predictive value in experimental conditions. It also has intuitive appeal, and clearly relates to practices in industrial relations such as comparability studies. However, there are many areas of ambiguity both in findings and application. Where the assumed comparison process results in inequity in an advantageous direction ('over-payment') subjects' responses have been theoretically less well predicted and less marked. More generally, it is not clear as to how people choose particular comparison groups, why and how comparison groups change or which factors are designated as 'costs'. In other words, the rationale for the choice of comparison group, and the content and dynamics of the comparison process, are not explicit within the theories. In this respect close study of the choices used by actual industrial groups in field settings would be helpful and provide some guidelines. However, the possibility that perceived equity is as much a process of rationalization as of determination cannot be dismissed. Useful reviews and discussions of this area are provided by Delafield (1979) and Pritchard (1969).

Psychological approaches to perceptions of felt pay while subject to important limitations nevertheless can contribute to the understanding of people's attitudes and behaviour in relation to pay. They broaden the discussion by moving it away from the view that income maximization is the sole motivating force, to the recognition of comparative and normative factors.

Bargaining and Negotiation

Bargaining behaviour is to some extent present in all interactions between workers and managers, but within industrial relations the focus is on collective bargaining: bargaining between *representatives* of each side. Such bargaining can take place in the workplace, at company, regional, or industry level. Some industrial relations writers describe the structure and extent of collective bargaining in the U.K. (e.g., Clegg, 1979; Jackson, 1977; Anthony, 1977) and in the U.S.A. (e.g., Kochan, 1980b). These writings are important in providing a social context for understanding psychological studies of bargaining. In particular they help to assess the extent to which results from experimental studies can be generalized to industrial settings.

This topic has produced more extensive psychological research than any other. One aspect on which psychologists have focussed is the study of the processes of negotiation. Here they have examined the perceptions, goals and decision-making strategies of negotiators. Since bargaining involves interaction over a divisive issue to find a mutually acceptable outcome, much of the research has focussed on the tactics adopted by each party in pursuit of their own objectives. The language of economic motive is widely employed in describing the target point (goal aimed for) and resistance point (point beyond which the party would break off negotiations). It has been found that bargainers try to disguise their own position and guess at the other's position. The work by Balke, Hammond, and Meyer (1973), however, suggested that in practice negotiators may not be entirely clear about their own position, let alone the other party's. Nevertheless, they are often very confident that they understand the other party's position. As well as the deliberate artifice, then, there is evidence of significant misperception. In studying strategy, some investigators have examined the circumstances under which a party will engage in concession-making, i.e., moving away from the original target point (see Magenau and Pruitt, 1979).

Experimental studies of bargaining have been valuable in isolating situational variables which influence behaviour. For example, Morley and Stephenson (1977) point to the influence of formality on the bargaining process. This has the effect of emphasizing commitment to own group and reducing empathic understanding between negotiators. Also, they found that the presence of a third party, as an observer or as a mediator, had the effect of making negotiators more ready to make concessions.

Some studies have also been conducted to elucidate the characteristics of a good negotiator. For example, Rackham and Carlisle (1978, 1979), in observational studies, found that effective negotiators tested and summarized opponents statements more than ineffective negotiators, who often left issues in an ambiguous state in their concern to achieve an agreement.

Finally, we should note the work, based on observation studies, which points to the development of phases or stages in the negotiation process (Douglas, 1962; Morley and Stephenson, 1977). Douglas, for example, found that the early stages of effective negotiation were characterized by an exaggerated emphasis on party loyalty. This was the phase of establishing the bargaining range. Later, issues were considered in more detail and only towards the end of negotiations was commitment to decisions made.

Useful reviews of social psychological work on bargaining are provided by Morley (1979, 1981) and Stephenson (1978, 1981), see also Chapter 4. These show it to be an approach which promises to refine understanding of the nature and outcomes of negotiations. However, this potential has yet to be fully realized. At present there are two important limitations. First, the experimental laboratory basis of much of the research calls into question the legitimacy of generalizing findings to industrial settings. In this respect McGrath's (1966) suggestions for making experiments more realistic are valuable. Second, the research has emphasized interpersonal bargaining—where there are no constituents to whom the negotiators have to refer or to whom they are accountable. In practice interparty bargaining is the more relevant occurrence (see Morley and Stephenson, 1977).

Trade Unions

Psychologists have investigated membership attitudes to trade unions and, more recently, there has been some interest in the functioning of trade unions as organizations. The literature on why employees join and remain in unions is diverse and to some extent contradictory. One focus of research has been whether there is a relationship between union membership and work attitudes. Although it is often thought that union membership is related to low morale or lack of job satisfaction, much of the existing evidence does not support this. Maxey and Mohrman (1980) and Gordon, Philpot, Burt, Thompson, and Spiller (1980), for example, fail to find a negative relation between work satisfactions and union commitment. Gordon, Philpot, Burt, Thompson, and Spiller (1980) suggest there may be some relationship between job dissatisfaction and interest in the union where workers are unorganized (since union involvement may bring about desired changes in the organization), but that where management has recognized a union, and negotiates with it, the relationship will be insignificant.

Union membership has also been investigated in relation to demographic and personality characteristics. The research by Gordon, Philpot, Burt, Thompson, and Spiller (1980) on union commitment is typical in finding union interest pervasive among shopfloor workers regardless of factors such as department, marital status, and seniority. The only exception was that males were more active in the union than females, although this is unsurprising given the tendency of women to bear domestic responsibilities. They also found stronger interest in the union where co-workers and friends were members. Research has also shown that members have a variety of motives for joining a union, from instrumental to ideological (Tagliocozzo and Seidman, 1956). Nicholson (1976) examined the factors influencing the decision to become a shop steward, and found that some stewards were internally motivated (for example by a belief they could do the job well or wanted to take it on for ideological reasons). Many, however, were externally motivated (for example, no-one else would take on the job). Interestingly this study showed that steward responsibilities were heavy and that a number of stewards suffered from considerable role stress.

More widely, Gordon, Philpot, Burt, Thompson, and Spiller (1980) suggest that attention needs to be paid to organizational and situational characteristics, as in research on organizational commitment. Spinrad (1960) argued that features such as small plants, urban workforces, and a workforce mixed in terms of occupation, were conducive to high rates of union involvement. The work by industrial relations researchers such as Brown, Ebsworth, and Terry (1978) indicates that the attitude of the employer to unions, and the size of the plant, can be significant in union workplace development, having a particular effect on the degree of shop steward organization.

The development of studies of unions from an organizational behaviour perspective is relatively recent. Brett (1980) reviews some areas developing in the U.S.A. These include the study of union democracy, organizing for union recognition, and the relationship between participation and collective bargaining effectiveness. In the U.K. too there has been considerable interest of this nature. Nicholson, (1981) studied a large white-collar union branch, finding a range of degrees of involvement, with some members selectively active on particular issues and with a tendency for greater participation on the part of higher status members. Influence processes in unions, because they are voluntary organizations, are two-way between leaders and rank and file. This can sometimes lead to contradictory pressures to be flexible and administratively effective as opposed to being effective in the representation of members' views. Child, Loveridge, and Warner (1973) and Hyman and Fryer (1975) discuss these pressures.

Industrial Democracy and Worker Participation

Participation has been defined as a situation:

'. . . where workers (as individuals or through the union or other organization) have a share in reaching managerial decisions in enterprises' (Clarke, Fatchett, and Roberts, 1972).

Participation in industrial organizations can be a sensitive political issue, since it potentially involves a transfer of power and control. Unions and employers may see participation differently, emphasizing varied, and often conflicing objectives.

A range of ways are available to increase worker involvement and control, and a number of these are described by industrial relations writers such as Poole (1975), Fatchett (1979), Clarke, Fatchett, and Roberts (1972), and Wall and Lischeron (1977). A useful distinction is between direct and indirect participation. Direct, or task-centred, participation refers to the involvement of the individual or workgroup at the level of the job. Interaction, communication, and influence take place directly with management, rather than through representative channels. It includes such practices as participative departmental meetings and action planning groups. Psychologists have done much work in this area and the main studies are reviewed by Wall and Lischeron (1977). In one empirical research project they undertook in a local authority, action planning groups were established in departments which could consider and make recommendations on any issue that concerned the workers to other decision-making bodies. Both management and workers became more aware of the problems and constraints each side operated under, because of improved communications. The importance of management attitudes to direct participation was highlighted in a study by Warr, Fineman, Nicholson, and Payne (1978) which consisted of action research in a steel works. Project groups established for problem-solving were most successful where management were enthusiastic about the objectives of the groups and the involvement of the workers in managerial decision-making.

Indirect, or power-centred, participation involves worker representatives, at various levels in the plant or company, becoming engaged in managerial decision-making. It includes such schemes as worker directors in the U.K. and rather more far-reaching schemes such as supervisory boards in other European countries (see Poole, 1975). Such formal schemes often make use of representation through pre-existing trade union structures. Psychologists have done less field-work in this area than in studying direct representation. However, some experimental work on communication and decision-making is relevant here. For example, Mulder (1971) investigated the hypothesis that where there are large differences in the expert power of members of a system then participation *increases* those power differences. In a small group laboratory discussion and decision-making exercise, he found that those with more information (more expert power) tended to dominate the decision-making and their influence increased with the length of the discussion. Where differences in expert power were low there were no differences in participation rates and all parties exerted more equal influence. This study could have implications for representative participation since managers and specialist staff have both more expertise and more information. Indeed, in an observational study of Yugoslav works councils Kolaja (1965) found that managers and particularly experts, such as accountants and engineers, put forward the majority of the proposals that were accepted by the councils. This suggests that possibly, from a trade union perspective, no participation may be better than bad participation, and that ways need to be sought to overcome expert power differences if participation is to be valuable for workers, or indeed if it is to become participative at all. Indirect participation has mainly been studied by industrial relations researchers (see for example, Fatchett, 1979; also Brannen, Batstone, Fatchett, and White, 1976). The two forms of participation should perhaps be seen as complementary rather than conflicting.

Other Areas

Strauss (1979) and Nicholson (1981) mention further issues amenable to psychological investigation, for example research on attitudes including the study of ideology, investigation of impasse resolution (using third-party intervention through mediation or arbitration), and research on conflict management. Within organizational behaviour there has been, in recent years, a growing interest in issues relevant to industrial relations, especially an increasing preparedness to address issues such as power in organizations (e.g., Pfeffer, 1981; Bacharach and Lawler, 1981), and the political processes underlying organizational behaviour. The willingness to explore conflicts of interest within the organization and an increased preparedness to research genuinely social issues, rather than simply individual or small group behaviour, may facilitate a rapprochement between psychology and industrial relations.

To illustrate psychological work in greater depth let us now turn to consider its contribution to the understanding of industrial conflict.

INDUSTRIAL CONFLICT

Conflict within organizations occurs in many forms. Interpersonal conflict, including so called 'personality clashes', may be common. Conflict within management teams, or between different functions such as sales and production, also often arise, and indeed have provided a focus for students of organizational behaviour (see for example Schein, 1980; Rhenman, Stromberg, and Westerlund, 1970). Industrial conflict is rarely discussed or researched. In the context of industrial relations, however, the primary focus is on the conflict between managers and managed. Kornhauser, Dubin, and Ross (1954) define industrial conflict as:

'... the total range of behaviour and attitudes that express opposition and divergent orientation between industrial owners and managers on the one hand and working people and their organizations on the other' (Kornhauser, Dubin, and Ross, 1954, p. 13).

This definition is extremely broad, and it is evident that industrial conflict can take many forms and is influenced by a variety of factors. In an attempt to capture this diversity the area will be discussed from several different perspectives. First we shall examine values and assumptions about conflict, since these have a significant effect on the way in which it is approached and conceptualized. We shall then explore definitions of industrial conflict and describe the forms in which it may be manifested. Of these the strike is a marked example and one on which most information is available. It is thus considered in more detail. Then we shall introduce psychological and industrial relations perspectives on conflict generation, and consider what happens when a strike is in progress. Finally, we address the question of how conflict may be resolved.

Values About Conflict

One reason for the neglect of industrial conflict by psychologists may lie in the different values and assumptions they hold compared to industrial relations researchers (Kochan, 1981; Strauss, 1979; Nicholson, 1981). We examine these values and assumptions because they influence how issues are defined and researched and affect ideas about the means by which conflict is resolved. Given that industrial conflict related to wider issues of conflict, stability, and change in society more generally, this is particularly important.

The classic paper by Fox (1973) discusses the different perspectives, or frames of reference, of researchers and practitioners in the field of industrial relations. Fox described three frames of reference: the unitarist, the pluralist, and the radical. The unitarist frame of reference assumes that workers and managers have common goals in the enterprise and that they can and should work co-operatively to achieve these joint aims. Adherents of the unitary perspective make liberal use of 'team' and 'family' metaphors about the organization. Organizational behaviour writers often hold a unitary frame of reference, emphasizing the need to work co-operatively to achieve organizational goals.

In contrast, recognition of divergent and opposing interests is the hallmark of the pluralist and the radical frames of reference. The pluralist sees the organization as a coalition of individuals and groups with goals which may coincide but often do not. Collaboration and compromise is achieved by bargaining and negotiation and the establishment of agreed rules about the ways in which the parties should relate to each other. The pluralist perspective sometimes assumes that there is an approximate balance of power between the parties. Many industrial relations specialists can be described as pluralists. The radical frame of reference is based on a similar notion of divergent interests, but there is an assumption of a more extreme power imbalance between parties (in favour of management) and that collaboration between parties is based on the assertion of managerial power, with workers and their trade unions resisting where they feel able to. The radical frame of reference also locates the sources of divergent interests in the material conditions of the wider society. Fox's work is also described by Jackson (1977). Hyman (1975) provides an analysis of industrial relations using a radical frame of reference.

The different assumptions about the interests of the parties (joint or opposing) has consequences for values and assumptions about conflict. With their predominantly unitarist perspective, it is not surprising that organizational behaviour specialists have typically expressed an antipathy to industrial conflict. Since workers and managers have similar goals then conflict between them must be a symptom of poor organizational functioning, stemming from irrational forces within individuals or groups or from misperceptions by parties of their own interests or the other party's intentions. Such views on the destructive, and quite unnecessary, aspects of conflict can be found in the work of a number of writers in organizational behaviour and social psychology, either explicitly or implicitly. By contrast, industrial relations writers, whether adopting a pluralist or radical frame of reference, see conflict as an inevitable outcome of goals which are at least sometimes divergent. Conflict may occur over different goals, and even where there are joint goals there may be a divergence in how reward should be apportioned. For example, in an employment contract, both parties may agree that there should be an exchange of material reward for work undertaken, but this is indeterminate on the effort side, so that bargaining and conflict may occur over effort. Conflict, then, does not represent an abnormality in the smooth functioning of business, but should be anticipated as inevitable on occasions. It is legitimate for conflict to be expressed and for grievances to be heard and for employees to attempt to restrain the power of management.

It is significant that Fox's frames of reference have been widely and sometimes heatedly debated by industrial relations researchers, but that the discussion has barely been raised within psychology. The implicit acceptance of the unitarist perspecive has made debate unnecessary. Yet the debate is important, influencing the values associated with conflict, and here psychologists could learn much from writings in the industrial relations field.

Which frame of reference seems most realistic to adopt? In this chapter we would like to start with the assumption that worker and management interests can be different and that therefore conflict and disputation may follow. Conflict should not therefore be seen as necessarily and inevitably bad. This is not to say that the parties' interests never converge, but that often they will not. To develop a perspective away from unitarism is a significant development for many psychologists; whether one then accepts pluralism or radicalism may depend on the individual's outlook.

Definitions of Conflict

Conflict is a multi-faceted, ambiguous, and value-laden term and a number of writers have discussed its meanings (see for example, Schmidt and Kochan (1972) on organizational conflict and Edwards (1979) on industrial conflict). Pondy (1967) in talking of organizational conflict, notes that it is used in at least two ways. First it can refer to the antecedent conditions of conflict (scarce resources or incompatible goals), which may be called a conflict of interests or latent conflict. Second, it can refer to overt conflict (i.e., expressed in behaviour). For conflict to become overt, argues Pondy, antecedent conditions must not just simply exist, they must be perceived by the parties. The perception of a conflict of interest may often be accompanied by negative feelings such as tension, stress and hostility. Pondy stresses that the material conditions for conflict (antecendents) are not inevitably translated into overt conflict, but are mediated by perceptions. The same point was made by Kornhauser, Dubin, and Ross (1954):

'The reality of opposed interests *as seen by the parties* is, of course, the decisive fact. And the *perceived* relationship obviously depends not only on the 'economic facts of life' but also on the social interpretations current among the people involved. It is possible that, at least for limited periods of time, workers and managers may falsely believe that they have conflicting interests when in fact, no objective basis for such beliefs exists. Conversely, they may accept a doctine of complete harmony even though genuine grounds for conflict are present' (Kornhauser, Dubin, and Ross, 1954, p. 14).

This statement provides a firm justification for the place of social psychology in understanding industrial conflict. It is not sufficient to assume that conflict will be expressed where preconditions are favourable for it. Equally, Kornhauser, Dubin, and Ross go on to warn against the dangers of a purely subjective approach. They argue that attitudes and beliefs of groups must be studied 'along with economic analyses of their material interests'. Psychology must team up with other disciplines to provide an explanation of conflict based on more than one level of analysis.

Manifest conflict is expressed through behaviour, but how do we know the individual or group is acting in a manner hostile to the other party, or whether they are simply behaving in a manner which does not suit the other party's goals? In other words, there may be no intention to engage in conflict when A's behaviour thwarts B's plans. Pondy (1967) suggests that whether behaviour is categorized as manifest conflict depends on the context in which it takes place:

'In other words, knowledge of the organizational requirements and the expectations and motives of the participants appear to be necessary to categorize the behaviour as conflictful' (Pondy, 1967 p. 303).

He also argues that:

'. . . behaviour should be defined to be conflictful if, and only if, some or all of the participants perceive it to be conflictful' (Pondy, 1967 p. 303).

This ignores the difficulty of how to interpret behaviour which is not self-consciously conflictful but which takes place where a conflict of interests exists. In this chapter we will exclude such types of behaviour, although some would argue for a wider definition.

Forms and Incidence of Industrial Conflict

Before examining the causes and consequences of industrial conflict we must note the forms that industrial conflict may take. What behaviours are we trying to explain and how often and where do they occur? To obtain this information, we must rely largely on the industrial relations literature.

Kornhauser, Dubin, and Ross (1954) and Kelly and Nicholson (1980b) document the main forms of industrial conflict. Strikes are the most spectacular and easily identifiable form of action but other types exist. The withdrawal of co-operation by workers through overtime bans, go-slows, and work-to-rules are also considered to be manifestations of conflict. Action by management may take the form of a lock-out, where work is suspended and workers sent home. Managerial sanctions also may include stopping overtime opportunities, withdrawing worker privileges, threatening to cancel investment, or to close plant. 'Unorganized conflict' is the term sometimes used to refer to behaviour at the level of the individual worker which surfaces in 'hostile' behaviour towards management. Some writers argue that turnover and absenteeism are expressions of unorganized conflict, and sometimes accidents and sabotage are also included in this category. It can be seen that there is a great variety of forms of action purportedly expressing conflict.

We will examine briefly the arguments and evidence about unorganized conflict, since there is some debate about how far absenteeism and turnover should be viewed as conflict behaviours. Kelly and Nicholson (1980b) discuss the arguments and the evidence for viewing these behaviours as conflict. In the view that absenteeism and turnover are a form of conflict, two hypotheses about their relationship to collective manifestations of conflict (notably strikes) exist. The compensation or alternative hypothesis proposes that if discontent exists within a particular work group and it does not find expression in collective action then it will 'seep out' through individual behaviour. This suggests that where dissatisfaction is high and collective action, for whatever reason, cannot be organized, workers will express hostility to management through high absence and labour turnover rates. The additive hypothesis suggests that individual conflict will be highly correlated with strikes since workers who express discontent will do so in a variety of ways. In other words, where workers engage in a high level of strike activity they will also take days off and have high resignation rates.

Although the two hypotheses have generated some research there are conceptual and empirical difficulties with them. Absence and turnover can occur for a variety of reasons, some being involuntary (due to genuine illness, leaving the area, etc.). Clearly involuntary behaviour should not be counted as conflictful. Yet how can the degree of voluntariness be assessed? Even where absence and turnover are relatively voluntary, one cannot assume that they are manifestations of conflict.

Does the individual have to understand the 'underlying' reason for his/her absence or turnover, or is it simply legitimate for researchers to infer that this behaviour expresses conflict? The danger of including absenteeism and turnover within the definition of conflict is that it requires inference about the nature of individual's motivation. If they are included, the concept of conflict as an analytical tool is considerably weakened. Where would the boundaries around conflict be drawn? Should any behaviour not in immediate pursuit of management goals be labelled conflict behaviour? To resolve this difficulty we can return to Pondy's (1967) notion that the term conflict should only be used where some or all participants perceive the behaviour to be conflictful. This suggests that absenteeism and turnover may have different meanings for workers and management according to the organizational context and that sometimes absenteeism and turnover can be seen as conflictful although they will not always be so. Edwards and Scullion (1982) also suggest that such behaviour must be interpreted according to the organizational context. In their study of forms of conflict in seven factories they found that absenteeism had a different meaning for workers according to the settings they were in, and specifically according to the degree of managerial control over the work and the job. In plants with close supervision and a low level of job control by employees, absenteeism was seen as an escape from work pressures and frustrations, did not necessarily imply a challenge to managerial control, and was not therefore essentially conflictful.

Despite difficulties of definition and inference absenteeism and turnover could be described as conflict if at an empirical level they showed a clear and systematic relationship with other forms of conflict expression, for example, strikes. The conclusion of Kelly and Nicholson (1980b) in their review of empirical studies investigating the relationship between absenteeism and strikes was that an inverse relationship (high absenteeism associated with a low strike record and vice versa) was found only in the methodologically weaker studies, with the more rigorous studies, such as that of Turner, Clack, and Roberts (1967) of the British car industry, finding no significant relationship.

In conclusion, absenteeism and turnover will not be discussed further as a behavioural expression of conflict. The conceptual problems outlined above, along with the unsupportive empirical findings do not justify their inclusion. However, it is important that readers become familiar with the arguments, even where they are ultimately rejected in their simple form, since the debate about the relationship between 'organized' and 'unorganized' conflict continues. For a more detailed discussion of unorganized conflict, the book by Edwards and Scullion (1982) should be consulted.

It is difficult to gather information about industrial action short of strikes (overtime bans, go-slows, and work-to-rules are the main restraints on production short of stoppages). Such actions may not be easy to detect, even by management, because the behaviour is often a covert restraint on production rather than an open expression of hostility. Work behaviour continues but in a modified form. Additionally, no official statistics are regularly collected for such behaviours in the way that they are for strikes. Knowledge in this is extremely scarce and is based on work-place surveys. Illustrative of findings in this area, however, are those from the recent Warwick survey of manufacturing plants (Brown, 1981). It was found that action short of strikes by manual workers in the two years before the survey was reported by 29% of establishments.

What can be learned from looking at the relationship between the use of restraints on production and the use of strikes? Clegg (1979) suggested that the former represent 'low cost action' since they do not incur major financial or job security penalties for employees, while still being effective forms of action. There is some evidence that the application of sanctions, such as overtime bans, requires a high degree of workforce cohesion and discipline which is difficult to encourage where there is little existing trade union organization (Edwards and Scullion, 1982). The Warwick survey (Brown, 1981) found that strikes were highest in firms with low union density, presumably because well-organized workforces are able to apply sanctions short of strikes in pursuance of their demands.

Strikes have been the focus of much industrial relations research and have been the form of conflict behaviour most intensively studied. The book by Hyman (1972) explores a number of issues concerning the incidence, and causes of strikes and is essential background reading, providing a context for social psychological analyses. Information about strikes in the U.K. is mainly derived from official statistics collected by the Department of Employment (the Bureau of Labour Statistics research equivalent in the U.S.). The U.K. statistics include only larger strikes in their definition and have been criticized for under-recording small stoppages of less than one day or those involving less than ten people (see especially Edwards, 1983, but see also Kelly and Nicholson, 1980b). However, they are useful for examining strike trends over time and the incidence of larger strikes.

A complementary source of evidence is to be found from workplace surveys based on interviews with managers and sometimes trade union officials. These confirm the criticism of official statistics with respect to under recording since they reveal a higher level of strikes (Daniel, 1974; Parker, 1974). In the most recent Warwick survey (Brown, 1981) of British manufacturing plants employing more than 50 workers, it was found that 46% of plants reported strikes and other forms of industrial action by manual employees in the previous two years. One-third of plants (33%) had experienced strike action specifically.

Both official and workplace survey statistics indicate that the incidence of strikes is unevenly distributed across plants. Some plants are 'strike-prone' and others free of strikes. The difference between the two could be an area of particular interest to social psychologists who could usefully explore attitudinal and behavioural differences between plants. The study of the parties' attitudes towards each other, their frames of reference, the level of trust, their perceptions of their relative power could all be profitably examined along with, among other things, analyses of economic factors and industrial relations procedures.

In turning now to examine how conflict is generated, we will concentrate the discussion on strikes. However, there is clearly much work to be done in the area of industrial action short of strikes; on how it is organized and why certain actions are preferred or chosen in particular contexts. Why is a strike organized rather than an overtime ban for example? Such questions would require detailed studies of workplace organization and management strategy. Edwards and Scullion (1982) have addressed these issues but much work could be undertaken in this area by psychologists.

Psychological Theories of Conflict Generation

As discussed earlier psychological researchers have tended to bypass industrial relations issues. As a result they have conducted little work specifically on industrial conflict. However, they have carried out extensive research on social conflict in other settings through experimental studies of interpersonal conflict based on a variety of game matrices (see Deutsch, 1973). Farr (1979) reviews these studies in relation to industrial conflict and concludes that much of the work has only marginal relevance in applied settings. In this section some of the main psychological approaches to conflict are described. These can be divided into those based on analysis at the individual level and those which focus on the group (Skinner, 1979).

At the individual level an early formulation is that developed by Dollard (1939). Based on a biological approach to motivation this postulates that where an individual aspires to achieve a goal, and the path to the goal is blocked, the resulting frustration is channelled into aggression and conflict. This frustration–aggression perspective was widely explored in animal studies in the early period of the development of psychology. From that source and clinical research it obtained some support. However, its explanatory value is necessarily limited. This is because the approach specifies neither the level or kind of frustration which will impel aggressive behaviour, nor the target or form that behaviour will take. As Pepitone (1976) argues, there are considerable social influences on the display of aggression and these may be more important determinants of behaviour.

The view that job dissatisfaction is a determinant of industrial conflict is, in effect, a modern derivative of the above approach. Although this has not been developed into an explicit theoretical model the view is prevalent in many quarters, for example in the media and among managers and social scientists of a 'human relations' persuasion. Those who advocate the enlargement or enrichment of jobs, for instance, often imply that the resultant expected increase in job satisfaction will decrease industrial strife. Myers' book in this area, *Managing Without Unions* (1978), exemplifies the view. The author describes his work as:

> '. . . a source book for improving management, so members of the organization can achieve their personal goals through the achievement of organizational goals, and thus make unions unnecessary' (Myers, 1978).

Here is a clear expression both of a unitarist view and that 'bad management' lead to dissatisfaction which in turn encourages trade union activity and conflict.

Some accounts of strikes offer support for the above view, in that they focus on boredom, monotony, and punishing physical conditions as conducive to the outbreak of collective action. However, closer examination of the avilable evidence results in a less convincing picture. Kelly and Nicholson (1980a) point out that high levels of strike activity are often found among skilled workers for whom job satisfaction is typically higher than average. Turner, Clack, and Roberts (1967) reported that strikes in vehicle manufacturing plants occurred least often for those in the most repititious task areas. Beynon (1968) analysed a strike in a vehicle manufacturing plant and found that it was powerlessness in the face of managerial decision-making, rather than job dissatisfaction, which was the determining factor. And, as mentioned earlier (p. 54), cross-sectional studies have not consistently shown job attitudes to be related to trade union commitment. Thus, while frustration, or job dissatisfaction, may contribute to industrial conflict and even strikes, it is clearly not a sufficient or complete explanation. It is at best one element among many.

Sherif's theory of group conflict

Sherif and his associates developed a major theory of inter-group conflict in their field experiments with American boys attending summer camps. Sherif's work was a landmark, not just for its methodology (it marked a change from contrived, laboratory-based studies) but because he located the causes of conflict in the relationships between groups rather than in the motivations and frustrations of individuals. He predicted that where groups were in competition for mutually incompatible goals, conflict would arise and where groups engaged in tasks which needed inter-dependent behaviour, co-operation would ensue. Moreover, he argued that the inter-group antagonism and intra-group solidarity which would arise would be founded on differences in real material interests between the groups. This was a sufficient condition for conflict to occur. The best description of the work is in Sherif (1966) although useful, shorter, accounts are available (Skinner, 1979; Tajfel and Fraser, 1978). Sherif's programme of research, begun in 1949, consisted of three sets of experiments, each lasting about three weeks and with different subjects and in different locations. Most accounts summarize the findings of all three experiments together, as a composite. The subjects were carefully selected to be well-adjusted eleven to twelve year old American boys, with no previous friendships with one another and with no pronounced differences in cultural background or physical appearance. The careful selection of subjects was to avoid any alternative individual-based explanations of the results, for example that the subjects were maladjusted. The boys attended camps and were isolated from outside social contacts. Camp personnel, unknown to the boys, were all trained observers and experimenters. There were three stages of group interaction: group formation, inter-group conflict, and the reduction of conflict, the conditions for which were manipulated by the experimenters to test their hypotheses.

The stage of group formation started when, on arrival, the boys were divided into two groups, with contact between the groups being prevented until the next stage. Over about a week, group cohesion developed, friendships formed, status, and roles developed within the group.

In the second stage, of inter-group conflict, the groups were brought into functional contact whereby they competed for goals which both groups valued but which only one group could win (for example, competitive team games.) Inter- and intra-group attitudes and behaviour during the second stage (of competition) revealed consistencies in all the experiments (even where friendships developed in the first stage were broken by placing friends in separate groups for the second stage). Unfavourable attitudes to the out-group developed, and contact with members of the other group decreased sharply. Derogatory traits were attributed to the other group and lower estimates made of, and value placed on, their achievement (even where the experimenters were able to take covert objective measures which showed no difference in the performance of the two groups). The hostility and conflict between the two groups could be very intense (the second experiment actually had to be abandoned because the level of hostility between the groups was so high!). While social distance from the other group increased, at the same time solidarity and co-operativeness within each group increased, with interpersonal conflict minimized. Members tended to over-estimate the achievements of their own group.

In the third stage, of the reduction of inter-group conflict, conditions which encouraged inter-group co-operation were introduced: situations where valued goals could only be achieved by both groups acting co-operatively (for example, helping to pull a truck to get it started). Initially, inter-group hostility and tension remained high and it was only after a *series* of such tasks that friendly social interaction between the groups took place and the negative traits attributed to the other group were gradually replaced by more positive ones. Over time interaction with the other group members became as desired as interaction with members of one's own group. The reduction in conflict was not due simply to increased interaction between the groups: where that had occurred verbal and physical abuse remained high. Sherif and his associates demonstrated that inter-group hostility could be reduced only through the presence of goals and tasks which both groups desired and which neither group could achieve alone.

Sherif's theory has been tested in laboratory-based experiments and with temporary working groups. Blake and Mouton (1962), for example, working with a variety of groups including both managers and trade unionists, showed that conflict could be induced where groups competed for outcomes attainable only by one (in experimental gaming terms these were zero-sum games), and co-operativeness could be stimulated by jointly working on common or superordinate goals. The work of Blake and Mouton has become popular in organizational behaviour, where the key lesson taken is that the provision of common goals eliminates conflict, although the notion of joint goals as the only means to conflict elimination ignores the conflict of interests between managers and employees which we have discussed earlier. Also, it is important to recognize that Blake and Mounton's work derived from training workshops which present somewhat artificial, and temporary, tasks and groups.

Although a number of writers have pointed to the relevance of Sherif's work to understanding industrial conflict (e.g., Kelly and Nicholson, 1980a; Skinner, 1979), Sherif himself was cautious. He placed two caveats on the application of his work to industrial settings. Firstly, he noted that an interdisciplinary understanding of conflict was essential: '... not all problems pertaining to groups and their relations are psychological' (p. 62). Like Kornhauser, Dubin, and Ross (1954) he suggested that analysis was needed at more than one level. Secondly, he pointed out that in industrial settings:

> '... it is important to specify differences from the model of our experiments ... (a) salient difference is that some groups in industry possess notably more power than others' (Sherif, 1966, p. 100).

For Sherif, this suggested that the development of superordinate goals might not always be sufficient to reduce inter-group conflict. Many organizational behaviour writers have ignored this caveat in their exhortations to management to develop common goals with their workforce as a principal means of conflict reduction.

Tajfel's theory of social competition

The work of Tajfel and his associates (Tajfel, Billig, Bundy, and Flament, 1971; Tajfel and Fraser, 1978) extended theory about inter-group conflict. They suggested that while Sherif's theory is empirically supported, it is incomplete as an explanation of group conflict because, they argue, inter-group conflict can be caused without the difference in the material interests of groups. Tajfel proposed that the simple fact of belonging to a group was significant for group members in terms of social identity. Brought into interaction, or even just the presence of another group, group members will tend to evaluate their own group in positive terms and out-group in negative terms. Also they will prefer to interact with and reward their own group members. This, Tajfel suggests, is sufficient for conflict to occur, through discrimination and reduced interaction with out-group. Once conflict, is initiated, it takes a similar course, in terms of attitudes, perceptions, and behaviour, for the groups, as that described by Sherif. Tajfel calls his a theory of social competition, to distinguish it from Sherif's theory of real or material competition. Tajfel thus extends the causes of inter-group conflict, although he does not contradict the work of Sherif.

The evidence for Tajfel's ideas of social identity and social comparison in groups derives from a set of laboratory experiments. The 'minimal group experiment' (e.g., Billig and Tajfel, 1973) consisted of subjects who were assigned to groups on the basis of insignificant criteria. Subjects were unaware of the basis for their group assignment, although they knew which group they and the other subjects were in. They were then asked to award points to members of their own or the other group over a series of trials (although the subjects did not meet, as this might have confounded the experiment by introducing personal preference influences). Where in-group and out-group members were paired, reward tended to be allocated to create maximum difference between the groups while favouring their own group (even where this meant that the in-group received less than their maximum available reward). Although this minimal group experiment did not model conflict behaviours, it does indicate that identification with a group can be sufficient to cause discriminatory behaviour between groups, and we can infer that the discrimination may exacerbate existing tensions.

While other experiments have been conducted (see Turner and Giles, 1982), these have largely been laboratory-based and are not necessarily indicative of how groups in industrial settings might behave. In other words, the external validity of the experiments is low. With no other information to go on than group membership, subjects may have discriminated in favour of their own group for a variety of reasons (although the trials with same group members to some extent controlled for this). Also a theory developed in a laboratory is able to present subjects with clear and unambiguous group categories, which may be less than realistic, given the muliple membership an individual has of groups in real life. However, the theory is important in pointing to the importance of inter-group perceptions, group identification, and relative status, and how these interact to sustain and magnify differences of objectives and perceptions.

The theories of Sherif and Tajfel are similar in seeing the group, rather than the individual, as the basis of conflict. Both seem useful in understanding how industrial conflict, and strikes in particular, may develop and escalate. The attitudinal and behavioural correlates of inter-group hostility may help to explain why, when conflict has started, it is difficult to stop. Both theories are valuable in emphasizing the importance of perceptions and attitudes in the development of conflict, which Kornhauser, Dubin, and Ross (1954) and Pondy (1967) note as a significant element in manifest conflict.

On their own, however, these theories cannot provide a complete explanation of conflict generation if divergent interests between management and workforce are accepted. Sherif's theory is unable to explain why strikes and other forms of action are not more widespread. Tajfel's notion of group identification and social competition also has difficulies, given widespread class and occupational differentiation in industry, in explaining why conflict is not more prevalent than it is. Psychological theories of conflict need to be able to explain *industrial peace*, as well as industrial conflict. Additionally, such theories must take account of the fact that strike levels change over time and that certain industries and plants are more strike-prone than others (see p. 170). Sherif's point that power is a salient component of industrial relations has not been pursued by psychologists, although there is increasing interest in perceptions of power as a dimension of inter-group relations. These criticisms should not be taken to suggest that social psychological theories of conflict are inappropriate; they can be valuable when integrated with explanations at other levels of analysis.

Other Levels of Analysis of Strike Causation

Social, economic and political variables can have a strong influence on facilitating or suppressing strike action and they may explain better the observed variations in strike frequency over time and between organizations. Theories abound, ranging from explanations in terms of industrialization through to the explanations at the level of the individual (the latter we have already discussed). Kelsall (1958) and Kelly and Nicholson (1980a) discuss a variety of such explanations. These are not mutually exclusive, since different levels of analysis are being employed. They draw on economics, sociology and the study of industrial relations institutions. If we are to understand strike generation we need to have some awareness of:

1. National trends.
2. Inter-industry comparisons.
3. Intra-industry comparisons.

We will briefly examine each in turn.

National trends

Strike trends have been investigated through examination of official statistics collected about strikes. Many analyses have been made of U.K. strike trends (see for example, Edwards, 1983). In the 1950s, in many countries including the U.K. and U.S.A., there was a declining strike rate. However, in the U.K. between 1960 and 1970, there was a steady increase in the number of strikes outside coal-mining. During the 1970s the incidence fluctuated but remained above the 1970 level. From 1980 onwards strike activity has dropped dramatically (Edwards, 1983). (Coal-mining is often excluded from analyses because of its unusual strike patterns.) Additionally, for the U.K., two features are apparent. Firstly, the duration of strikes has increased over the last decade. Secondly, large strikes involving a large number of workers has increased, particularly in the public sector.

Economic forces have generally been viewed as having a major impact on strike levels. Knowles (1952) suggested that strikes were related to the business cycle, with an increase in the number of strikes and a decrease in their length when union's bargaining power is at its greatest (i.e., during an economic boom). Recession brings a decline in the number, and an increase in the duration of strikes. Edwards (1983) and Clegg (1979) discuss this relationship for the U.K. Incomes policies and inflation have both been discussed as possible causes of high strike levels (Clegg, 1979; Edwards, 1983). In the late 1960s, it was popular to assert that the observed dramatic increase in workplace (as opposed to national) level bargaining had contributed to a breakdown in formal industrial relations structures, and that this was a cause of the increased strike activity. While this partially fitted strike trends in the 1960s, it proved inadequate in the light of strike incidence during the 1970s and 1980s. During these years workplace organization and bargaining continued to develop but the rate of strikes decreased. However, for a while it was a popular theory, consistent with the Ross and Hartmann (1960) notion that encouraging formal collective bargaining would reduce strike levels.

Inter-industry comparisons

Certain industries, notably coal, iron and steel, shipbuilding, motor vehicle manufacture, and docks have high levels of strikes. Others, notably retail and distribution, footwear, and railways have low strike rates. The ranking of industries over time has changed very little, and some (though not all) of these industries, have similar rankings in international inter-industry comparisons. The differences across industry may provide clues as to why strikes occur. Technology has been suggested as a variable, although this fails to explain satisfactorily the often dramatic variations within industries. Union density and strength have also been put forward as an explanation, although the evidence is not clear on this point. As suggested earlier, strong unions may not need to resort to strikes to pursue their goals, preferring the use of sanctions. Clegg (1979) suggests that high strike rates characteristic of certain industries may perhaps be explained by the presence of fluctuating earnings (caused, for example, by being on piece rates) and the existence of fragmented bargaining (with frequent opportunities to bargain at the point of production). This would explain high levels of strikes in coal-mining (and their more recent decline with the introduction of new pay schemes and bargaining arrangements) although it does not fit all industries. However, it suggests that there may be pressures which could be converted to grievances or demands through collective action.

Intra-industry comparisons

There is a considerable variation in the strike records of plants within an industry, for example across different coalmines in the U.S.A. (see Brett and Goldberg, 1979). The recent survey of manufacturing industry in the U.K. (Brown, 1981) found that 4% of plants accounted for 49% of incidents of strikes and other actions. Strikes seem to be unevenly distributed with some plants consistently strike-prone while at the other extreme, others are strike-free. A major influence, suggested by the Warwick workplace survey (Brown, 1981) was that of size, which was positively correlated with strikes. Larger plants experienced a higher number of strikes and a greater number of working days lost per worker. Similar results have been found with official statistics also (e.g., Prais, 1978). While the effect of size is marked, it is not clear what organizational or inter-group processes are associated with it, for example whether it influences inter-group communications, attitudes, or decision-making.

Brett and Goldberg (1979) suggested that within coal-mines, strikes occurred less often where managers are able to solve problems and grievances at local level, without referring them to higher levels of management. The survey by Brown (1981) analyses other variables thought or found to be related to intra-industry differences in strike rates.

Some of the above ideas are concerned with explaining the susceptibility of certain types of plant to strike action, rather than the reasons for a stoppage in a particular plant. They had been based on aggregate statistics and give an indication of variables which *facilitate* strike action. To understand why strike action is taken by a particular workgroup we have to use disaggregated data, based on case studies of individual plants or workshops.

Case Studies of the Nature, Processes, and Outcomes of Strikes

We have so far considered a range of general or nomothetic explanations of strike causation, from the psychologcial to the economic. These inevitably omit two issues from consideration. First, they have little to say about how discontent is transformed into strike action. Second, they cannot highlight the often unique or idiographic nature of strikes. Eldridge (1968) and Nicholson and Kelly (1980) warn against treating strikes as a uniform social phenomenon. It may be that they are homogeneous only in that they involve a stoppage of work. An important alternative perspective is therefore provided by observational case studies, and illustrative work of this nature will be briefly described here.

Batstone, Boraston, and Frenkel (1978) observed 25 stoppages or near stoppages in a large U.K. plant of about 4,500 manual workers engaged in vehicle manufacture. An interesting feature of their account is that although a strike might appear to be an obvious and highly visible phenomenon, there are certain difficulties in defining it. When is a 'pause for discussion' or a union meeting which extends beyond the meal-break seen as a strike? A stoppage may not develop into a strike and Batstone, Boraston, and Frenkel (1978) describe several such incidents as well as some which lead to strikes. They found that management played a crucial role in strike definition. On occasions management preferred not to define a stoppage as a strike but rather to work on ways of overcoming the dispute, especially where there were production pressures. This suggests that the definition of a stoppage as a strike is a *social process*, dependent on the relationship between the parties and their organizational context. Here we might in passing also note the point made by von Beyme (1980), among others (e.g., Eldridge, 1968), that strikes and other forms of industrial action are not always a cost to management. Management may provoke, or allow a strike in order to discredit the union, or arrange that, if inevitable, it occurs at a time which suits them, or use a strike to avoid wage costs in times of slack product demand.

The focus of Batstone, Boraston, and Frenkel's (1978) work was how an event or situation was defined by the workgroup as a problem and how collective action was organized. They found that workers had to develop a rationale in support of strike action (see also Hiller, 1928). In order to develop support for a strike someone has to put forward arguments to convince people, firstly that there is a problem, and secondly, that it would best be solved by strike action. The authors call these justifications 'vocabularies of action', and found that they varied from an appeal to immediate sectional interests to arguments based on union principles. Generally, more than one type of argument was used to propose strike action. The authors observed that minor frustrations have to be built up into a coherent interpretation of events, 'to mould and shape workers perspectives' (Batstone, Boraston, and Frenkel, 1978, p. 61). Vocabularies in opposition to strike action were also framed; often by convenors and the more-experienced shop stewards.

Additionally, in this study it was found that stoppages and near-stoppages were not randomly distributed through their observation period of 75 days but were clustered. A third of the incidents occurred in just three days. Although the issues were not obviously interrelated in this period, they occurred close to days when there were mass meetings about the annual wage negotiations. The authors suggest that during this time, the workers were more conflict-oriented and 'bargaining-aware'. In other words, the perceptions of the potential strikers, and the organizational context were important, as Kornhauser earlier suggested.

With respect to the roles of individuals Batstone, Boraston, and Frenkel found that shop stewards were the main category of worker employing arguments to persuade others to support strike action; they initiated twelve out of 25 stoppages or near-stoppages. There were differences in strike initiation between types of shop steward. In an earlier book Batstone, Boraston, and Frenkel (1977) had distinguished between *leader* and *populist* shop stewards. Populists reflect rather than mould their members' opinions while leaders are more ready to adopt policies and strategies which are initially contrary to those desired by their constituency. In the study described here the researchers found that the leader steward was more likely to restrain sectional interests, and to be more strategic:

'. . . he tends to use the strike weapon more carefully and to time its use with greater skill' (Batstone, Boraston, and Frenkel, 1978, p. 73).

Strikes were often avoided by convenors and the more experienced shop stewards close to them. These people were able to use other means, such as informal talks with management, to resolve issues. They were also more aware of the dangers of sectional disputes to a strong union organization and so were prominent in arguing against strikes. However, their part was crucial in the development of support for a large strike which almost took place.

The major role played by certain individuals in orchestrating collective support for action is also seen in the description of a short, wild-cat stoppage among coal-miners, described by Paterson and Willett (1951). However, this should not be seen as confirming an 'agitator' view of the instigation of strikes. Hyman (1972) and Kelly and Nicholson (1980a) dismiss this as a plausible theory since agitation requires a pre-existing level of discontent. Individuals may shape discontent towards particular action but persuasion is their only means.

The above research has been valuable in adding to our knowledge about how a dispute between managers and workers arises in a particular context, and the social processes involved in initiating collective action. How far it is possible to generalize from that U.K. vehicle manufacturing plant to other types of employing organization or to other countries remains to be demonstrated, since little additional evidence is available, although Hiller (1928) has emphasized the considerable amount of planning and organization which must go into generating the collective action of a strike. This is the area where the theories of Sherif and Tajfel may be most appropriate—where the development of group identity and cohesion is essential to the collective organization involved in strike mobilization, and where the attitudinal and behavioural correlates of conflict, so carefully documented by Sherif, may be significant in escalating conflict. Work could extend beyond these two theories, incorporating psychological expertise in the areas for example, of attribution theory, theories of leadership, expectancy theory about the perceptions of the rewards and costs of taking industrial action.

An early case study of a wild-cat strike in a gypsum mining and processing plant is that presented by Gouldner (1954) and highlights another feature of strikes: that simple monocausal explanations are inadequate. There had been no previous industrial conflict in the plant. Relations between the workforce and management had been relaxed, characterized by an 'indulgency pattern', which meant that the management did not impose close supervision on the job and allowed some job discretion, lateness, and absenteeism. Additionally, wage rates were slack, with plenty of overtime so that wages were high. The worsening economic climate and a change of works manager resulted in a downturn in wages and also increased managerial control over working methods and times. The strike was called over a wage claim. This Gouldner calls the '*manifest*' issue, although the underlying '*latent*' cause, he suggests, was the violation of workers' expectations about the indulgency pattern caused by changed economic and organizational circumstances. This raises the more general point of strike causation, that the actual focus of activity may not be the underlying cause or causes. It is to this that Kelly and Nicholson (1980a) refer when they distinguish between 'triggers' and 'issues'.

Hartley, Kelly, and Nicholson (1983) analysed the causes of the 13-week U.K. steel strike in 1980 and suggest that the trigger for the lengthy dispute was the low wage offer, seen by the unions as derisory. However, this needs to be understood in the light of the underlying issues: the decline in real wages and the dramatic increase in redundancies in the company over the previous decade. Beynon (1968) gives a vivid example in his description of a short stoppage in a Liverpool car manufacturing plant: a strike over lay-off pay occurring against a background of dissatisfaction with managerial treatment of grading grievances.

Some case studies have focussed upon group processes underlying strikes (Lane and Roberts, 1971). In Hartley, Kelly, and Nicholson's (1983) study it was clear that the strike committees set up to co-ordinate activities developed increased solidarity and cohesiveness over time—much as would be predicted by Sherif's work discussed earlier (pp. 165–7). However, to use Walton and McKersie's (1965) term, there was also much intra-party bargaining. That is to say, many adjustment bargaining and influence processes occurred *within* the group of strikers since unanimity of beliefs about strategies proved difficult to maintain over the extended period.

The outcomes of strikes have also been described. While these are commonly considered in terms of the degree to which each party has achieved, or failed to reach, its 'stated' objectives, it is clear that other effects ensue. Thus Kelly and Nicholson (1980a) suggest that strikes have substantive and procedural outcomes as well as an industrial relations climate outcome. Substantive change concerns the issues in question. Procedural outcomes concern how the relationship between the parties will be conducted in the future. The impact of a strike on industrial relations climate can be varied. Purcell (1979) suggests that, in some companies, a strike can 'clear the air', leading to a more co-operative relationship between the parties. In other situations, relations between workers and management may become bitter and mistrustful for some time (Hartley, Kelly, and Nicholson, 1983). Finally, a strike may have consequences for intra-party processes (see Hartley, Kelly, and Nicholson, 1983; Brett, 1981; Kochan, 1981). For example, after the steel strike there was considerable interest by certain rank and file workers in creating structural changes in their union, and making union policy more accountable to the shopfloor (Hartley, Kelly, and Nicholson, 1983).

Conflict Resolution

Having examined theories about conflict generation, focussing on theories of strike causation, we turn now to consider how industrial conflict might be resolved. Here we consider not simply strikes but the wider area of industrial action.

How conflict is resolved is crucially dependent on theories as to how conflict occurs. The view of conflict causation predicates the available solutions. Returning to the earlier discussion of values about conflict, and the unitarist, pluralist, and radical frames of references as described by Fox (1973), we can see that each frame of reference provides different prescriptions for the major means of conflict resolution. Within a unitarist framework, conflict is caused by failure or unwillingness by certain individuals or parties to perceive common goals. This suggests that human relations techniques for developing inter-party trust and loyalty will resolve conflict and prevent further outbreaks. The pluralist and radical frames of reference argue that there is an inherent, structural conflict of interests between managers and the workforce, which will not be simply resolved by shared perceptions and increased communication about organizational goals. The conflict of interests means that manifest conflict is inevitable and will only be resolved through structural change. For the radical, this means changes in the form of changes in industrial ownership and managerial control. For the pluralist, differences can be channelled, and temporarily resolved, through the establishment of particular industrial relations procedures and structures, notably collective bargaining.

We have already noted how strikes, and other forms of industrial conflict, require multi-causal explanation, so that conflict resolution might be expected to occur on several levels. Conflict resolution could occur through the elimination of manifest conflict, through settlement on conflict demands, through settlement on the underlying issues or through changes in the perceived or actual relations between parties. Resolution of these different aspects of conflict would require different strategies.

Both Kornhauser, Dubin, and Ross (1954) and Pondy (1967) as we have seen, emphasize the significance of perceptions in the understanding of conflict, while recognizing that an underlying conflict of interests is crucial. It is not a question of choosing whether conflict is structural or perceptual since both can co-exist. This was clearly demonstrated in Sherif's work which noted the psychological concomitants of inter-party conflict based on material competition. The existence of a structural cause for conflict was associated with intra- and inter-party changes which increased social distance, fostered distrust and hostility, and reduced inter-group communication. Even with the removal of competitive tasks, hostility did not decrease, because of the attitudinal and perceptual changes which had occured. It was only over a series of collaborative tasks that conflict and hostility gradually decreased.

Approaching conflict resolution through structural and social-psychological change is well illustrated in a case study of conflict in a small production plant engaged in filling gas cylinders in the U.K. (described by Donaldson and Lynn, 1976). Employing only 25 workers, the firm had a history of poor industrial relations climate, with a high level of grievances, and a series of bitter and protracted conflicts. There was discontent over the payment system and level of reward, and distrust of management which was seen to be remote, unreliable, and unwilling to reward effort. A change in plant manager brought both structural and human relations changes, which gradually led to improvements in relations over a ten-month period. Key elements in the formal, structural changes included increases in pay and leisure time for extra production, and a more flexible approach to the payment system and hours of work. Additionally, there were social-psychological changes including increasing the amount of contact between management and workers, sharing information, management keeping its word, and developing trust. The interpersonal and inter-group changes, mainly initiated by the new plant manager, were at first treated with suspicion by the workers (as Sherif would predict). Over time, however, in conjunction with material changes in job arrangements and financial reward they were accepted.

Conflict between parties may be incapable of resolution where positions are entrenched or there is little incentive to reach agreement. Sometimes third party intervention may be called for: mediation, conciliation, or arbitration (see Dickens, 1979 for an explanation of the differences in these processes). Arbitration, where the third party's decision is binding on both parties, is particularly prevalent in the U.S. Kochan (1981) discusses the types of third party intervention which may occur, and their behavioural implications for the parties and their relationships, using evidence from both laboratory and field-based studies.

In passing, we should briefly note conflict *prevention* strategies which can also take structural and social-psychological forms. The development of formal, recognized collective bargaining procedures to contain and channel potential conflict has been advocated by a number of writers (e.g., Clegg, 1979). This could include the development of a fast and effective grievance procedure to handle discontent where it surfaces (e.g., Brett and Goldberg, 1979). However, Batstone (1979) warns that such procedures may only institutionalize conflict if the underlying conflict of interests is not resolved. Organization development may also help to prevent certain aspects of conflict occurring, through the development of effective working groups and decision-making teams.

Before trying to eradicate the expression of conflict from the workplace, however, we should note that the absence of conflict is not necessarily better than its presence. Batstone (1979) warns of the dangers of being complacement about industrial peace:

'. . . The lack of dramatic forms of conflict does not mean that opposition does not exist; the balance of power may be such that the subordinate group is presently unable or unwilling to challenge the dominant group. Or apparent peace may indicate that temporary accommodations have been reached but that each party is permanently organized and ready to engage in forms of conflict expression' (Batstone, 1979, p. 55)

CONCLUSIONS

In this chapter we have examined the contribution of psychology to industrial relations in general, and industrial conflict in particular. Two conclusions may be drawn from this review. First, it is clear that psychological research has tended to neglect industrial relations issues. This we have suggested is at least partly due to a generally unitarist perspective on the part of psychologists. The consequence is that certain psychological contributions to this area of enquiry have been indirect, and incompletely formulated. They are thus of unproven utility. However, the area of industrial relations psychology is currently enjoying a revival. The second point is that there exists immense potential for psychological contributions. It is clear from accounts of bargaining, strikes and other aspects of industrial relations, that people's perceptions, values, attitudes, group membership, and other factors play an important part in accounting for the processes and outcomes which arise. Here is particularly fertile ground for empirical research and the development of theory from a psychological standpoint.

The argument, however, is not for an isolated psychological input to industrial relations. Rather, as it is hoped the chapter makes clear, it is for psychological methods, techniques, and theories to be used to complement those more firmly established in the area. It should be now be evident that industrial relations behaviour, such as a strike, is affected by a variety of factors which operate and must be simultaneously considered at differing levels of analysis. To understand the causes, nature and effects of industrial relations phenomena a multi-disciplinary approach is required. It is perhaps time that psychologists broadened their views, took on board what is inevitably a difficult though valuable task, and joined their colleagues already active in the area. Some psychologists have already done so, but others are needed to achieve the 'critical mass' necessary to make a substantial advance.

REFERENCES

Adams, J. (1965) Inequity in social exchange, in Berkowitz, L. (ed.), *Advances in Experimental Social Psychology*, Academic Press, New York, Vol. 2.

Anthony, P. D. (1977) *The Conduct of Industrial Relations*, IPM, London.

Bacharach, S., and Lawler, E. J. (1981) *Bargaining: Power, Tactics and Outcomes*, Josey-Bass, San Francisco.

Bain, G. S. (1983) *Industrial Relations in Great Britain*, Blackwell, Oxford.

Bain, G. S., and Clegg, H. (1974) A strategy for industrial relations research in Great Britain. *British Journal of Industrial Relations*, **12**, 91–113.

Balke, W. M., Hammond, K. R., and Meyer, G. D. (1973) An alternative approach to labour management relations. *Administrative Science Quarterly*, **18**, 311–327.

Batstone, E. (1979) The organization of conflict, in Stephenson, G., and Brotherton, C. (eds.), *Industrial Relations: A Social Psychological Approach*, Wiley, Chichester.

Batstone, E., Boraston, I., and Frenkel, S. (1977) *Shop Stewards in Action*, Blackwell, Oxford.

Batstone, E., Boraston, I., and Frenkel, S. (1978) *The Social Organization of Strikes*, Blackwell, Oxford.

Beynon, H. A. (1968) A wild-cat strike. *New Society*, **September 5**, 336–337.

Billig, M., and Tajfel, H. (1973) Social categorization and similarity in inter-group behaviour. *European Journal of Social Psychology*, **3**, 27–52.

Blake, R., and Mouton, J. (1962) The inter-group dynamics of win-lose conflict and problem-solving collaboration in union-management relations, in Sherif, M. (ed.), *Inter-group Relations and Leadership*, Wiley, New York.

Brannen, P., Batstone, E., Fatchett, D., and White, P. (1976) *The Worker Directors: A Sociology of Participation*, Hutchinson, London.

Brett, J. M. (1980) Behavioural research on unions and union-management systems, in Staw, B., and Cummings, L. (ed.), *Research in Organizational Behavior*, **2**, 177–213.

Brett, J. M., and Goldberg, S. B. (1979) Wild-cat strikes in bituminous coal mining. *Industrial and Labour Relations Review*, **32**, 465–483.

Brotherton, C., and Stephenson, G. (1975) Psychology in the study of industrial relations. *Industrial Relations Journal*, **6**, 42–50.

Brown, W. (1973) *Piece-work Bargaining*, Heinemann, London.

Brown, W. (1979) Social determinants of pay, in Stephenson, G., and Brotherton, C. (eds.), *Industrial Relations: A Social Psychological Approach*, Wiley, Chichester.

Brown, W. (1981) *The Changing Contours of British Industrial Relations*, Blackwell, Oxford.

Brown, W., Ebsworth, R., and Terry, M. (1978) Factors shaping shop steward organization in Britain. *British Journal of Industrial Relations*, **16**, 139–159.

Child, J., Loveridge, R., and Warner, M. (1973) Towards an organizational study of trade unions. *Sociology*, **7**, 71–91.

Clarke, R., Fatchett, D., and Roberts, B. (1972) *Workers' Participation in Management in Britain*, Heinemann, London.

Clegg, H. (1979) *The Changing System of Industrial Relations in Great Britain*, Blackwell, Oxford.

Daniel, W. (1976) *Wage Determination in Industry*, Political and Economic Planning, London.

Delafield, G. (1979) Social comparisons and pay, in Stephenson, G., and Brotherton, C. (eds.), *Industrial Relations: A Social Psychological Approach*, Wiley, Chichester.

Deutsch, M. (1973) *The Resolution of Conflict*, Yale University Press, New Haven.

Dickens, L. (1979) Conciliation, mediation and arbitration in British industrial relations, in Stephenson, G., and Brotherton, C. (eds.), *Industrial Relations: A Social Psychological Approach*, Wiley, Chichester.

Dollard, J., Doob, L., Miller, N., Marer, O., and Sears, R. (1939) *Frustration and Aggression*, Yale University Press, New Haven.

Donaldson, L., and Lynn, R. (1976) The conflict resolution process: the two-factory theory and an industrial case. *Personnel Review*, **5**, 21–28.

Douglas, A. (1962) *Industrial Peace-making*, Columbia University Press, New York.

Dubin, R. (1976) *Handbook of Work, Organization and Society*, Rand McNally, Chicago.

Dunlop, J. (1958) *Industrial Relations System*, Holt, New York.

Dunnette, M. D. (1976) *Handbook of Industrial and Organizational Psychology*, Rand McNally, Chicago.

Edwards, P. K. (1979) The 'social' determination of strike activity: an explication and critique. *Journal of Industrial Relations*, **21**, 198–216.

Edwards, P. K. (1983) The pattern of collective industrial action, in Bain, G. S. (ed.), *Industrial Relations in Great Britain*, Blackwell, Oxford.

Edwards, P. K., and Scullion, H. (1982) *The Social Organization of Industrial Conflict*, Blackwell, Oxford.

Eldridge, J. (1968) *Industrial Disputes*, Routledge and Kegan Paul, London.

Farr, R. M. (1979) The relevance of experimental gaming studies to industrial relations, in Stephenson, G., and Brotherton, C. (eds.), *Industrial Relations: A Social Psychological Approach*, Wiley, Chichester.

Fatchett, D. (1979) The form of participation in Stephenson, G. and Brotherton, C. (eds.),

Industrial Relations: A Social Psychological Approach, Wiley, Chichester.

Flanders, A. (1965). *Industrial Relations: What is Wrong with the System?,* Faber, London.

Fox, A. (1973) Industrial relations: a social critique of pluralist ideology, in Child, J. (ed.), *Man and Organization,* Allen and Unwin, London.

Gordon, M. E., and Burt, R. E. (1981) A history of industrial psychology's relationship with American unions: lessons from the past and directions for the future. *International Review of Applied Psychology,* **30,** 137–156.

Gordon, M. E., Philpot, J. W., Burt, R. E., Thompson, C. A., and Spiller, W. E. (1980) Commitment to the union: development of a measure and an examination of its correlates. *Journal of Applied Psychology,* **65,** 479–499.

Gouldner, A. (1954) *Wild-cat Strike,* Harper, New York.

Hartley, J., Kelly, J., and Nicholson, N. (1983) *Steel Strike,* Batsford, London.

Hiller, E. (1928) *The Strike,* Arno Press, New York.

Homans, G. (1976) *Social Behaviour: Its Elementary Forms,* Harcourt Brace, New York.

Hyman, R. (1972) *Strikes,* Fontana, London.

Hyman, R. (1975) *Industrial Relations: A Marxist Introduction,* Macmillan, London.

Hyman, R., and Brough, I. (1975) *Social Values and Industrial Relations,* Blackwell, Oxford.

Hyman, R., and Fryer, R. (1975) Trade Unions as Organizations, in McKinley, J. (ed.), *Processing People: Cases in Organizational Behaviour,* Holt, Rhinehart and Winston, London.

Jackson, M. (1977) *Industrial Relations,* Croom Helm, London.

Kelly, J., and Nicholson, N. (1980a) The causation of strikes. *Human Relations,* **33,** 853–883.

Kelly, J., and Nicholson, N. (1980b) Strikes and other forms of industrial action. *Industrial Relations Journal,* **11,** 20–31.

Kelsall, E. P. (1958) A theoretical setting for the study and treatment of strikes. *Occupational Psychology,* **32,** 1–20.

Knowles, K. (1952) *Strikes—A Study of Industrial Conflict,* Blackwell, Oxford.

Kochan, T. A. (1980a) Collective bargaining and organizational behaviour research, in Staw, B., and Cummings, L. (eds.), *Research in Organizational Behavior,* **2,** 129–176.

Kochan, T. A. (1980b) *Collective Bargaining and Industrial Relations,* Irwin, Homewood, Illinois.

Kochan, T. A. (1981) An American perspective on the integration of the behavioural sciences into industrial relations, in Thomson, A., and Warner, M. (eds.), *The Behavioural Sciences and Industrial Relations,* Gower Press, Aldershot.

Kolaja, J. (1965) *Workers' Councils: the Yugoslav Experience,* Tavistock, London.

Kornhauser, A., Dubin, R., and Ross, A. (1954) (eds.), *Industrial Conflict,* McGraw-Hill, New York.

Lane, T., and Roberts, K. (1971) *Strike at Pilkingtons,* Fontana, London.

McGrath, J. E. (1966) A social psychological approach to the study of negotiation, in Bowers, R. (ed.), *Studies on Behavior in Organizations,* University of Georgia Press, Georgia.

Magenau, J. M., and Pruitt, D. G. (1979) The social psychology of bargaining, in Stephenson, G., and Brotherton, C. (eds.), *Industrial Relations: A Social Psychological Approach,* Wiley, Chichester.

Margerison, C. J. (1969) What do we mean by industrial relations? A behavioural science approach. *British Journal of Industrial Relations,* **7,** 273–286.

Maxey, C., and Mohrman, S. A. (1980) Worker attitudes toward unions: a study integrating industrial relations and organizational behaviour perspectives.

Proceedings of the 33rd Annual Meeting of the Industrial Relations Research Association, 326–333.

Morley, I. (1979) Behavioural studies of industrial bargaining, in Stephenson, G. and Brotherton, C. (eds.), *Industrial Relations: A Social Psychological Approach*, Wiley, Chichester.

Morley, I. (1981) Negotiation and bargaining, in Argyle, M. (ed.), *Social Skills and Work*, Methuen, London.

Morley, I., and Stephenson, G. (1977) *The Social Psychology of Bargaining*, Allen and Unwin, London.

Mulder, M. (1971) Power equalisation through participation? *Administrative Science Quarterly*, **16**, 31–38.

Myers, C. S. (1933) *Industrial Psychology in Great Britain*, (2nd Edn.), Cape, London.

Myers, M. S. (1978) *Managing Without Unions*, Addison-Wesley, New York.

Nicholson, N. (1976) The role of the shop steward. *Industrial Relations Journal*, **7**, 15–26.

Nicholson, N. (1981) Motivation: a test case for the integration of psychology and industrial relations, in Thomson, A., and Warner, M. (eds), *The Behavioural Sciences and Industrial Relations*, Gower Press, Aldershot.

Nicholson, N., and Kelly, J. (1980) The psychology of strikes. *Journal of Occupational Behaviour*, **1**, 275–284.

Nicholson, N., Ursell, G., and Blyton, P. (1982) *The Dynamics of White-collar Unionism*, Academic Press, London.

Parker, S. (1974) *Workplace Industrial Relations*, HMSO, London.

Paterson, T., and Willett, F. (1951) Unofficial strike. *Sociological Review*, **43**, 57–94.

Pepitone, A. (1976) Toward a normative and comparative biocultural social psychology. *Journal of Personality and Social Psychology*, **34**, 641–653.

Pfeffer, J. (1981) *Power in Organizations*, Pitman Publishing, Marshfield, Massachusetts.

Pondy, L. (1967) Organizational conflict: concepts and models. *Administritive Science Quarterly*, **12**, 296–320.

Poole, M. (1975) *Workers' Participation in Industry*, Routledge and Kegan Paul, London.

Prais, S. J. (1978) The strike proneness of large plants in Britain. *Journal of the Royal Statistical Society*. Series A (General), 141, 368–384.

Pritchard, R. (1969) Equity theory: a review and critique. *Organizational Behavior and Human Performance*, **4**, 176–211.

Purcell, J. (1979) The lessons of the Commission on Industrial Relations' attempts to reform workplace industrial relations. *Industrial Relations Journal*, **10**, 4–22.

Rackham, N., and Carlisle, J. (1978) The effective negotiator, I: The behaviours of successful negotiators. *Journal of European Industrial Training*, **2**, 6–11.

Rackham, N., and Carlisle, J. (1979) The effective negotiator, II: Planning for negotiations. *Journal of European Industrial Training*, **2**, 2–5.

Rhenman, E., Strömberg, L., and Westerlund, G. (1970) *Conflict and Co-operation in Business Organizations*, Wiley, London.

Ross, A., and Hartmann, P. (1960) *Changing Patterns of Industrial Conflict*, Wiley, New York.

Runciman, W. (1966) *Relative Deprivation and Social Justice*, Routledge and Kegan Paul, London.

Schein, E. H. (1980) *Organizational Psychology*, 3rd Edn., Prentice-Hall, Englewood Cliffs, New Jersey.

Schmidt, S. M., and Kochan, T. A. (1972) Conflict: towards conceptual clarity. *Administrative Science Quarterly*, **17**, 359–370.

Sherif, M. (1966) *Group Conflict and Co-operation*, Routledge and Kegan Paul, London.

Skinner, M. (1979) The social psychology of inter-group conflict, in Stephenson, G., and

Brotherton, C. (eds.), *Industrial Relations: A Social Psychological Approach*, Wiley, Chichester.

Spinrad, W. (1960) Correlates of trade union participation: A summary of the literature. *American Sociological Review*, **25**, 237–244.

Stagner, R. (1956) *The Psychology of Industrial Conflict*, Wiley, New York.

Stagner, R., and Rosen, H. (1965) *The Psychology of Union-management Relations*, Tavistock, London.

Stephenson, G. (1978) Negotiation and collective bargaining, in Warr, P. B. (ed.), *Psychology at Work* (2nd Edn.), Penguin, Harmondsworth.

Stephenson, G. (1981) Intergroup bargaining and negotiation, in Turner, J. C. and Giles, H. (eds.), *Inter-group Behaviour*. Blackwell, Oxford.

Stephenson, G., and Brotherton, C. (eds.), (1979) *Industrial Relations: A Social Psychological Approach*, Wiley, Chichester.

Strauss, G. (1979) Can social psychology contribute to industrial relations? in Stephenson, G. and Brotherton, C. (eds.), *Industrial Relations: A Social Psychological Approach*, Wiley, Chichester.

Tagliacozzo, D. L., and Seidman, J. (1956) A typology of rank and file union members. *American Journal of Sociology*, **61**, 546–553.

Tajfel, H., Billig, M., Bundy, R., and Flament, C. (1971) Social categorization and inter-group behaviour. *European Journal of Social Psychology*, **1**, 149–177.

Tajfel, H., and Fraser, C. (1978) *Introducing Social Psychology*, Penguin, Harmondsworth.

Thomson, A., and Warner, M. (1981) *The Behavioural Sciences and Industrial Relations*, Gower, Aldershot.

Turner, H., Clack, G., and Roberts, G. (1967) *Labour Relations in the Motor Industry*, Allen and Unwin, London.

Turner, J., and Giles, H. (1981) *Inter-group Behaviour*. Blackwell, Oxford.

Von Beyme, K. (1980) *Challenge to Power*, Sage, London.

Walker, K. (1979) Psychology and industrial relations: a general perspective, in Stephenson, C. and Brotherton, C. (eds.), *Industrial Relations: A Social Psychological Approach*, Wiley, Chichester.

Wall, T. D., and Lischeron, J. (1977) *Worker Participation*, McGraw-Hill, London.

Walton, R. E., and McKersie, R. B. (1965) *A Behavioural Theory of Labour Relations: An Analysis of a Social Interaction System*, McGraw-Hill, New York.

Warr, P. B., Fineman, S., Nicholson, N., and Payne, R. (1978) *Developing Employee Relations*, Saxon House, Farnborough.

Williams, R., and Guest, D. (1969) Psychological research and industrial relations. *Occupational Psychology*, **43**, 201–211.

Social Psychology and Organizational Behaviour
Edited by M. Gruneberg and T. Wall
© 1984 John Wiley & Sons Ltd

Chapter 8

Social Psychology and Organizational Change

D. E. GUEST

Almost all aspects of the application of social psychology to the study of organizations can imply change—for example, change to produce more effective leadership, change to increase satisfaction, or change resulting from conflict resolution. Inevitably, therefore, in this chapter we will re-trace ground that has already been partly covered in earlier chapters. At the same time, the focus on change in organizations can provide a useful integrating framework. However the subject of change is important in itself; indeed the 'problem of change', what to change, how to change, and resistance to change, can become a central pre-occupation within organizations.

There is no single integrative social-psychological approach to change in organizations. Instead, there are several approaches, each offering a different emphasis in defining both the nature of the problem and the appropriate method of bringing about change. This chapter starts by describing these approaches to organizational change and assessing some of the methods of change associated with them. Several attempts have been made to integrate the various approaches and three of these—organization development, the quality of working life, and employee participation—are examined in the following section. Finally the questions of strategy and evaluation are used as a basis for a more critical assessment of the contribution of social psychology to organizational change.

SOCIAL-PSYCHOLOGICAL MODELS AND ORGANIZATIONAL CHANGE

For the present purpose, eight social-psychological approaches to change can be identified. These are: the human relations model, field theory, systems theory, counselling, attitude theory, social learning theory, expectancy theory, and contingency theory. They have a number of features in common: each is based on a clearly identifiable theoretical perspective which exists independently of its application in industrial organizations; each defines the focus of change, and the aims and methods of change; each has been extensively applied in industrial organizations. It might also be added that each has particular strengths and weaknesses, and attracts its strong advocates and critics. It is therefore essential to analyse the assumptions underlying them and the evidence used in their support. The eight models and their implications for organizational change are summarized in Table 1. This section examines each in turn, identifying the key features of the approach, illustrating it with examples which have been used as demonstrations of its success in the introduction of change and assessing its strengths and weaknesses.

The Human Relations Model

The human relations model is based on the work of Elton Mayo and his Harvard colleagues (Mayo, 1933, 1945; Roethlisberger and Dickson, 1939). Mayo was an industrial psychologist who brought to the study of organizational behaviour the methodology and perspectives of clinical psychology and social anthropology. These were reflected in his views of the relationships between individuals, groups, and organizations—views formed on the basis of the now famous 'Hawthorne Studies' (see Chapter 3 and Chapter 7). An important outcome of this early field research was to highlight the importance of the social system, and the informal rather than formal structure, as determinants of employee attitudes and behaviour. The assumption was that improvements in the social system, resulting in cohesive social groups and an integration of management and worker goals, would lead to increases in satisfaction, morale, and commitment—and hence to improved performance. The improvements in the social system, in turn, were seen as being made possible by changing leadership style, building up communications and by recognizing and allowing for the influence of social groups.

Inevitably, over the years the Hawthorne Studies have attracted considerable and legitimate criticism (see Chapter 3). Nevertheless, in their day they provided an important counterbalance to the emphasis of scientific management, and offered a basis for a new strategy of organizational change. Perhaps the most coherent example of such development is that offered by Likert (1961, 1967). It contains several features. First, it advocates a highly participative style of management which is labelled 'System Four'. Second, it develops the linking-pin principle of organizational integration whereby each individual belongs to one or two hierarchically and horizontally linked groups who will ideally take participative group decisions. A supervisor will therefore belong to one group in which he is the supervisor and, along with other supervisors, to a second group in which he is a subordinate. The third feature is an advocacy of human asset accounting, a sophisticated system for taking positive account of human capital. This strategy of change involves the use of survey feedback and organizational

Table 1. Social psychological approaches to organizational change

Model	General focus of analysis	Aims/outcomes	Focus for change	
			What to change	How to change
1. Human relations	Social system Social relations	Social integration Satisfaction → improved performance	Social relationships	Alter leadership style, communication, consultation and develop group working
2. Field theory	Social values	Change in values Commitment to new goals	Individual values Group values	T-groups Group participation
3. Systems theory	'Production' systems	Joint optimization of social and technical goals	The socio-technical system	Introduce autonomous work groups
4. Counselling	Socio-emotional state	Improved mental health and socio-emotional competence	Individual's mental health	Individual or group therapy
5. Attitude theory	Attitudes. Beliefs	Attitude change → behaviour change	Attitudes	Present new information Persuasive communication
6. Learning theory (including social learning)	Competence in skill and knowledge	Improved competence → improved individual performance	Skill and knowledge	Training and education
7. Expectancy theory	Motivation	Improved motivation	The link between effort, performance and rewards	Alter rewards, job design and controls, perceptions
8. Contingency theory	Contextual variables	Appropriate context → effective performance	Contextual variables	Rational analysis → management introduction of changes

re-structuring together with training programmes to develop more participative management and open communication. He recognizes that change takes time and involves risks; therefore part of the use of human asset accounting is to widen the consideration of benefits to the organization to include such things as reduced labour turnover and absenteeism.

Likert's strategy of change with its focus on the whole organization, is highly sophisticated. Yet it contains some of the central problems of the human relations approach. Firstly it uses a doubtful model of satisfaction and performance in which satisfaction is seen as a causal influence on performance (see Brayfield and Crockett (1955) for a critique of this assumption). Second its focus on the social system exists at the expense of a concern for other key variables such as the production system and power relationships. Finally the focus on integration ignores the possibility of fundamental conflicts of interest between management and workers. These factors mean that the range of contexts in which this strategy can successfully be applied are likely to be limited.

Field Theory

Field theory, as developed by Lewin (1952) has several features, only a few of which will be discussed in the present context. Essentially, it is a dynamic theory which views behaviour as a function of the interaction between the individual and his environment. That environment may be variously conceptualized, but for Lewin, its important characteristics are those perceived by the individual—his life space or bounded field of perception. A key feature of all individual behaviour is that it takes place in, and will be influenced by, the social environment and more particularly the various groups to which an individual belongs. Therefore attempts to introduce change should concentrate not on the individual *or* the environment but on the individual *in* his social environment. The unit for change will therefore be the social group to which the individual belongs and from which he derives his values.

Another central feature of Lewin's theory is the concept of valence which is concerned with the attractiveness of certain goals. The stronger the valence the greater the force or motivation impelling the individual towards the goal. Whether the individual attains the goal or is frustrated depends on the barriers in the environment. Developing this into an analysis of the pressures for and against change in behaviour, Lewin utilized the concept of force field analysis. An important part of the field will be the social groups from which the individual derives his values. The general strategy for change, therefore, should be to use the group as a context to alter the individual's values and commitments, because group commitment serves to increase the pressures for and reduce the pressures against change.

Lewin (1952) demonstrated the value of this approach with his attempt to persuade women in American to purchase unpopular meats such as beef hearts and kidneys. A lecture programme, directed at individuals, persuaded only 3% to start buying the meats; group discussions, involving individual commitment in the context of a social group resulted in 32% changing their habits.

An attempt to apply these principles in the work context was reported in another classic study by Coch and French (1948) at the Harwood garment factory. Changes in the product and its packaging necessitated new work methods and a potential threat to incentive earnings. In two groups, each operator participated in group discussion of the need for change, the problems of change, and decisions about the change. A third group appointed representatives to participate on their behalf and a fourth group, a control group, simply had a meeting at which the details of the changes were announced. In the two participative groups, it took four days to return to the pre-change levels of production and it eventually settled down 14% above its earlier level. The group with a representative reached pre-change levels after 14 days and stayed at that level. Finally the fourth group showed a considerable drop in output, displayed aggression towards management and after considerable labour turnover was eventually disbanded.

Some years later, French, Israel, and Ås (1960) attempted to repeat this study using groups of men in a Norwegian footwear factory. Both the more and less participative groups returned to the same level of production and reported no change in job satisfaction; the only difference was that the participative groups returned to the previous production levels more quickly.

This second study can be used to criticize the viability of the approach. However, it can be interpreted within the context of Lewin's notion of force field analysis, in the sense that the pressures for change did not significantly outweigh the barriers to change. More specifically, the changes were seen as trivial and of doubtful value; and the method of direct participation in change was seen to cut across the highly valued representative role of the trade union.

A more recent study by Juralewicz (1974) in South America also failed fully to replicate the Coch and French findings. On the other hand, Fleishman (1965), using sewing machine operators who were given extensive scope for group decision-making reported highly positive results. In a recent re-appraisal, Bartlem and Locke (1981) criticized the failure to distinguish between the benefits derived from the process of participation and effects of the participative decisions. Indeed they prefer to interpret both the Coch and French and Fleishman results in terms of variations in the perceived fairness of the new rates of pay.

Even this reinterpretation does not deny the value of the process of participation and field theory is more concerned with the process than with the content of change. By highlighting the negative forces leading to resistance to change which develop when changes are externally imposed, together with the benefits of commitment to change, field theory focusses on the need to change values by using the social environment and in particular the social groups from which the individual derives these values.

The method of change has two main aims. The first is concerned with changing individuals. For effective change in individuals, which must mean a change in cognitions and values, the most appropriate setting is the type of social context from which so many values are derived (Benne, 1976). The preferred vehicle for this is a temporary training group—or what has come to be known as a T-group. The second aim is concerned with organizational change and here it is argued that the appropriate unit of analysis is the group rather than the individual, therefore group participation methods, along the lines of the Coch and French study, should be used. Finally Lewin pioneered the use of action research in organizations. This is a process whereby academics, making conscious use of behavioural science theory, intervene in organizations to introduce change, at the same time evaluating the impact of the intervention and therefore the validity of the theory. The Coch and French study is an excellent illustration of action research. Many of the approaches derived from field theory appear under the label of 'organization development', a more general approach to change which is discussed in a later section.

There are a number of problems in using field theory as a basis for organizational change. In many respects these problems are similar to those facing human relations. Firstly the concern for the social environment means that it can underplay the significance of the technical system. At the same time the emphasis on process can result in a tendency to ignore key features of the content of change. Secondly it plays down conflict and in particular ignores the economic and power-related bases for differences of interest. Thirdly Lewin and some of his followers displayed values which quite clearly favoured democratic and participative processes. However, this was a limited view, which under-emphasized representative democracy and it may have influenced their interpretation of some of the studies. Finally the methods of change are susceptible to the charge of being a sophisticated form of manipulation. This is a particular risk where careful and selective use is made of individuals' perceptions to lead them towards acceptance of change. (For a fuller discussion see Sofer, 1972). Despite the force of some of these criticisms, the approaches developed out of field theory have had perhaps the greatest influence on organizational change of all the social-psychological theories.

Systems Theory

Systems theory has a well-established basis in the physical sciences and in disciplines such as biology. It has also been adapted for use in the behavioural sciences. Talcott Parsons, for example, in his major work on the analysis of society, described it as 'the social system' (Parsons, 1951). Within psychology, Rice, of the Tavistock Institute has suggested that:

'An individual may be seen as an open system. He exists and can exist only through processes of exchange with his environment' (Rice, 1969, p. 574).

One of the important contributions to social psychology, and particularly organizational psychology is the major text by Katz and Kahn (1978). They use as their framework the concept of an open system. This, they believe, enables them to present a social psychology of organizations which extends beyond analysis at the level of the individual and group to consider questions of social structure as well as influences exerted from outside the organization. Von Bertalanffy (1968), distinguishing between open and closed systems, defined a closed system as existing independently of its environment while an open system interacts with its environment within a framework of inputs, transformations, and outputs. Clearly individuals and organizations should be viewed as open systems. One consequence of accepting the concept of an open system and the dynamic and selective nature of the interaction with the environment, is that in any change there is choice. A key issue therefore is to identify the range of choices and the influences upon the system.

The value of systems theory lies in providing insights of this type and presenting a useful and, within social psychology probably the most useful framework for the description and analysis of behaviour in organizations. Because of this, a general systems approach does not provide a specific strategy for change. However, researchers from the Tavistock Institute have developed a somewhat narrower, more applied approach known as socio-technical systems theory.

The pathfinding case which influences the development of socio-technical systems theory was reported by Trist and Bamforth (1951) on the basis of a study in coal-mining. The problem they investigated was the failure of new technology and the associated new organization of work to provide the expected benefits in terms of higher productivity. They concluded that the concentration on the technical aspects of production had occurred at the expense of the social aspects. This was a particular problem in mining where close-knit social groups had a tradition of shared concern for safety, allocation of work, and rewards. The solution, the benefits of which they were able to demonstrate through higher productivity, was to reconceptualize the production process in terms of a socio-technical system. The emphasis should be neither on the social or the technical aspects alone but on the optimal balance between them.

The coal-mining study had concentrated on the workplace and group level analysis and was reinforced by further work in the same industry some years later by Trist and his colleagues (Trist, Higgin, Murray, and Pollock, 1963). Subsequent studies, more particularly those by Rice (1958) in the Ahmedabad textile mills concentrated more on the organizational level. More recent work at different levels in a number of organizations in Norway (Emery and Thorsrud,

1976) has helped to consolidate this into a significant and highly influential strategy for change.

The focus of the socio-technical approach to change, is the 'production' system, what Rice (1958) terms the 'primary task' or main reason for the existence of a group of workers. The aim in considering changes is to achieve joint optimization of the social and technical systems and it is therefore these systems that have to be changed. In practice this means that jobs, departments, and sometimes whole production systems and organization structures will have to be changed. However, the unit of analysis is invariably the group and work is organized around the concept of the semi-autonomous work group. This is examined in more detail in a later section.

There are a number of practical and conceptual problems with socio-technical systems theory. For example the concept of joint optimization can present difficulties, depending upon how the goals are defined, but it could, in theory, point to the need for reduced autonomy. The use of the group level of analysis may limit the application of the approach. The motivational basis for the advocacy of the approach (Emery and Thorsrud, 1976) is unclear and unsubstantiated. Finally it is not clear how the technical system should be analysed. As a result of these factors, what has emerged in some of the more recent work is a rather normative view of organizational change. However, any criticism of socio-technical systems theory, as applied in practice, should not detract from the value of open systems theory as an analytic framework.

Counselling

Counselling is well-established within psychology and psychiatry as a means of facilitating individual change and within organizational psychology has been extensively applied in the form of vocational, career, and more recently retirement counselling. In addition counselling has been used in organizations for two more general purposes (Hopson, 1978). The first is to help individuals to change. This is an extension of clinical counselling and may involve the removal of fears and anxieties or the facilitation of learning. The second is to help individuals to adjust to external change and pressure. One illustration is assistance in developing methods of coping with stress.

Although counselling is not normally considered as a strategy for organizational change, a number of Tavistock Institute workers have used it for this purpose. The influences on this approach, as Sofer (1972) has noted, are both psychoanalytic and sociological and include the ideas of Bion (1968) who developed a method of group counselling where the group and the health of the group is the focus of analysis rather than the individual. Sofer (1961) has described his role in bringing about change through a form of client-centred therapy in which the unit of analysis is the organization or some part of it. He illustrates how, while not attempting to remove conflict, his intervention exposed conflicts, opened up organizational issues for discussion through a form of reality testing and thereby facilitated change. Variations on this approach are reported by Jaques (1951) at the Glacier Metal Company and by Menzies (1960) in a hospital setting.

The use of the group and organization, as well as the individual, as the unit of analysis places this kind of counselling within the ambit of social psychology. As a strategy of change, the general focus is on what might be termed the socio-emotional state of the organization and the groups and individuals within it and underlying this is a view of individual mental health and organizational health which is the goal of the intervention. To bring about change in socio-emotional competence, the form of counselling used, for example by Sofer, has two basic approaches. One is to reduce conflict and tension; the other is to permit growth and learning. Indeed one of the criteria of organizational health is that such growth can occur.

There are a number of problems with this approach to organizational change. Firstly it is based on a normative view of mental and organizational health which has its roots in psychoanalytic theory. Secondly the methodology seems to be unsystematic and there is a risk that key structural and more particularly economic variables may be ignored. Thirdly it places considerable emphasis on the authority and expertise of the change agent with respect to diagnosis, change strategy, and evaluation.

Attitude Theory

The study of attitudes and attitude change has always been a central topic in social psychology. The traditional model described attitudes in terms of three components; a cognitive, an affective, and a conative or action tendency. Implicit in the concept of an attitude is a causal link between beliefs and values and behaviour. If information can be presented which changes beliefs and values, then this may be an effective path to changes in behaviour. Furthermore it reflects a rational view of organizational life in which change is the result of information which convinces the receiver of the case and persuades him to change his views.

Hovland, Janis, and Kelley (1953) brought together much of the early work in social psychology which reflected this view. They used a form of information processing model in which attention was focussed on the communicator, the nature and organization of the presentation of the message and the receiver of the material. While acknowledging a number of problems, they concluded that in general a convincingly argued case, with good quality information deriving from a credible source would persuade the target to reassess his position and accept change. In organizations, much of the use of technical consultants and information-based education courses reflects this strategy. It also helps to explain why organizations place such emphasis upon the content and process of communication.

In essence, therefore, this strategy focusses on attitudes and on the assumption that a change in attitude will facilitate a change in behaviour. It seeks to change behaviour indirectly by changing attitudes first and it does this mainly through the presentation of new and persuasive information. It is popular in industrial organizations because it reflects the ideology of scientific management and the implied rationality underlying these organizations.

In practice there are many reasons why this is a grossly over-simplified picture. Firstly the concept of attitude and more particularly the link between attitudes and behaviour have come under critical scrutiny. Fishbein and Ajzen (1975) have argued that the term attitude should only refer to the affective or evaluative dimension of, for example, like–dislike or good–bad, and both beliefs and actions should be treated separately. They go on to suggest that the link between attitudes and behaviour will be determined by their correspondence and specifically in terms of the nature of the action, the target of the action, the context and the time (Ajzen and Fishbein, 1977). All too often these are ignored. Indeed the rather general surveys of the link between job satisfaction and performance (Brayfield and Crockett, 1955; Vroom, 1964) show an average correlation of only 0.14. When rather more specific issues are explored, the correlation improves. This was found, for example, in the link between organizational commitment and labour turnover (Mowday, Porter, and Steers, 1982) and between specificity of personally set goals and attainment of the goals (Umstot, Bell, and Mitchell, 1976).

A second problem is that at its simplest the model seeks to explain behaviour in terms of a single explanatory variable and to treat the receiver of information as essentially passive. Yet, as Festinger's (1975) theory of cognitive dissonance indicated, the individual may be faced with a conflict between existing ideas and the new information and the way in which he resolves these conflicts is not always predictable or rational. Kelman (1961) described a three-stage process of attitude change which identifies coercion, compliance, and commitment. Information is essentially directed towards compliance in the first instance; however, recognition of the difficulties of bringing about change in this way has led to the use of information directed at the emotions. A common example of this is the use of a certain amount of fear-arousal in safety and accident prevention campaigns.

A third, and linked problem with this strategy is that it can under-estimate the importance of the social context. Researchers have identified the importance of an individual's reference group, (Hyman, 1960) of communications networks (Shaw, 1954), and of opinion leaders (Katz and Lazarsfeld, 1955). Indeed a recognition of the importance of opinion leaders, or what Lewin (1952) termed 'gatekeepers', leads to the notion of a two-step flow of information in which the key initial targets are these opinion leaders.

All the research on information and attitude change serves to highlight the complexity of the subject. It does not negate the strategy but it does raise serious doubts about the extent of its feasibility and effectiveness. The more telling criticism comes from those who dispute the causal link between attitude and behaviour. An alternative model might emphasize the dynamic nature of the interaction; behaviour and experience may then become a major path to attitude change.

Social Learning Theory

Social learning theory (for an overview, see Bandura, 1977) proposes that almost all behaviour and more especially social behaviour is learned. The learning may be systematic or haphazard. In practice the key, and often rather haphazard process is socialization which, if successful, involves identification with a model and then the modelling or copying of the behaviour of that model. Other forms of learning can coexist as the parent or member of the work organization provides encouragement, guidance, and reinforcement for the appropriate form of response. If all behaviour is learned, then the strategy for change is one in which the key is to arrange structured learning and ensure that it is successful.

Socialization into a work organization can involve some complex processes of adjustment and change. Bloom (1956) has shown how learning can be considered in terms of hierarchies of complexity, the appropriate methods of instruction being of necessity geared to the nature of the material to be learned. The early experiences in a new organization, what Van Maanen (1976), in his review of organizational socialization, termed accommodation, are critical. For example Berlew and Hall (1966) found that the subsequent performance of managers depended to a great extent upon their initial socialization and early experiences in the organization. In common with others, their subjects used trial and error learning in the face of often stressful ambiguity and conflict. Social learning theory argues for a more structured and helpful approach to facilitate what can often be a stressful change. Not only will this remove some of the stress, but it will have long-term benefits in terms of commitment and effectiveness.

The strategy seeks a change in social skills and knowledge through training. This will occur either at the initial period of induction and socialization or later as a form of developmental training or re-learning. This second strand is based on the assumption that inappropriate skills are learned; the problem therefore is to unlearn inappropriate skills and to learn more appropriate ones. The emphasis on learning theory implies close attention to the methods of learning, to avoid the usual less conscious modelling or trial and error. One of the best known examples of this is social skills training (SST). Several approaches to SST have been developed (for a review, see Argyle, 1981), ranging from the conventional lecture to the encounter group. They have been based on careful analyses of social interaction in a range of work contexts (Rackham and Morgan, 1977), on developments in our understanding of non-verbal communication (Ekman and Friesen, 1975) and on more general attempts to classify human interaction (see for example Harris, 1973).

Two issues are central to SST. The first concerns the nature of 'effective' social behaviour, which can be difficult to define independently of the context in which it is displayed. While it can be relatively straightforward to define anti-social behaviour, the difference between barely acceptable and highly effective social skills in a work context is more difficult to identify. One approach is to validate effective behaviour against criteria of success such as number of sales, duration of meetings, or number of customer complaints. Another, which recognizes the dynamics of social interaction, presents broad normative guidelines about what constitutes appropriate behaviour as a framework for learning. This leads into the second point, namely the most effective form of training. Using the conventional principles of learning, the need to provide for practice and transfer point to the advantages of learning in a group. Therefore while the model of 'effectiveness' lies outside the group, practice within the group, using feedback as a source of evidence rather than pressure, provides a convenient context for technically and economically efficient development of individual social skills.

Argyle (1981) is critical of the rather general, often poorly evaluated packages for SST. Instead he has developed what he terms the 'Oxford' approach which he claims is distinctive in its careful development out of social psychological knowledge, particularly in areas such as non-verbal communication, sequence analysis and the study of social situations. The core method is role playing, the process whereby individuals can try out social skills in a safe environment. The particular form of role playing will depend upon the training need.

The concern for individual learning, even if it takes place in the context of a social group, limits the scope of this strategy by omitting structural variables. However, even within these limits there are the problems, discussed earlier, of defining what constitutes appropriate behaviour and the assumption that individuals have the motivation to learn it. At a more technical level, much of the learning of social skills takes place off the job and there are problems of transfer back to the workplace. Social learning theory therefore provides a potentially effective but strictly limited approach to organizational change which has nevertheless proved attractive to organizations employing workers such as salespersons, police, and airline stewards whose success depends to a considerable extent upon effective social skills.

Expectancy Theory

Expectancy theory is essentially a theory of motivation, but unlike certain other motivation theories which have attracted wide attention in work organizations (see for example Maslow, 1943; Herzberg, 1966) and which have a clinical bias linked to a concern for mental health, it leans heavily upon the social context for the derivation and adaptation of goals and behaviour. Indeed one of the earlier and best known formulations (Vroom, 1964) acknowledges a considerable debt to Lewin. Building on Vroom's work the theory has developed considerably in complexity and sophistication. However, the theoretical development has tended to run ahead of the methodology to test it, a point acknowledged even by Lawler (Lawler and Suttle, 1973), who has also presented one of the most sophisticated formulations (Lawler, 1971).

Taken at a fairly simple level, the theory suggests that effort or motivation will be a function of three factors. First the extent to which the individual believes that effort will lead to performance; second the belief that high performance will lead to rewards; and third the belief that attractive rewards are available, which outweigh the costs of obtaining the rewards. The theory goes further in suggesting that the link between effort and performance will be mediated by the individual's skill and ability and by the accuracy of his perception of his role requirements.

There have been numerous attempts to test expectancy theory. The number of variables involved means that most studies only test part of the theory. Campbell and Pritchard (1976) in a review of many of the earlier studies found that correlations between the independent and dependent variables rarely exceed 0.30. Furthermore the use of the multiplicative relationship between the independent variables only slightly improved the correlation. They conclude that while the model is not a powerful basis for explaining behaviour, it does have heuristic value. This suggests that if used cautiously the model could provide a basis for identifying some approaches to organizational change.

The focus of expectancy theory is on the need to change behaviour by changing (increasing) the level of motivation and, as a secondary factor, by improving the effort–performance linkage. The model points to several possible variables that might be changed to increase motivation. The first and most popular focus for change is the design of jobs to improve the link between effort, performance, and rewards. The second possibility is to change the nature of the rewards to provide the type or level of rewards that are more highly valued by the workforce. The third type of change is concerned with employee perceptions. This might include attempts to alter perceptions of the link between effort, performance and reward, perceptions of equity and perceptions of the most appropriate social role. Finally the changes might concentrate on selection and more particularly training to improve the skills, ability, and understanding necessary to translate high motivation into effective performance.

Expectancy theory has been widely criticized. The first, and major group of criticisms concern its complexity, the problems of testing it, and the consequent inadequacy of the methods employed in many of the studies which have attempted to examine it. Locke (1975), in particular has added a second type of criticism in expressing concern about the implicit hedonism and some of the other assumptions which underpin the theory. Finally, others have noted the difficulties in operationalizing the theory. For example Campbell and Pritchard (1976) identified the problems in using the concept of 'effort' and Wallbank

(1980) has reported several different ways in which 'effort' can be operationalized.

The complexity of the theory can also be an advantage; it highlights the range of variables influencing behaviour, thereby reinforcing both the complexity of change and the possibility of choice of strategy. Nevertheless its primary concern for individual behaviour imposes severe limitations on its value as a general framework for organizational change. In practice it has been found most useful in areas such as pay policy and job redesign. In particular, it provides the basis for the job characteristics model of job design which was first presented by Hackman and Lawler (1971) and has subsequently been developed both theoretically (Hackman and Oldham, 1976) and as a strategy for change (Hackman and Oldham, 1980). This proposes that the presence of certain core job characteristics leads to the existence of critical psychological states which result in high internal motivation. The aim is therefore to redesign jobs to build in these core

The key to the theory lies in the correct identification of the core job characteristics. This was based on a comprehensive literature review and guided by the central tenets of expectancy theory. A major influence was earlier work by Turner and Lawrence (1965) who had attempted to relate the objective characteristics of jobs to job satisfaction. Hackman and his colleagues adapted the dimensions and measures developed by Turner and Lawrence, in the process cutting out the dimensions of social interaction, and produced a set of standardized descriptive measures for diagnosis and evaluation. The model suggests that the potential for internal motivation is a function of five task dimensions, related to each other as follows:

$$\text{Motivating potential score} = \left[\frac{\text{skill variety} + \text{task identity} + \text{task significance}}{3}\right]$$

$$\times \text{ autonomy} \times \text{job feedback}$$

Skill variety, task identity, and task significance are linked because they are all associated with the critical psychological state of experienced meaningfulness of work. Autonomy leads to experienced responsibility for work outcomes while feedback is associated with the third psychological state of knowledge of the actual results of job activities. Since all three critical psychological states are considered essential for high internal motivation, their relationship is multiplicative. The final element in the model is an acceptance of the necessity for individuals to possess a strong higher order need strength, that is, the potential to be motivated by these factors and there is an acceptance that individual differences in higher order need strength might limit the effectiveness of the model.

may make its use in the introduction of organizational change more difficult. Hackman and Oldham are pragmatic about the type of change strategy needed to bring about job redesign and see factors such as power relationships and union strength as contingency factors helping to point to the appropriate strategy. They do, however, insist on careful diagnosis using the job diagnostic survey; thereafter they prefer the strategy most conducive to getting the change introduced properly, irrespective of whether it results in individual or group forms of job design and irrespective of whether participative or autocratic methods of introducing the change are used.

A careful study by Wall, Clegg, and Jackson (1978) and an experimental study by Orpen (1979) both gave partial but by no means clear support to the approach. More field experiments are necessary before a full evaluation is possible. A model which makes such clear statements about the important diagnostic dimensions and is at the same time so vague about the process of change (Clegg, 1980) is an easy target for criticism by those concerned with organizational change. Wall (1980) reporting an action research programme in which he considered the use of a form of the model found that it failed to fit the experience of the actors and their views of the important variables such as technology and management practices. In other words, its utility as a credible model for change was called into question. Nevertheless it does point to the choice of method of job redesign and makes it possible to advocate job enrichment without basing it on the now largely discredited (Locke, 1976), though still influential motivator-hygiene theory developed by Herzberg (1976).

Contingency Theory

Contingency theory was developed initially by sociologists interested in the impact of structural variables on other features of structure and behaviour in organizations. However, it has been adapted for use in areas of considerable interest to organizational social psychologists such as the design of payment systems (Lupton and Gowler, 1969) and the identification of appropriate leadership styles (Vroom and Yetton, 1973) see Chapter 2.

One of the earliest and most influential pieces of empirical work using contingency theory was reported by Woodward (1965). After surveying a number of organizations, she concluded that the nature of the technology had a major bearing upon the shape of the organizational hierarchy and structure. By implication certain designs were more appropriate for certain technologies; in her case she distinguished mass production, batch, and process industries.

A second U.K. study, by Burns and Stalker (1961), identified the nature of the market as the key contingent variable. They argued that organizations operating in a stable market environment were likely to be most effective if they utilized a 'mechanistic' or highly structured organization design. In contrast those organizations operating in turbulent markets, where swift adjustment to changing circumstances was required, would be more successful if they had an 'organic' or flexible, project-based structure.

A final illustration at the organizational level is the work of Lawrence and Lorsch (1967) on the importance for the success of large and medium sized organizations of achieving the right level of differentiation and integration. By differentiation, they mean sufficient specialization of function; by integration they mean the ability of the organization to create structures to integrate the activities of the various departments and direct them towards a common organizational goal.

The difficulty with each of these approaches is their focus on a narrow range of variables. This difficulty is reflected in the increased complexity of the range of contextual or contingent variables used when the analysis is moved 'down' a level to issues of more concern to social psychologists. For example, the model used by Lupton and Gowler (1969) to identify the appropriate payment system contains 21 variables ranging from degree of automation to number of trade unions and level of labour turnover. Vroom and Yetton in their contingency theory of leadership identify seven situational variables although the earlier formulation by Fiedler (1967) concentrated on three variables, namely leader–member relations, task structure, and leader position power to arrive at the most appropriate leadership style.

As a strategy of change, contingency theory seeks to provide a rational analysis of the independent variables to point to the most appropriate form of organization design, payment system, or leadership style. It should be based on an analysis of the choices available and can, in principle, be applied to any situation. Since the contingent variables are usually taken as given, the focus for change is the dependent variable. Because the principle of contingency theory can be applied at all levels, it is impossible to specify the precise variables which will be the focus of change. A contingency approach could also be used to identify the most appropriate form of implementation of the change. In practice this is often left open and it is assumed that the logic of the argument and the strength of the analysis will make the change widely acceptable.

Contingency theory shares some of the attractions and the problems of expectancy theory. It has also received widespread attention and considerable criticism (see Child, 1977). There are three main types of criticism. First it is difficult to demonstrate what the key contingent variables should be and also how great their influence is likely to be. Secondly most studies are essentially correlational and yet reach conclusions about cause and effect. Furthermore they are often vague about the dependent criterion. Research by Rumelt (1974) and more particularly Pennings (1975) shows little relationship between structural fit and specific definitions of organizational effectiveness. This leads to the third problem with contingency theory, namely the search for a 'best fit' in the face of what can sometimes be complex and perhaps competing contingencies. In practice there are usually a number of choices.

Despite its limitations, by recognizing that the contextual circumstances can determine the most appropriate form of change, contingency theory is more analytic and less prescriptive than most other approaches in identifying what should be done. Its attractions are reflected in Child's view that it is currently the 'dominant paradigm in the field of organizational design' (Child, 1977, p. 165).

Discussion of the Eight Approaches

Eight social-psychological approaches have been outlined, reflecting different frameworks for analysis and diagnosis and different assumptions about the nature of the key issues and problems. These assumptions often point to the type of variables that need changing and to the most appropriate process for introducing change. There are obvious attractions in being able to utilize a framework and it provides a degree of certainty in indicating what to do, particularly in a highly unstable and uncertain organizational environment. However, there can also be costs. Several of the approaches are partial, in that they may help to solve certain organizational problems and not others. The difficulty arises when enthusiasts use them as a starting point to analyse organizational problems for which they are inappropriate.

A brief review is sufficient to identify limitations in each theoretical perspective and its associated methods if it is used as a general approach to organizational change. Recognizing this, social psychologists have gone beyond specific methods to develop broader approaches to organizational change which, although they may be biased towards one of the models of change nevertheless try to embrace several of them. In this sense they are attempts to present an integrative approach to organizational change. These integrative approaches also reflect a move away from a narrowly social-psychological view of change to embrace wider organizational factors. Three of the main examples of an integrative approach are examined in the next section, organization development, the quality of working life movement, and employee participation.

INTEGRATIVE APPROACHES TO ORGANIZATIONAL CHANGE

Organization Development

Organization Development (OD) is an attempt to bring together the various social-psychological approaches to change under one broad label and to apply them in the organizational context. It is both a technology of change, focussing in particular (but by no means exclusively) upon the process of change in individuals and small groups, and a set of values amounting to what has been described as the 'OD movement'. Because it deliberately encompasses a range of approaches, it is difficult to describe OD in succinct yet comprehensive terms.

Indeed Kahn (1974), in a widely quoted critical review, suggested that 'OD is only a convenient label for a bunch of activities'. However, it is more than this, and the best idea of the approaches and philosophy underlying OD can be found in the early volumes of a series of books published by Addison-Wesley and written by some of the leading OD practitioners (Blake and Mouton, 1969; Walton, 1969). Reviewing developments in OD and reflecting the view of its early advocates, French and Bell (1973) described OD, in its ideal form, as:

> '. . . a long-range effort to improve an organization's problem-solving and renewal processes, particularly through a more effective and collaborative management of organizational culture—with special emphasis on the culture of formal work teams—with the assistance of a change agent, or catalyst, and the use of the theory and technology of applied behavioural science, including action research' (French and Bell, 1973, p. 15).

Building on French and Bell's description, the key characteristics of OD can be identified.

1. OD reflected the growing confidence, felt in the 1960s, in the ability to apply the behavioural sciences to solve organizational problems and help organizations become more effective. At the same time it attempted to integrate the different levels of analysis within the behavioural sciences. Indeed one of the early books in the Addison-Wesley series, by Lawrence and Lorsch (1969), dealt with organizational contingency theory and was mainly sociological in approach. Nevertheless the continuing emphasis on intra-group change processes means that social-psychological perspectives have dominated.
2. OD is an expression of a set of values built around the motivation models of Maslow (1943) and McGregor (1960). In particular, as reflected forcefully in the views of Argyris (1964), it provides a means to integrate the individual and the organization, based on the potential complementarity of individual and organizational growth. The philosophy is integrative, optimistic, and growth oriented. As such, it reflects the values of its advocates, of the organizations in which it found its earliest application and of the economic and social climate of the 1960s out of which it emerged. Finally, it reflects the notion that change is a continuing activity which should be viewed as a positive opportunity rather than as something outside individual control and understanding and therefore to be feared.
3. OD makes deliberate use of a change agent. Typically, the 'trainer' moves out of his university and into the organization. In the organization he can adopt a variety of consultancy roles such as catalyst, expert, or irritant. However, because of the academic background of so many OD consultants and the emphasis on feedback and learning, one role will often be that of action-researcher.

4. OD attempts to improve processes, and more particularly intra- and inter-group processes as the means of bringing about change. For example, the OD practitioner is far less concerned with the substance of decisions than with the process of decision-making.
5. All the previous points accept the view that the locus of change should be within the organization.

OD in Practice

French and Bell (1973) identify three stages in any OD programme. The first is diagnosis, in which an attempt is made, often through some systematic form of data collection, to describe the organizational context and climate and to identify problems and opportunities for change. Perhaps the best known method of diagnosis is the opinion survey. The second and major phase is action to bring about change. For example Mann (1961) and Likert (1967) have made extensive use of survey feedback to obtain commitment to change. Other methods of change include the managerial grid and T-groups, although the emphasis would be on the application of T-groups to 'intact' organizational groups. Still other methods include educational activities or deliberate attempts to alter the distribution of power. The final stage can be termed process maintenance. This consists of building up and maintaining an OD activity within the organization and creating an acceptance of change as a continuing process. In practice, most of the emphasis is likely to be put on the second stage at the expense of the first and third.

T-Groups

One of the best known methods of change falling within the general ambit of OD is the T-group. The T-group is an unstructured group, without an agenda, usually comprising eight to 14 individuals and usually lasting for several days. Its aims, as summarized by Campbell, Dunnette, Lawler, and Weick (1970), include providing the individual with insight into his or her own behaviour towards others and its impact upon them; helping participants to learn how to listen; fostering increased understanding and tolerance of the behaviour of others; and providing a setting within which new forms of interaction can be tried out. The individuals in the group provide the models of behaviour and the sources of pressure for change. The composition of the group is therefore of some importance; so, too, is the role and competence of the trainer. This role can vary. In the type of T-group developed at the National Training Laboratories at Bethel in the USA, the trainer is very much a part of the group and plays an active participant role. A variation on this format has been developed by the Tavistock Institute which adopts a more clinical approach in which the trainer stands outside the group and comments upon its behaviour.

T-groups have aroused much controversy and much research. Studies have attempted to assess the reactions of individuals to the experience of the T-group and to assess its impact on their behaviour in general and on their behaviour in the work setting in particular.

Any evaluation of the impact of T-groups is fraught with difficulty (for a review of the problem, see Harrison, 1971) and interpretation of the results seems to reflect personal values. The more thorough and sympathetic reviews (see for example Blumberg and Golembiewski, 1976) are uncontroversial in reporting that the great majority of participants evaluate the experience of the T-group positively. However, the activities within a T-group, which encourages individuals to explore their social behaviour and emotions, can be stimulating for some but a source of anxiety and stress for others. Occasionally there are casualties, but there is controversy over the casualty rate. Lieberman, Yalom and Miles (1973) concluded that a casualty rate of 7.5% was realistic where a casualty is defined as someone who has suffered some sort of psychological injury after, and presumably as a result of the T-group. Blumberg and Golembiewski (1976) found only 1% reporting persisting or substantial negative experiences and Kaplan, Obert and Van Buskirk (1980) set the figure at 2%.

Turning to the longer-term effects, Smith (1980) reviewing the evidence, concludes that, as far as participants are concerned:

'Their own behaviour is often perceived by others as changed. Changes most frequently noted are improved communication skills and more warmth and concern. Follow-up studies show that these changes do not all persist. The effect which shows the strongest persistence is a more favourable evaluation of oneself' (Smith, 1980, p. 54).

A number of studies have specifically evaluated the impact of T-groups on subsequent performance at work. Bunker (1965) compared 229 T-group trainees and 112 control subjects who had not undergone training by obtaining completed questionnaires from the individual and work colleagues assessing the nature of any change; 67% of the trainees compared with 33% of the controls reported corroborated changes six to eight months after the T-group. The changes occurred in a number of areas such as greater interpersonal skills, greater openness and tolerance, and improved understanding of self and others. A broadly similar trend of findings was reported by Boyd and Elliss (1962) using Canadian managers, and by Moscow (1971) with British and Dutch groups. Both of these studies went further than the Bunker study in comparing T-groups with other forms of training and in showing their superiority compared with conventional training programmes.

Full reviews of the impact of T-groups in organizations have been provided by Campbell and Dunnette (1968) and Cooper and Mangham (1971). Campbell and Dunnette in particular are critical of the methodology used in many evaluative studies, with its potential for bias in favour of the T-group. For example, trainees may be an atypical group, they may be identified as trainees to corroborative raters, and they may have discussed changes among themselves. Furthermore most of the evaluation is post-training without comparative pre-training measures.

Two persistent concerns have resulted in a decline in the use of the T-group as a vehicle for change in organizations. One is the anxiety about the potentially harmful effect on a small minority of trainees of training which focusses on emotions as a path to changes in behaviour. The second and more serious are doubts about the significance of the changes brought about by T-group training. The problems centre around the difficulty of transfer and reinforcement of behaviour changes following a return to the workplace. One approach which attempts to overcome both of the major problems with the T-group is Blake and Mouton's (1964) managerial grid. This is a multi-stage approach to organizational change starting from an off-the-job training course based on exercises designed to assess behaviour along the two dimensions of the grid, namely concern for production and concern for people. The focus is on behaviour, while acting either as a group leader or group member engaged on specific tasks, and this helps to provide it with higher face validity among managers. Subsequent stages are concerned with change in organizational teams and ultimately in organizational structure and functioning although very few organizations have taken it this far. Unfortunately very little systematic evaluation of managerial grid programmes has been reported.

The Impact of OD

Much has been written about the nature and potential of OD, yet until recently, for an approach which emphasizes action research, surprisingly little systematic research has been reported on its effectiveness. A cursory review of the available literature might suggest that OD interventions are usually successful. However, much of the available data is of poor quality. Porras and Berg (1978a, b) attempted to overcome this by excluding most partial or inadequate evaluations. The data from the relatively few remaining studies (35 out of 160) was rather negative. They concluded that in general OD does not increase individual satisfaction, only occasionally changes group processes, seldom affects task variables, and has its main impact on the individual rather than the organization. Other less comprehensive reviews have attempted to identify the features distinguishing successful from unsuccessful OD interventions. Two of these represent the work at the Michigan Institute of Social Research. Franklin (1976) concentrating on the context, concluded that interventions were more likely to succeed if they had a specific focus, support from the top and a careful selection and use of internal change agents. Bowers (1973) looking at methods of intervention, concluded that survey feedback was the most successful and the T-group the least. The limited impact of T-groups is reinforced by Porras and Berg while the value of more participative methods, including survey feedback, is the main conclusion of a review by Dunn and Swiercjek (1977). Finally a more limited review by Greiner (1967) emphasizes the importance of the first and third stages in an OD programme. Greiner, for example, emphasizes the importance of internal and external pressures for change. In other words, the method of intervention is insufficient, in itself, to ensure success. This conclusion justifies the emphasis within OD on organizationally based change rather than the earlier external more method-based approaches favoured by many social psychologists.

OD in Retrospect

It is clear from this review that OD has failed to live up to the early over-optimistic claims of its advocates. At the same time OD has itself been undergoing change. Alderfer (1977) has indicated how OD has been applied in a wide range of organizational contexts outside industry. In industry it has spread down the organization to embrace blue-collar groups and in so doing has had to confront sectional interests and power as key issues. This has resulted in a challenge to the values of the earliest practitioners and in particular the failure of most to give sufficient weight to the pervasiveness of power and organizational politics (Pettigrew, 1975). Finally, the subject matter of OD has expanded; for example two of the more recent volumes in the Addison-Wesley series deal with job design (Hackman and Oldham, 1980) and the physical environment of work (Steele, 1973). While advocates of OD, such as Alderfer, see these developments as signs of healthy adaptation and growth, others (Jones and Pfeiffer, 1977) have begun to question the utility of the concept. In practice, as long as it continues to provide a broad umbrella for the application of a variety of methods within the behavioural sciences, its future seems assured.

Quality of Working Life

Quality of working life (QWL) is a term used to denote approaches to the re-design of the social and physical conditions of work, of tasks, and sometimes of whole factories and offices, to give workers greater responsibility, autonomy, and well-being. It shares with OD the difficulty of being a broad umbrella concept and also the ability to attract almost evangelical enthusiasm in some of its advocates. In other respects, however, it contrasts quite strongly with OD. First, it is concerned with the content of change rather than, though not in exclusion to, the process. Thus it presents a set of goals, relating in particular to the design of tasks but also to the terms and conditions of work. Second, the main locus of action is the shopfloor or office rather than management levels. Third, it is the structure, content and to some extent the context of work that is changed to meet the needs of individuals and groups rather than vice versa. Finally, it is more ambitious than OD in the sense that it has sought action at the national and even international level as well as in the organization.

The impetus for the QWL movement can be found partly in the social upheavals and student movements of the years around 1968; partly in the belief that the younger generation of workers are less prepared to accept the limitations and controls of narrow, repetitive jobs (Sheppard and Herrick, 1972); and partly in the value certain social scientists placed on social improvement through changes in the workplace (Work in America, 1973). Subsequently, concern for the need to improve productivity, particularly in the USA where Japanese competition has been a potent factor, shifted the emphasis from the early concern of behavioural scientists for social goals to the more managerial concern for productivity and sometimes towards a trade union concern for job security.

The principal method of improving the quality of working life is based on the application of socio-technical systems theory, developed by social psychologists at the Tavistock Institute. The particular attraction of this is the notion of joint optimization, whereby technical, economic, social, and psychological goals can all be met through the appropriate re-design of tasks. This re-design invariably results in autonomous work groups in which tasks are grouped together around a major activity. The best known example is probably car assembly where individual fragmented tasks are replaced by the complete sub-assembly by work groups, for example, of the engine, the gear system, or the electrical circuit (Lindholm and Norstedt, 1975). The work requires interdependence within the group and provides the group as a whole, and each worker within it with responsibility, autonomy, feedback, and the opportunity to practise existing skills and learn new ones. The changes are generally introduced using an outside consultant, who will have fairly clear views on the criteria for appropriate task design but who will use participative methods to achieve it. Some of the earliest 'demonstration' cases, using this approach were carried out in Norway (Emery and Thorsrud, 1976) and the rationale linking socio-technical systems theory to QWL activities has been elaborated by Trist (1981).

The possession of a theoretical base, a technology of change and apparently successful demonstration cases was not enough in itself to guarantee success for the QWL as a force for change. In 1972 a conference was held (Davis and Cherns, 1975), attended largely by behavioural scientists, at which an international QWL movement was launched and where the problem of diffusion was a key concern. This concern was stimulated in particular by the apparent failure of the demonstration cases to provide a bridgehead for wider QWL activity in Norway (Herbst, 1976). In considering how to bring about change, Lawler (1976) posed the question, should QWL be legislated? Using an expectancy theory framework, he argued that employers will only adopt it if they see positive pay-offs; therefore those elements which result in social rather than economic benefits may only be introduced with pressure from legislation or some other sources such as the trade unions.

In the event, QWL was adopted by the Swedish Employers Federation (SAF) with such enthusiasm that there were soon reports of major innovations at green field sites and over 500 workplace programmes (SAF, 1975). In the U.S.A. a number of major employers also introduced QWL programmes which quickly attracted the public eye. Governments became interested in QWL, attracted by the prospects of joint optimization and government bodies were set up and research initiated in most western industrial countries. The subject also attracted the attention of international organizations such as the OECD, EEC, NATO, and the ILO. In several countries legislation has been passed on a number of QWL issues; these cover the more social aspects such as equal rights, shift work, working hours, safety, and employee participation but also, in certain cases, the design of work. In Norway, a change in emphasis on the part of QWL advocates, help to lead to the 1977 Work Environment Act, which, among other things, required organizations to take account of human factors in job design.

The Impact of Quality of Working Life Changes

In parts of Europe, the high level of interest in QWL was a temporary phenomenon of the 1970s and activity has now subsided, while in North America it is more persisting. In addition to the many reports of individual cases, there have been several attempts to review and evaluate the evidence on the impact of QWL programmes (Taylor, 1977a, b; Cummings, Molloy, and Glen, 1977). These have met problems similar to those encountered in attempts to evaluate OD. The research design and the quality of the data are often inadequate and the use of action research creates problems of independence. To combat these deficiencies, the major Michigan ISR Quality of Work Programme is both developing improved evaluation methodologies (Lawler, Nadler and Camman, 1980) and conducting a number of change programmes (Goodman, 1979; Nadler, Camman, and Mirvis, 1980). In general, and whatever the methodological problems, the results in both Europe and North America point to improvements in job satisfaction and more particularly in productivity. The criterion of joint optimization has therefore usually been met.

Two major problems arise in many of the existing studies. The first is the problem of attributing causality of change. Changes in task design are often associated with other changes such as the introduction of new participative schemes, new forms of supervision and alterations in payment. It is therefore difficult to identify which factor led to the changes. The second problem lies in the explanation of changes. Increases in productivity may be the result of workers displaying increased motivation in the context of new, more stimulating tasks; or the changes may have led to more efficient organization coupled with work intensification. The early 'demonstration' cases reported by Emery and Thorsrud (1976) point to the second explanation (Bolweg, 1976). An analysis of many of the major applications of socio-technical systems theory suggests that it is particularly suited to conditions where workloads vary and where group working enables manning levels to be adjusted down (Kelly, 1978). Such cases provide some basis for the radical critiques which see job design as simply another form of managerial manipulation of employees (Braverman, 1974). Certainly the motivational theory underlying advocacy of autonomous work groups (Emery and Thorsrud, 1976) is vague both in nature and origins.

In 1981, a second international conference on QWL attracted 1,700 participants of which 1,000 were managers (Jenkins, 1981). A review of QWL innovations in Europe (Lupton and Tanner, 1980) indicated that the major and most successful examples resulted from initiatives by engineers rather than social scientists or personnel managers. As the evidence illustrates the economic benefits, and the emphasis shifts from social to economic goals, so the influence of social psychological concerns is diminished.

Employee Participation

Employee participation, like OD and QWL, can be defined in numerous ways. In practice it is a process whereby employees are provided with more influence over certain decisions, either through a process of consultation, joint regulation or delegation. Employee participation can be viewed either as a means of bringing about changes and improving outcomes such as employee satisfaction and productivity, or as an end in itself. It is with the former that we are primarily interested in the present context rather than the wider debate on industrial democracy.

Employee participation can be analysed in terms of its form, the level at which it operates in the organization, the subject matter it covers and its aims. It may be either individual or representative in form. Individual participation enables each employee to exert influence or control through his job and within his department and could include autonomous work groups, job enrichment, problem-solving groups, and possibly two-way briefing groups and survey feedback activities. Representative participation, as its name implies, involves a representative who acts on behalf of a group of employees. It may therefore involve worker directors, supervisory boards, works councils, joint consultation, and even collective bargaining. Clearly, therefore, participation can operate at different levels in the organization ranging from the local job level, to the more distant organization level. The issues covered by participation can range from very short-term executive decisions, as in the case of job enrichment, to long-term policy decisions in the case, for example, of supervisory boards.

This brief outline indicates how participation can be used as an integrating framework for many of the types of change advanced by social psychologists. Both OD, more particularly when the method of change is survey feedback and QWL programmes emphasize the role of employee participation. Indeed, setting aside job redesign, the introduction of a form of participation has sometimes been a central feature of programmes carrying the QWL label. One well-known illustration is the development of joint consultation and problem-solving activities at Tarrytown (Guest, 1979).

Any analysis which recognizes the range of forms and levels of participation will also accept the potential choice of method of bringing about change. The actual choice will depend upon careful diagnosis and a clear understanding of aims. It will also reflect the varying views of employer–employee relations as primarily integrative or distributive (Walton and McKersie, 1965). Social psychologists, particularly in North America, have tended to favour changes at the job or unit level, using an integrative orientation. In Europe the choice is partly constrained because most countries have introduced legislation to ensure that employee participation is practised, more particularly at plant and company level. Indeed analysis of the process whereby participation is introduced highlights the importance of external pressures and, paradoxically, the limited amount of participation by many of the eventual participants.

The Impact of Participation

The extensive literature on employee participation consists largely of general analyses and descriptions of various forms of participation (e.g., I.D.E., 1980, Crispo, 1978) or surveys of attitudes towards participation and the desire for participation (for a review see Wall and Lischeron, 1977). There are also numerous surveys of reactions to participation. Far less has been written about the impact of participation on the process of change. However, it is possible to identify and distinguish studies concerned mainly with the relationship between the introduction of participation and changes in satisfaction and performance; and studies concerned with the role of participation in facilitating change.

In the first category, from which we shall omit job redesign studies, one of the best-known experiments was conducted by Morse and Reimer (1956). In two divisions of an insurance company, white-collar employees were encouraged to participate in various aspects of decision-making while in a further two, hierarchical control was maintained and even increased. After a year the staff in the more participative divisions showed increased satisfaction and in the hierarchical divisions they reported decreased satisfaction. However, all groups showed increased productivity, with the hierarchically controlled divisions showing the largest increase. This result can be explained partly in terms of the measure of productivity; labour turnover was higher in the hierarchical division and staff who left were not always replaced. At the same time, it does raise questions about the short-term benefits of attempts to introduce more participative management.

Strauss (Whyte, 1955) has reported a rather different change among a team of women spraying paint on dolls that were carried along by a moving belt. Low morale and poor quality work was reported and in a rather desperate attempt to remedy the problem, the women were allowed to set the pace of the moving belt. Within three weeks they were operating at 30% to 50% above their expected levels. Both the speed of their work and their level of bonus earnings caused such problems among other workers that the participation was revoked. As a result labour turnover among the team rose and production fell. One of the lessons for social psychologists is the importance of taking into account the wider production and reward systems in designing group changes.

Concern for the impact of participation on the process of change has attracted more attention in Europe. A notable exception is the study by Coch and French (1948), cited earlier, which appeared to demonstrate the advantages of participation in bringing about change. However, the replications in Norway (French, Israel, and Ås, 1960) and South America (Juralewicz, 1974) failed to produce the same positive outcome, raising questions about the influence of the cultural context. The Coch and French study illustrates the temporary use of participation to facilitate a specific change. This is likely to raise problems in many contexts, although short-term project groups are not unusual. One example of this was found in the joint committees set up by ICI in the U.K. to introduce more local participation (Roeber, 1975).

A further variant which has been used with some success is the problem-solving group, established on a permanent basis and embracing more than the formal employee representatives, which meets regularly to discuss a wide range of issues. West (1980) has shown how this helped to facilitate change in the port transport industry. Wall and Lischeron (1977) have reported a similar participation scheme in a local authority recreation department. A recent, albeit more limited variant of this approach is the quality control circle, which is currently receiving considerable attention (JETRO, 1981)

Studies of the impact of participation at plant and company level have been generally conducted by sociologists rather than social psychologists. Brannen, Batstone, Fatchett, and White (1976) while reporting generally negative results on the impact of worker directors in the British Steel Corporation did find a generalized view at board level that the presence of worker directors could contribute to the quality of certain decisions, particularly where they would result in changes affecting the workforce. A more provocative study (Jacobs, Orwell, Paterson, and Weity, 1977) compared the approach to change of organizations in West Germany and the UK. Through an analysis of case studies they concluded that the use of participation had a major bearing on the outcome. U.K. managers tended to avoid disclosure to the unions and workforce of any more information than was necessary, thereby storing up later opposition. In West Germany the detailed discussions that took place in the statutory works councils ensured that most of the contentious issues were aired and resolved at an early stage leading to a more satisfactory eventual outcome.

Employee Participation: Some Conclusions

The use of employee participation as an integrating framework illustrates some of the limitations of the social-psychological approach to the analysis of organizational change. First, there is the understandable but not inevitable tendency to focus on and perhaps elevate changes at the individual and group level on the shop or office floor at the expense of higher levels in the organization. Second there has been a tendency to concentrate on integrative forms of participation at the expense of a more conflict-oriented or distributive perspective. This has been particularly true of American work. It opens up advocates of integrative, consensual forms of participation to the criticism of being overly managerial. For this reason there are benefits in presenting a more concrete definition of participation using the concept of control (Guest, 1979a). Finally, the benefits of participation—and indeed of OD and QWL programmes—are not clearly demonstrated. This calls for a more sophisticated analysis to classify the range of possible change strategies and the criteria which help to determine which is the more appropriate in specific organizations.

CHANGE: PROCESS, EVALUATION AND RESISTANCE

The Process of Change

Social psychologists have focussed largely on processes of change through people—through changes in their values, perceptions and relationships and through changes in the social and to a lesser extent the technical aspects of work. However, such approaches can usefully be set in a wider context of strategies of change. There are various classifications of such strategies, but one of the most valuable is presented by Chin and Benne (1976) who outline three general strategies for planned organizational change which they label empirical–rational, normative–re-educative, and power–coercive.

In the empirical–rational approach, change comes about as a result of analysis and presentation of new information. This may take the form of, for example, a research survey, an annual appraisal or a consultant's report. The information results in a reasoned and rational case for change. Since the dissemination of information can be crucial to this strategy, education, and communication have a central role to play. Within social psychology there is a long tradition of research on the impact of communication of information which has typically used as a standard model an analysis of the sender of the information, the nature of the information and the receiver (Hovland, Janis, and Kelley, 1953). The success of the strategy depends upon an acceptance of the rationality of the case for change and, as Chin and Benne argue, there is a tendency to underestimate the role of the receiver who may ignore or reject the information for a number of reasons. One illustration of this is the Norwegian work on job redesign (Emery and Thorsrud,

1976) which initially used the empirical–rational strategy of presenting successful demonstration cases in the hope that other organizations would see their merit and follow their lead. As Herbst (1976) acknowledges, this approach failed to convince an uncommitted audience. Despite this, the strategy has a major role in bringing about change in industrial organizations.

The second approach is the normative–re-educative strategy. This starts from a view of man as acting upon his environment rather than passively receiving information. Therefore, as Lewin in particular argued, change should be a collaborative activity involving both the change agents and those being changed. However, this approach also starts out from theories of human behaviour, which, while largely embedded in behavioural science research, are normative in character. The approach therefore attempts to bring about change in values as well as perceptions and cognitions by utilizing the participants. The obvious illustration is Organization Development and it will be seen from this outline that much of the work of social psychologists described in this chapter falls within this category.

Chin and Benne's third approach, which they consider to be widely found throughout industry, is the power–coercive strategy. This involves the use of power, and especially economic and political sanctions to obtain consent to change. In organizations this may be manifested in the arbitrary imposition of change by an established elite. Where there are countervailing forces, collective bargaining may become the means of bringing about change. From outside the organization legal sanctions may be used, as illustrated by legislation on equal opportunities. While there are attractions to power holders in this approach, its potential divisiveness and the repercussions of this must be taken into account in assessing its viability.

Thurley and Wirdenius (1973) have identified a fourth general approach to change which they have described as the action–centred strategy. This is essentially a problem-solving approach to practical problems. The strategy may therefore consist of setting up committees or working parties involving those with a stake in the outcome. This group may become the focus of some sort of training activity centred around the development of competence to solve the immediate problem. As such, it is a more pragmatic, step by step approach than the empirical–rational strategy and it lacks the normative element of the normative–re-educative strategy. It can be illustrated by some of the problem-solving approaches appearing in the previous section on participation (e.g., Wall and Lischeron, 1977). While this strategy can be used on a piecemeal basis one of the potential drawbacks, particularly in large bureaucratic organizations is that the setting up of committees may in fact be a means of postponing rather than facilitating change.

The four strategies outlined above are ideal types and it is relatively rare to find one strategy used in isolation over any period of time. However, they help to highlight the choices for change in organizations, choices which may be based on a range of factors including the nature of the organization's structure, technology, culture, history, and goals, an assessment of power relationships, dominant coalitions and interest groups, and the motives, orientations, and abilities of individuals. Implicit in each of the strategies, therefore, is a model of change involving several stages; there are analysis and diagnosis; objective setting; choice of strategy; implementation; and evaluation. In practice this cycle may be repeated several times. This essentially empirical–rational sequence applies in particular to planned organizational change. In practice much change in organizations is unplanned and accidental.

Table 2. The relationship between social-psychological models of change and the strategy of change

Model	Strategy
1. Human relations	Normative–re-educative
2. Field theory	Normative–re-educative
3. Systems theory	Normative–re-educative (empirical-rational)
4. Counselling	Normative–re-educative
5. Attitude theory	Empirical–rational (normative–re-educative)
6. Learning theory	Empirical–rational (normative–re-educative)
7. Expectancy theory	Empirical–rational
8. Contingency theory	Empirical–rational (power–coercive)

The dominant strategy is presented with a subsidiary strategy included in brackets where appropriate.

As Table 2 shows, the contribution of social psychologists to organizational change falls predominantly, though not exclusively within the normative–re-educative strategy. Given the nature of much of the research in social psychology and the concern identified by Chin and Benne for people rather than things, this is not surprising. However, it is questionable how widespread and how effective this strategy is. For example the evaluations of organization development cases highlighted the limited impact of T-groups, which are clearly normative–re-educative and the strength of survey feedback which in some respects is closer to the empirical–rational strategy. Even when method-based approaches such as socio-technical systems analysis are used, which could fall within the empirical–rational strategy, close analysis shows that the methods used, for example, to analyse the technical system, are weak and that the normative element emphasizing human motives and the benefits of autonomous work groups predominates.

There has also been too little contribution from social psychology to the analysis of the power–coercive strategy. Psychology has become increasingly concerned with power both at the individual level, see for example McClelland's (1975) work on the need for power, at the group level, illustrated by French and Raven's (1960) analysis of social power and at the organizational level where Pfeffer (1981) has recently reviewed the nature, sources and operation of power in organizations. Nevertheless Pettigrew's (1975) criticism of the failure to consider power in the context of organization development has considerable force and none of the analyses listed above have addressed themselves directly to the question of organizational change. One exception is the work of Walton and McKersie (1965) on the distinction between distributive and integrative bargaining in labour relations which is, in effect, a distinction between the power–coercive and the other strategies of change (see Chapter 7). There is, therefore, a need for social psychologists to widen their area of concern, not just in terms of the level of analysis, as Katz and Kahn (1978) have illustrated, but also in terms of the range of concerns in the field of organizational change.

Evaluation of Change

Any social-psychological analysis of change must be concerned with the question of evaluation. In this final section, three aspects of evaluation will be examined. The first concerns the choice of evaluation criteria; the second concerns the quality of evaluation data; and the third concerns the problem of resistance to change.

Choice of evaluation criteria

Hesseling (1966) has outlined a pragmatic framework in which the method and focus of evaluation will depend upon who is doing the evaluating and for whom. This approach recognizes that the evaluation of organizational change is inevitably a political process and also recognizes that in the absence of formal and systematic evaluation, those involved in and affected by the change will inevitably arrive at their own judgements and attributions of the success of the changes.

Organizational change is often initiated and controlled by management. Management therefore sets the objectives and to some extent pre-determines the formal criteria for evaluation. Social scientists may add further criteria and may contribute by insisting upon the importance of careful measurement of the criteria of change. In this sense they are often evaluating for other social scientists, to whom they may wish to communicate the results, as well as for management.

The importance of control over objective setting, the management and therefore the evaluation of change is one of the issues identified by advocates of an extension of employee participation who argue the need to extend control over organizational change to employees as a whole, particularly in relation to matters which have an impact on their well-being. Some support for this position comes from an analysis of the literature on organizational effectiveness which is a central concept in any evaluation of organizational change. Reviews of approaches to organizational effectiveness (Goodman and Pennings, 1977; Campbell, Bownas, Peterson, and Dunnette, 1974; Steers, 1975) highlight two factors. One is the range of criteria used to define and measure organizational effectiveness; the other is the absence of worker-related and more particularly worker-centred criteria. In this latter respect, Steers (1975) is an exception in arguing for the inclusion of job satisfaction. The absence of worker-centred criteria would seem to reinforce the view of management as what Cyert and Marsh (1963) term the dominant coalition that establishes the goals of change and the criteria of evaluation.

The absence of worker-centred criteria may seem surprising in the light of the focus on employee behaviour in the social-psychological approaches to organizational change outlined in this chapter. It does not mean that criteria such as job satisfaction, reduced stress and improved well-being are invariably ignored but rather that they are treated by organizations, if not by social psychologists, as intervening variables, linked to reduced absenteeism, higher output, and other criteria considered by the dominant coalition to be important indicators of organizational effectiveness. The central contribution of the social-psychological perspectives therefore appears to be that of facilitating change and it is surprising that more attention has not been paid to criteria such as the time taken to introduce change, the level of conflict and opposition engendered, and other process criteria.

There have been two significant attempts by social-psychologists to confront and broaden managerial criteria of organizational effectiveness. One is to build upon the existing framework by developing the concept of human asset accounting. This attempts to set a financial value on having a workforce which is highly trained, satisfied, and co-operative (Likert, 1967). There is little or no evidence to suggest that management has been persuaded by this perspective. The second approach is the use of the concept of quality of working life in an attempt to convince management of the importance to the organization, to the workforce and to society as a whole of worker-centred goals for change. (Work in America, 1973; Sheppard and Herrick, 1972). Here again, however, as Lawler's (1976) analysis indicates, management is unlikely to introduce change to benefit the workforce unless it is convinced that the organization also benefits. Changes which have a significantly greater benefit to the workforce may require legislation or a framework of employee participation. Indeed Kelly's (1978) review of studies evaluating the impact of autonomous work groups suggests that they are seldom introduced unless they meet managerial goals first and employee goals second and the major evaluation criteria reflect an acceptance of this view.

In summary, the evaluation of organization change of the type to which social psychology has made a contribution is often centred around managerial criteria. While social psychologists have recognized the importance of worker-centred goals for change (see for example the work of Bradburn, 1969, and Warr and Wall, 1975, on the concept of well-being) there is little evidence that in practice organizational change of any significance has been directed towards these goals. In short there is still a need in the context of organizational change to answer the critique by Baritz (1965) of social psychologists as 'servants of power'.

The quality of evaluation data

Social psychologists face several problems in obtaining data of good quality, even where sophisticated measures are available. The first problem is one of access. Few have the good fortune to have full management and union co-operation in monitoring and evaluating change in an ideal way. Gardell (1981) for example, commenting on the job re-design and quality of working life programme encouraged by the Swedish Employers Federation and claimed by them to be a great success says that:

> 'As a social scientist I regret that it has been part of employer policy not to identify these efforts as scientific research or to call in social scientists to assist in field experiments, or evaluations. Possibly as a result of this policy, documentation has not met acceptable scientific standards and there are difficulties for outsiders who wish to make more independent evaluations of what has been achieved' (Gardell, 1981, p. 4.).

In this context, the more carefully controlled and monitored Michigan quality of working life programme is to be welcomed.

A second problem of evaluation is the difficulty faced by social psychologists who are both change agents and evaluators, a problem which is particularly acute in OD and QWL programmes. This may be compounded by the ambiguities and complexities of the change process which make attribution of cause and effect difficult. There may also be a bias in favour of successful change programmes. In an attempt to demonstrate that as much can be learned from failure, Mirvis and Berg (1977) have produced an insightful account of failures in OD.

A third problem concerns the time dimension and the difficulty of judging when a change is complete. There is pressure on the researcher to collect data and publish results as swiftly as possible. Yet Likert (1967) has argued that the study by Morse and Reimer (1956), which failed to show clear benefits for the more participative system of organization, did so because it was evaluated over too short a time-frame. He argues for a period of four to five years to evaluate the real impact of organizational change. Support for this view comes from a study by Blackler and Brown (1980) of a QWL programme in Shell UK. An earlier evaluation (Hill, 1971) had concluded that the change had proved successful. Blackler and Brown, returning some years later, found that the programme had largely collapsed and that the introduction of a new plant manager, who had little sympathy for the changes, was sufficient to undo the seemingly fragile changes introduced by the Tavistock consultants.

A fourth and more conventional problem concerns the biases created by the process of evaluation. There is a tendency to assume that changes which are of central concern to management or to the social psychologist are of equal importance to the workforce. Guest, Williams, and Dewe (1980) explored this issue by asking workers what changes had occurred as a prelude to the more conventional approach of gauging their reactions. Only 72% cited the 'significant' changes which were the primary focus of the study. One way round this is to use repeat measures over time without reference to the changes and preferably using a control group. In this way Paul, Robertson, and Herzberg (1969) were able to demonstrate the benefits of job enrichment at ICI. Another approach is to use objective criteria. Seashore (1975) has argued for both objective and subjective measures of quality of working life, suggesting that:

'. . . the individual . . . is in important respects incapable of optimum judgement of his own life situation' (Seashore, 1975, p. 107).

The potential problem with this approach, which again raises the questions posed by Hesseling of by whom and for whom the evaluation should be conducted, is that a conflict between objective and subjective criteria may well place the worker on the periphery of the evaluation process, something which a social-psychological perspective should seek to discourage.

Resistance to change

In attributing success and failure in organizational change, it is tempting to explain success in terms of effective management of the change process and failure in terms of resistance to change. While this may provide a partial explanation, it can often obscure the reasons for resistance to change. Furthermore it tends to focus on resistance to change among individuals or groups when an analysis of features of the organization may be more appropriate.

Legge (1978) in her evaluation of the effectiveness of personnel managers argues that they are often ineffective because of the nature of the personnel role. The need, therefore, is to consider change in the role. A vivid picture of organizational constraints on change has been provided in studies of large bureaucracies such as Warwick's (1975) examination of the U.S. Department of State and Burn's (1977) examination of the BBC in the U.K. Crozier (1964) on the basis of his work on two large French bureaucracies, identified what he termed the 'bureaucratic phenomenon', a condition whereby the pressures to maintain the status quo, enhanced by the complex system of controls, makes progress towards change extraordinarily difficult.

Studies of change in bureaucracies reinforce the point made forcibly by Katz and Kahn (1978) that an effective social psychology of organizations and more particularly of organizational change must include analysis at the organizational level. It must also integrate the influence of and the impact of change on individuals. For example Holmes and Rahe (1967) have found a relationship between the amount of change an individual experiences in any sphere of life and his or her chances of illness. As change becomes a part of everyday life, it is therefore important that the social psychologist does not lose sight of the individual and of worker-centred concerns.

SUMMARY

In exploring the relevance of social psychology for the analysis of organizational change, this chapter has used social psychological theory as the starting point. Eight theories were selected using the criterion that they have been applied to the problem of organizational change. The eight are human relations, field theory, systems theory, counselling, attitude theory, learning theory, expectancy theory, and contingency theory. It is worth emphasizing that some social psychologists would feel uneasy with the classification of theories, the way in which they have been interpreted and more particularly the way in which they have been applied. There is a continuing and on the whole healthy tension between those primarily concerned with the development of theory and those who seek to solve organizational problems. There is a strong case for believing that this tension is particularly apparent with respect to the study of organizational change. Three reasons for this are reflected in themes underlying this chapter.

The first major difficulty for the social psychologist who is used to the rigours of controlled academic research is that organizational change is invariably a messy business. This chapter may create an illusory feeling of order. It presents eight social psychological theories, outlines three integrative approaches to organizational change—through organization development, quality of working life and worker prticipation—and describes a three stage process of change, moving from diagnosis, through choice of strategy to evaluation. In practice, however, it is usual to find uncertainty, ambiguity, and lack of clarity about goals and processes. As a result it is difficult to set boundaries, establish cause and effect and determine what to measure and when. One response is to steer away from involvement in the area. On the other hand, the 'problem' of change may be so apparent that the arguments in favour of some form of involvement may be overwhelming. These difficulties also go some of the way towards explaining some of the inadequacies of the evaluation studies described in this chapter.

The second source of tension for a disciplinary perspective and one which is discussed in the later sections of the chapter is the need to adopt an interdisciplinary approach to the study and analysis of organizational change. In addition to sociology and psychology, elements of political science and economics are often essential. The ability to use an interdisciplinary approach usually comes more easily to those who start from the problem rather than from the disciplinary base. Part of the case for an interdisciplinary perspective lies in the biases inherent in a narrow view of problem definition. For the social pychologist there is a danger that all problems of organizational change will be diagnosed in social psychological terms. Selected strategies for change may therefore be inappropriate and unsuccessful.

The final major tension lies in the potential conflict between the social psychologist as researcher, and as change agent. Throughout the chapter there have been illustrations of the contribution made by social psychology to the theory of organizational change and more particularly to the role of change agent. Indeed it can be argued that social psychology has made the dominant contribution among the social sciences to the development and understanding of the role of the change agent. However, as the later sections of the chapter implied, this is not without its problems. It raises questions concerning the values of the change agent, the models of the worker used by the change agent and the need to determine for whom the change agent is working. In this sense organizational change is inevitably a political question and at various points the naivety or perhaps the disingenuousness of some social psychologists has been noted.

In summary there is a need for continued learning among theory builders, applied researchers, and practitioners within social psychology as well as a need to recognize the value of an interdisciplinary perspective. The beginnings of the development of such a perspective can be detected in the integrative concerns for organization development, quality of working life, and employee participation, and in each case there is the potential for further development. The need for similar development in the areas of diagnosis, choice of change strategy, and evaluation must also be highlighted. Finally, if progress is to be made in tackling the problems of change, the issues of values and power are among those requiring the urgent attention of social psychologists concerned with organizational change.

REFERENCES

Ajzen, I., and Fishbein, M. (1977) Attitude-behaviour relations: a theoretical analysis and review of empirical research, *Psychological Bulletin*, **84**, 888–918.
Alderfer, C. P. (1977) Organization development, *Annual Review of Psychology*, **28**, 197–223.

Argyle, M. (1953) The relay assembly test-room in retrospect, *Occupational Psychology*, **27**, 98–103.

Argyle, M. (ed.) (1981) *Social Skills and Work*, Methuen, London.

Argyris, C. (1964) *Integrating the Individual and the Organization*, Wiley, London.

Bandura, A. (1977) *Social Learning Theory*, Prentice-Hall, Englewood Cliffs, N.J.

Baritz, L. (1965) *The Servants of Power*, Wiley, New York.

Bartlem, C. S., and Locke, E. A. (1981) The Coch and French study: a critique and reinterpretation, *Human Relations*, **34**, **7**, 555–566.

Beckhard, R. (1969) *Organization Development: Strategies and Models*, Addison-Wesley, Reading, Massachusetts.

Benne, K. D. (1976) The processes of re-education: an assessment of Kurt Lewin's views, in Bennis, W. G., Benne, K. D., Chin, R., and Corey, K. E. (eds.), *The Planning of Change*, (3rd. Edn.) Holt, Rinehart, Winston, London.

Bennis, W. G. (1969) *Organization Development: Its Nature, Origins and Prospects*, Addison-Wesley, Reading, Massachusetts.

Berlew, D. E., and Hall, D. T. (1966) The socialization of managers: effects of expectations on performance, *Administrative Science Quarterly*, **11**, 207–223.

Berne, E. (1964) *Games People Play*, Grove Press, New York.

Bion, W. R. (1968) *Experiences in Groups*, Tavistock, London.

Blackler, F. H. M., and Brown, C. A. (1980) *Whatever Happened to Shell's New Philosophy of Management?*, Saxon House, Farnborough, Hants.

Blake, R. R., and Mouton, J. S. (1964) *The Managerial Grid*, Gulf Publishing Co., Houston.

Blake, R., and Mouton, J. S. (1969) *Building a Dynamic Corporation Through Grid Organization Development*, Addison-Wesley, Reading, Massachusetts.

Bloom, B. S. (1956) *Taxonomy of Educational Objectives, Handbook I: Cognitive Domain*, McKay, New York.

Blumberg, A., and Golembiewski, R. T. (1976) *Learning and Change in Groups*, Penguin, Harmondsworth, Middlesex.

Bolweg, J. F. (1976) *Job Design and Industrial Democracy*, Martinus Nijhoff, Leiden.

Bowers, D. G. (1973) OD techniques and their results in 23 organizations: the Michigan ICL study, *Journal of Applied Behavioural Science*, **9**, 21–43.

Boyd, J. D., and Elliss, J. (1962) *Findings of Research into Senior Management Seminars*, Hydroelectric Power Commission of Ontario, Toronto.

Bradburn, N. M. (1969) *The Structure of Psychological Well-Being*, Aldine, Chicago.

Brannen, P., Batstone, E., Fatchett, D., and White, P. (1976) *The Worker Directors*, Hutchinson, London.

Braverman, H. (1974) *Labour and Monopoly Capital*, Monthly Review Press, New York.

Brayfield, A. H., and Crockett, W. H. (1955) Employee attitudes and employee performance, *Psychological Bulletin*, **52**, 396–424.

Bunker, D. R. (1965), The effect of laboratory education upon individual behaviour, in Schein, E. H., and Bennis, W. G. (eds.) *Personal and Organizational Change Through Group Methods*, Wiley, New York.

Burns, T. (1977) *The BBC: Public Institution and Private World*, Macmillan, London.

Burns, T., and Stalker, G. M. (1961) *The Management of Innovation*, Tavistock, London.

Campbell, J. P., Bownas, D. E., Peterson, M. G., and Dunnette, M. D. (eds.) (1974) *The Measurement of Organizational Effectiveness: A Review of Relevant Research and Opinion*, Navy Personnel Research and Development Centre, San Diego.

Campbell, J. P., and Dunnette, M. D. (1968) Effectiveness of T-group experiences in managerial training and development, *Psychological Bulletin*, **70**, 73–104.

Campbell, J. P., Dunnette, M. D., Lawler, E. E., and Weick, K. E. (1970) *Managerial*

Behaviour, Performance and Effectiveness, McGraw-Hill, New York.

Campbell, J. P., and Pritchard, R. D. (1976) Motivation theory in industrial and organizational psychology, in Dunnette, M. (ed.), *Handbook of Industrial and Organizational Psychology*, Rand-McNally, Chicago.

Channon, D. F. (1973) *The Strategy and Structure of British Enterprise*, Macmillan, London.

Child, J. (1977) *Organization*, Harper and Row, London.

Chin, R., and Benne, K. D. (1976) General strategies for effecting change in human systems', in Bennis, W. G., Benne, K. D., Chin, R., and Corey, K. E. (eds.), *The Planning of Change*, (3rd Edn.) Holt, Rinehart and Winston, London.

Clegg, C. W. (1980) The process of job redesign: signposts from a theoretical orphanage? *Human Relations*, **32**, 999–1022.

Clegg, C. W. (1982) Modelling the practice of job design, in Kelly, J. E., and Clegg, C. W. (eds.), *Autonomy and Control at the Workplace*, Croom Helm, London.

Coch, L., and French, J. R. P. (1948) 'Overcoming resistance to change', *Human Relations*, **1**, 512–32.

Cooper, C. L., and Mangham, I. L. (eds.) (1971) *T-Groups: A Survey of Research*, Wiley, London.

Crispo, J. (1978) *Industrial Democracy in Western Europe: A North American Perspective*, McGraw-Hill Ryerson, Toronto.

Crozier, M. (1964) *The Bureaucratic Phenomenon*, University of Chicago Press, Chicago.

Cummings, T. G., Molloy, E. J., and Glen, R. (1977) A methodological critique of 58 selected work experiments, *Human Relations*, **30, 8**, 675–708.

Cyert, R. M., and Marsh, J. G. (1963) *A Behavioural Theory of the Firm*, Prentice-Hall, Englewood Cliffs, N.J.

Davis, L. E., and Cherns, A. B. (1975) *The Quality of Working Life*, Free Press, New York, Volume I.

Drexler, J. A., and Lawler, E. E. (1977) A union-management co-operative project to improve quality of working life, *Journal of Applied Behavioural Science*, **13**, 373–387.

Dunn, W. N., and Swiercjek, F. W. (1977) Planned organizational change: towards grounded theory, *Journal of Applied Behavioural Science*, **12, 2**, 135–157.

Ekman, P., and Friesen, W. V. (1975) *Unmasking the Face*, Prentice-Hall, Englewood Cliffs, N.J.

Elliott, J. (1978) *Conflict of Cooperation? The Growth of Industrial Democracy*, Kogan Page, London.

Emery, F. E., and Thorsrud, E. (1976) *Democracy at Work*, Martinus Nijhof, Leiden, Holland.

Festinger, L. (1957) *A Theory of Cognitive Dissonance*, Harper and Row, New York.

Fiedler, F. E. (1967) *A Theory of Leadership Effectiveness*, McGraw-Hill, New York.

Fishbein, M., and Ajzen, I. (1975) *Belief, Attitude, Intention and Behaviour*, Addison-Wesley, Reading, Massachusetts.

Fleishman, E. A. (1965) Attitude versus skill factors in work group productivity, *Personnel Psychology*, **18**, 253–266.

Franklin, J. L. (1976) *Characteristics of Successful and Unsuccessful Organization Development*, Institute of Social Research, Ann Arbor, Michigan.

French, J. R. P., Israel, J., and Ås, D. (1960) An experiment on participation in a Norwegian factory, *Human Relations*, **13**, 3–19.

French, J. R. P., and Raven, B. H. (1960) The bases of social power, in Cartwright, D., and Zander, A. (eds.), *Group Dynamics: Research and Theory*, (2nd Edn.) Row, Peterson, New York, pp. 607–623.

French, W. L., and Bell, C. H. (1973) *Organization Development*, Prentice-Hall,

Englewood Cliffs, N.J.

Gardell, B. (1981) Strategies for reform programmes on work organization and work environment, in Gardell, B., and Johansson, G. (eds.) *Working Life: A Social Science Contribution to Work Reform*, Wiley, Chichester.

Goodman, P. S. (1979) *Assessing Organizational Change: The Rushton Quality of Work Experiment*, Wiley, New York.

Goodman, P. S., and Pennings, J. M. (1977) *New Perspectives on Organizational Effectiveness*, Jossey-Bass, San Francisco.

Greiner, L. E. (1967) Antecedents of planned organizational change, *Journal of Applied Behavioural Science*, **3**, 51–86.

Guest, D. (1979a) A framework for participation, in Guest, D., and Knight, K. (eds.), *Putting Participation into Practice*, Gower, Farnborough, Hants.

Guest, D. (1979b) Job design, industrial democracy and the quality of working life, *British Journal of Industrial Relations*, **17**, 119–122.

Guest, D., Williams, R., and Dewe, P. (1980) Workers' perceptions of changes affecting the quality of working life, in Duncan, K. D., Gruneberg, M. M., and Wallis, D. (eds.), *Changes in Working Life*, Wiley, London.

Guest, R. H. (1979) Quality of work life—learning from Tarrytown, *Harvard Business Review*, **July/August, 1979**, 76–87.

Hackman, J. R., and Lawler, E. E. (1971) Employee reactions to job characteristics, *Journal of Applied Psychology*, **55** 259–286.

Hackman, J. R. and Oldham, G. R. (1976) Motivation through the design of work: test of a theory, *Organizational Behaviour and Human Performance*, **16**, 250–279.

Hackman, R. J., and Oldham, G. R. (1980) *Work Redesign*, Addison-Wesley, Reading, Massachusetts.

Harris, T. A. (1973) *I'm OK, You're OK*, Pan Books, London.

Harrison, R. (1971) Research on human relations training: design and interpretation, *Journal of Applied Behavioural Science*, **7**, 71–85.

Herbst, P. G. (1976) *Alternative to Hierarchies*, Martinus Nijhoff, Leiden.

Herzberg, F. (1966) *Work and the Nature of Man*, World Publishing Company, New York.

Herzberg, F. (1976) *The Managerial Choice*, Dorsey, Homewood, Illinois.

Hesseling, P. (1966) *Strategy of Evaluation Research*, Van Gorcum, Assen.

Hill, P. (1971) *Towards a New Philosophy of Management*, Gower, London.

Holmes, T. H., and Rahe, R. H. (1967) The social re-adjustment rating scale, *Journal of Psychosomatic Research*, **11**, 213–218.

Hopson, B. (1978) Counselling in Work Settings, in Warr, P. B. (ed.), *Psychology at Work*, Penguin, Harmondsworth, Middlesex.

Hovland, C., Janis, I., and Kelley, H. (1953) *Communication and Persuasion*, Yale University Press, New Haven.

Hyman, H. H. (1960) Reflections on reference groups, *Public Opinion Quarterly*, **24**, 383–396.

I.D.E. (1981) *Industrial Democracy in Europe*, Oxford University Press, Oxford.

Jacobs, E., Orwell, S., Paterson, P., and Welty, F. (1977) *The Approach to Industrial Relations*, Anglo-German Foundation, London.

Jaques, E. (1951) *The Changing Culture of a Factory*, Tavistock, London.

Jenkins, D. (1981) *QWL—Current Trends and Directions*, Ontario Ministry of Labour, Ontario.

J.E.T.R.O. (1981) Productivity and quality control. The Japanese experience, *Now in Japan*, **1981**, 30.

Jones, J. E., and Pfeiffer, J. W. (1977) On the obsolescence of the terms Organizational

Development, *Group Organizational Studies*, **2**, **3**, 263–264.

Juralewicz, R. S. (1974) An experiment on participation in a Latin American factory, *Human Relations*, **27**, 627–637.

Kahn, R. L. (1974) Organizational development: some problems and proposals, *Journal of Applied Behavioural Science*, **10**, **(4)**, 485–502.

Kaplan, R. E., Obert, S. L., and Van Buskirk, W. R. (1980) The etiology of encounter group casualties: second facts, *Human Relations*, **33**, 131–148.

Katz, D., and Kahn, R. L. (1978) *The Social Psychology of Organizations*, (2nd Edn.), Wiley, London.

Katz, E., and Lazarsfeld, P. F. (1955) *Personal Influence: The Part Played By People in the Flow of Mass Communication*, Free Press, New York.

Kelly, J. E. (1978) A reappraisal of socio-technical systems theory, *Human Relations*, **31**, 1069–1099.

Kelman, H. C. (1961) Processes of opinion change, *Public Opinion Quarterly*, **25**, 57–78.

Klein, L. (1976) *New Forms of Work Organization*, Cambridge University Press, Cambridge.

Landsberger, H. A. (1958) *Hawthorne Revisited*, Cornell University Press, Ithica, N.Y.

Lawler, E. E. (1971) *Pay and Organizational Effectiveness: A Psychological View*, McGraw-Hill, New York.

Lawler, E. E. (1976) Should the quality of working life be legislated? *Personnel Administrator*, **January, 1976**, 17–21.

Lawler, E. E., Nadler, D. A., and Camman, C. (1980) *Organizational Assessment: Perspectives on the Measurement of Organizational Behaviour and Quality of Working Life*, Wiley, New York.

Lawler, E. E., and Suttle, J. L. (1973) Expectancy theory and job behaviour, *Organizational Behaviour and Human Performance*, **9**, 482–503.

Lawrence, P. R., and Lorsch, J. W. (1967) *Organization and Environment*, Harvard Business School, Boston.

Lawrence, P. R., and Lorsch., J. W. (1969) *Developing Organizations: Diagnosis and Action*, Addison-Wesley, Reading, Massachusetts.

Legge, K.(1978) *Power, Innovation and Problem-Solving in Personnel Management*, McGraw-Hill, London.

Lewin, K. (1952) Group decisions and social change, in Swanson, G. E., Newcomb, T. M., and Hartley, E. L. (eds.), *Readings in Social Psychology*, (2nd Edn.) Holt, New York, pp. 459–473.

Lieberman, M. A., Yalom, I. D., and Miles, M. B. (1973) *Encounter Groups: First Facts*, Basic Books, New York.

Likert, R. (1961) *New Patterns of Management*, McGraw-Hill, New York.

Likert, R. (1967) *The Human Organization*, McGraw-Hill, New York.

Lindholm, R., and Norstedt, J. P. (1975) *The Volvo Report*, S.A.F., Stockholm.

Locke, E. A. (1975) Personnel attitudes and motivation, *Annual Review of Psychology*, **26**, 457–480.

Locke, E. A. (1976) The nature and causes of job satisfaction, in Dunnette, M. D. (ed.), *Handbook of Industrial and Organizational Psychology*, Rand and McNally, Chicago, pp. 1297–1349.

Lupton, T., and Gowler, D. (1969) *Selecting a Wage Payment System*, Kogan Page, London.

Lupton, T., and Tanner, I. (1980) Work design in Europe, in Duncan, K. D., Gruneberg, M. M., and Wallis, D. (eds.), *Changes in Working Life*, Wiley, Chichester.

McClelland, D. C. (1975) *Power: The Inner Experience*, Irvington, New York.

McGregor, D. (1960) *The Human Side of Enterprise*, McGraw-Hill, New York.

Mann, F. C. (1961) Studying and creating change, in Bennis, W. G., Benne, K. D., and Chin, R. (eds.), *The Planning of Change*, (1st Edn.), Holt, Rinehart and Winston, New York.

Maslow, A. H. (1943) A theory of human motivation, *Psychological Review*, 50, 370–396.

Mayo, E. (1933) *Human Problems of an Industrial Civilization*, Macmillan, New York.

Mayo, E. (1945) *The Social Problems of an Industrial Civilization*, Harvard University Press, Cambridge, Massachusetts.

Menzies, I. E. P. (1960) A case-study in the functioning of social systems as a defence against anxiety: a report of a study of the nursing services of a general hospital, *Human Relations*, **13**, 2.

Mirvis, P. H., and Berg, D. N. (eds.) (1977) *Failures in Organizational Development and Change*, Wiley, New York.

Morse, N. C., and Reimer, E. (1956) The experimental change of a major organizational variable, *Journal of Abnormal and Social Psychology*, **52**, 120–129.

Moscow, D. (1971) T-group training in the Netherlands: an evaluation and a cross-cultural comparison, *Journal of Applied Behavioural Science*, **7**, 427–448.

Mowday, R. T., Porter, L. W., and Steers, R. M. (1982) *Employee-Organization Linkages: The Psychology of Commitment, Absenteeism and Turnover*, Academic Press, London.

Nadler, D. A., Camman, C., and Mirvis, P. M. (1980) Developing a feedback system for works units: a field experiment in structural change, *Journal of Applied Behavioural Science*, **16, 1**, 41–62.

Orpen, C. (1979) The effects of job enrichment on employee satisfaction, motivation, involvement and performance, *Human Relations*, **32**, 189–217.

Parsons, T. (1951) *The Social System*, Free Press, New York.

Paul, W. J., Robertson, K. B., and Herzberg, F. (1969) Job enrichment pays off, *Harvard Business Review*, **March/April, 1969**, 61–78.

Pennings, J. M. (1975) The relevance of the structural-contingency model for organizational effectiveness, *Administrative Science Quarterly*, **20**, 393–410.

Pettigrew, A. M. (1975) Towards a political theory of organizational intervention, *Human Relations*, **28**, 191–208.

Pfeffer, J. (1981) *Power in Organizations*, Pitman, London.

Porras, J. I., and Berg, P. O. (1978a) Evaluation methodology in organization development: an analysis and critique, *Journal of Applied Behavioural Science*, **14**, 151–173.

Porras, J. I., and Berg, P. O. (1978b) The impact of organizational development, *Academy of Management Review*, **April, 1978**, 249–266.

Rackham, N., and Morgan, T. (1977) *Behaviour Analysis and Training*, McGraw-Hill, London.

Rice, A. K. (1958) *Productivity and Social Organization: The Ahmadebad Experiment*, Tavistock, London.

Rice, A. K. (1969) Individual, group and intergroup processes, *Human Relations*, **22, 6**, 565–84.

Ritzer, G., and Trice, H. M. (1969) *An Occupation in Conflict*, Cornell University Press, Ithica, New York.

Roeber, J. (1975) *Social Change At Work*, Duckworth, London.

Roethlisberger, F. J., and Dickson, W. J. (1939) *Management and the Worker*, Harvard University Press, Cambridge, Massachusetts.

Rumelt, R. P. (1974) *Strategy, Structure and Economic Performance*, Harvard Business School, Cambridge, Massachusetts.

S.A.F. (1975) *Job Reform in Sweden*, S.A.F., Stockholm.

Schein, E. H. (1969) *Process Consultation: Its Role in Organization Development*,

Addison-Wesley, Reading, Massachusetts.

Seashore, S. E. (1975) Defining and measuring the quality of working life, in *The Quality of Working Life*, Volume I. (Eds. L. E. Davis and A. B. Cherns), Free Press, London.

Shaw, M. E. (1954) Some effects of problem solution efficiency in different communication nets, *Journal of Experimental Psychology*, **48,** 211–217.

Sheppard, J. L., and Herrick, N. Q. (1972) *Where Have All the Robots Gone?*, Free Press, New York.

Smith, P. B. (1980) *Group Processes and Personal Change*, Harper and Row, London.

Sofer, C. (1961) *The Organization From Within*, Tavistock, London.

Sofer, C. (1972) *Organizations in Theory and Practice*, Heinemann, London.

Steele, F. I. (1973) *Physical Settings and Organization Development*, Addison-Wesley, Reading, Massachusetts.

Steers, R. M. (1975) Problems in the management of organizational effectiveness, *Administrative Science Quarterly*, **20,** 546–558.

Taylor, J. C. (1977a) Experiments in work system design: economic and human results, Part I, *Personnel Review*, **6(3),** 21–34.

Taylor, J. C. (1977b) Experiments in work systems design: economic and human results, Part II, *Personnel Review*, **6(4),** 21–42.

Thurley, K. E., and Wirdenius, H. (1973) *Supervision: A Reappraisal*, Heinemann, London.

Trist, E. (1981) *The Evolution of Socio-Technical Systems*, Ontario Ministry of Labour, Ontario.

Trist, E. L., and Bamforth, K. W. (1951) Some social and psychological consequences of the longwall method of coal getting, *Human Relations*, **4, 7,** 13–38.

Trist, E. L., Higgin, G. W., Murray, H., and Pollock, A. B. (1963) *Organizational Choice*, Tavistock, London.

Trist, E., Susman, G. I., and Brown, G. R. (1977) An experiment in autonomous working in an American underground coal mine, *Human Relations*, **30,** 201–36.

Turner, A. N., and Lawrence, P. R. (1965) *Industrial Jobs and the Worker*, Harvard University Press, Cambridge, Massachusetts.

Umstot, D. D., Bell, C. H., and Mitchell, T. R. (1976) Effects of job enrichment and task goals on satisfaction and productivity; implications for job design, *Journal of Applied Psychology*, **61,** 379–394.

Van Maanen, J. (1976) Breaking-in: socialization to work, in Dubin, R. (ed.) *Handbook of Work, Organization and Society*, Rand and McNally, Chicago, pp. 67–130.

Von Bertalanffy, L. (1968) *General Systems Theory*, George Brazillier, New York.

Vroom, V. H. (1964) *Work and Motivation*, Wiley, London.

Vroom, V. H., and Yetton, P. (1973) *Leadership and Decision-Making*, University of Pittsburgh, Pittsburgh.

Wall, T. D. (1980) Group work redesign in context: a two-phase model, in Duncan, K. D., Gruneberg, M. M., and Wallis, D. (eds.) *Changes in Working Life*, Wiley, Chichester.

Wall, T. D., Clegg, C. W., and Jackson, P. R. (1978) An evaluation of the job characteristics model, *Journal of Occupational Psychology*, **51,** 183–196.

Wall, T. D., and Lischeron, J. A. (1977) *Worker Participation*, McGraw-Hill, London.

Wallbank, M. (1980) Effort in motivated work behaviour, in Duncan, K. D., Gruneberg, M. M., and Wallis, D. (eds.), *Changes in Working Life*, Wiley, Chichester.

Walton, R. E. (1969) *Interpersonal Peacemaking*, Addison-Wesley, Reading, Massachusetts.

Walton, R. E., and McKersie, R. B. (1965) *A Behavioural Theory of Labor Negotiations*, McGraw-Hill, New York.

Warr, P., and Wall, T. D. (1975) *Work and Well-Being*, Penguin, Harmondsworth, Middlesex.

Warwick, D. P. (1975) *A Theory of Public Bureaucracy: Politics, Personality and Organization in the State Department*, Harvard University Press, Cambridge, Massachusetts.

West, A. (1980) Introducing participation: an example from the British ports industry, *Journal of Occupational Psychology*, **53,** 97–106.

Whyte, W. F. (ed.) (1955) *Money and Motivation*, Harper, New York.

Wood, S. J. (1979) A reappraisal of the contingency approach to organization, *Journal of Management Studies*, **16,** 3.

Woodward, J. (1965) *Industrial Organization: Theory and Practice*, Oxford University Press, London.

Work in America (1973) *Report of a Special Task Force to the Secretary of Health, Education and Welfare*, MIT, Cambridge, Massachusetts.

Social Psychology and Organizational Behaviour
Edited by M. Gruneberg and T. Wall
© 1984 John Wiley & Sons Ltd

Chapter 9

The Conceptual, Methodological, and Ethical Foundations of Organizational Behaviour

A. K. KORMAN and D. J. VREDENBURGH

Organizational behaviour (OB) is concerned with how people behave in organizations and how organizations function. It is a diverse field of knowledge with indistinct boundaries which range from inter-organizational relations to individual psychological dynamics. It draws from such diverse academic disciplines as industrial engineering, occupational, and organizational sociology, and industrial and organizational psychology. From this background OB attempts to develop and examine theoretical frameworks for understanding the behaviour of individuals, groups, and organizations and then to use these theories in developing guidelines for management application.

In this chapter we will be concerned with both these goals of the field of OB, their historical significance and how they may be changing in importance in today's world. We will begin our discussion by first examining these goals in their traditional perspectives and then we will move on to more contemporary conceptual, methodological, and ethical issues and questions.

THE DEVELOPMENT OF ORGANIZATIONAL BEHAVIOUR

Historical Development of Theory in OB

Theory development has historically been a key activity for the field of OB because of its conceptual and applied significance. A theory consists of organized ideas, specifically concepts and their relationships, that purport to explain tentatively some phenomenon. There are good theories and poor theories. Often students and practitioners denigrate theory as idealistic and irrelevant to management practice, but it is important to remember that all managers operate from implicit theories or assumptions about how to motivate or lead people.

Managers often need to examine these assumptions and compare them to other ideas if they are to improve their effectiveness. To help in this examination is one of the purposes of behavioural science courses and textbooks. Among the criteria for a good theory are the following (Kaplan, 1964):

1. Correspondence—the theory fits the facts.
2. Coherence—the theory is structurally logical.
3. Parsimony—the theory explains efficiently.
4. Pragmatism—the theory predicts actual events.
5. Intuition—the theory appears plausible.

Unfortunately, most theories in OB do not meet these criteria but some do partially and others come close. In addition, even though most OB theories do not really meet the requirements of a 'good theory' in the sense that Kaplan (1964) defines them, some of the theoretical proposals have proved to be of value, nevertheless, in providing directions for research and, sometimes, management guidelines. Thus theories in OB have been of considerable value sometimes and may be even better in the future.

In this section we will review the historical development of theory in OB, a development that has evolved from four general perspectives. These are classical management theory, human relations theory, systems theory, and contingency theory.

Classical theory is generally divided into two groups, scientific management and administrative management. Scientific management, began with Frederick Taylor, an engineer and practising manager in the United States during the early part of the twentieth century. Taylor, who wrote a book entitled *Principles of Scientific Management* (1911), focussed on the management of work activities, particularly the efficiency of the individual production shop worker. The emphasis of Taylor and later writers has been on collecting data about separate tasks and motions and developing timed output standards. In addition to time and motion studies, scientific management writers advocate piece rate compensation systems, in which an individual is paid a designated amount per unit produced, rather than receiving remuneration based on time. This position reflects their assumption of a rational economic model of man, of people who behave rationally in accordance with their economic self-interest. Thus scientific management is essentially a prescriptive engineering approach to managing production operations that focusses on increasing efficiency through work methods, equipment design, and materials flow.

The other stream of classical thought, administrative management theory, is also prescriptive, but it concentrates on principles of organizational structure and managerial functions. Historically, it can be traced to the early twentieth century German social philosopher and sociologist Max Weber, who articulated the ideal structural and functional principles for the new emerging form of organization of the time, i.e., the bureaucracy. According to Weber (1947), a bureaucracy should:

1. Recruit and promote based on technical competence.
2. Structure itself through specialization or the division of labour, i.e., breaking down work into many component tasks and assigning a limited number of tasks to each employee.
3. Co-ordinate differentiated positions and units through a hierarchy of authority.
4. Develop rules and formal procedures for efficient task accomplishment.
5. Record the decisions, authority, procedures, and duties of positions and individuals.
6. Operate impersonally with respect to member–client and member–member interactions.
7. Separate owners' and managers' property.

If followed, these characteristics would, according to Weber, result in greater efficiency for the bureaucracy in its operations.

Other classical theorists have advocated certain principles as critical to organizing and managing large organizations. Fayol (1949) analysed public sector organizations in France during the second decade of this century, suggesting that division of work, unity of command, and centralization are integral guides to good management. Other administrative management writers have emphasized the differences between line and staff units, a limited span of control and the desirability of viewing management in fundamental functional terms such as planning, organizing, commanding, co-ordinating, and controlling.

This initial theoretical perspective in the applied field of OB, i.e., classical management theory, eventually generated a reaction known as the human relations movement. Whereas classical management theory underemphasized the behaviour of individuals and groups in organizations, the human relations orientation concentrated on just that. As a result of research studies during the 1930s at the Hawthorne plant of Western Electric Company (Roethlisberger and Dickson, 1939), much attention was paid during the next two decades to individual social and ego needs, group dynamics, the informal or nonformal organization (i.e., norms and activities not sanctioned by the organization's formal structure) and the nature of supervision. This human relations school tended to advocate employee centred, participative leadership (Likert, 1961). (See Chapter 3.)

The human relations orientation fostered two additional conceptual perspectives, the Carnegie school of behavioural decision-making and organizational development (OD). The Carnegie group has viewed organizations as essentially decision-making entities and has concentrated on studying information flows and individuals as problem solvers. The work of three individuals, namely H. Simon, J. March, and R. Cyert, all associated with Carnegie–Mellon University during this time and representing diverse academic disciplines, is typical of this group. They argued that organizational members, while intendedly rational, nevertheless possess limited rational and information processing abilities and therefore perceive stimuli rather selectively. These characteristics result in organizational decision making that is satisficing, i.e., searching for good enough or sufficient alternatives, rather than maximizing or searching for best alternatives. Similarly, these same characteristics cause people to seek and assign simple causes to events rather than complex ones. Another characteristic of the Carnegie decision-making school has been its interest in organizational structuring, viewing this as a process of developing operating programmes or sequences of activities to be evoked by some stimulus, for task accomplishment. These organizational programmes also serve to stabilize human behaviour and make interpersonal relationships more predictable.

The other outgrowth of the human relations school is the OD or organizational development perspective (see Chapter 8). OD consists of planned, action oriented behavioural science interventions that seek to change attitudes and/or behaviours in interpersonal relationships and groups in order to increase organizational effectiveness and health (Beckhard, 1969). The changes sought through OD programmes often concern job design, communication, organizational climate and norms, and organizational structure. One difference between these two outgrowths of the human relations group has been their basic goals. Whereas the decision-making school is largely descriptive, the OD school is normative. OD consultants tend to assume that organizations function better if:

1. Communication is open.
2. Mutual trust characterizes interpersonal relationships.
3. Groups or teams are treated as the basic building blocks of organizations.
4. Decision-making is participative.
5. Co-operation rather than competition characterizes inter-unit relationships within an organization.
6. Controls are viewed as interim measurements rather than the basis of managerial strategy (Beckhard, 1969).

Another difference is that while the Carnegie decision-making and OD approaches are both essentially behavioural or psychological in nature, the OD school emphasizes individual motivational processes from a humanistic perspective and the decision making school characterizes individuals in cognitive terms, i.e., as limited rational processors of information for decision making purposes. Both approaches, however, have viewed organizational functioning in terms of the behaviour of individuals. This is not the underlying focus of the third major OB theoretical perspective, systems theory.

The systems approach is an abstract, often intellectually stimulating but sometimes practically limited perspective that views organizations as open systems. The approach proposes that organizations go through input-throughput-output cycles during which they use human, material and information inputs to produce outputs via some transformation or productive technological process. The outputs, which are products or services sold or otherwise distributed to users, allow the system to acquire additional inputs, continuing the cycle and assuring the system's survival. Thus, organizations are open systems, which means their functioning is critically dependent on the environments in which they exist, including economic, political, technological, legal, and socio-cultural components. In addition, an organization, as a system, consists of interdependent, interacting subsystems which perform the functions necessary for the organization to acquire inputs, transform them into outputs, distribute the outputs, and meet longer run system needs to assure survival. According to Katz and Kahn (1978) the major subsystems of an organization are:

1. Production or technical subsystem—activities producing products or services.
2. Production support subsystem—activities that provide inputs and distribute outputs, e.g. purchasing and sales.
3. Maintenance subsystem—activities that preserve the functional capacity of the organization, e.g. personnel activities.
4. Adaptive subsystem—activities that monitor the environment and encourage appropriate adaptation, e.g. market research, research and development, and forecasting.
5. Institutional subsystem—activities that seek social support and legitimacy for the organization, e.g. public affairs.
6. Managerial subsystem—co-ordinating and conflict resolving activities.

As a general theory of organizations, the systems approach is mind broadening because of its emphases on environment/organization relationships and abstract subsystem activities *vis à vis* traditional functional departments, e.g. accounting or marketing. But, as we have mentioned, systems theory has limits. Thus, in OB, it has not delineated specific relationships between specific variables.

A fourth OB theoretical perspective has attempted to meet this last problem. While the phrase 'contingency theory' has been used in different ways in OB, its primary purpose is to specify how given relationships between two factors are affected, in turn, by another variable. It reflects an attempt by organizational behaviour researchers to examine complexity by analysing how the presence of a third variable affects the relationship between two other variables. For example, how does the effect of participative leadership on performance depend on the personalities of the people involved? While it is not always successful, contingency theory has clarified some of our basic relationships concerning leadership and technology. (See Chapter 2 for a discussion of contingency approaches to leadership.)

It is clear that OB as a field lacks an integrated, over-all theory. What has been described here is a set of schools or perspectives, (i.e., values, assumptions, and concepts) that are ways of perceiving organizational behaviour and functioning. OB does not possess grand theories of encompassing scope. What the field does contain are a number of relatively specific attempts to examine particular topics, a not surprising approach given the young age of OB. Nor is it a bad approach at this stage of our knowledge, since grand theories need more knowledge and require more measurement and research adequacy than we now have, as we shall see later.

Another point to make about the theoretical perspectives described here is that while they were presented in roughly the chronological order in which they emerged, the ideas contained in any of them ought not to be considered obsolete. Time and motion studies, piece rates, group dynamics, and technological constraints on organizational structure are all part of today's work world; and task design, individual needs, maintenance and adaptive processes, and environmental uncertainty remain important concepts in the study of organizational behaviour. Thus while the scientific and administrative management perspectives and the human relations school, as they developed and are described here, are not the theoretical perspectives currently used by most OB researchers and writers, many ideas and concepts from those perspectives remain pertinent to the practice and study of organizational behaviour. Similarly, systems theory remains an abstract, analytical framework of limited practical utility but is popular as a source of hypotheses for reasearch. Contingency theory's fundamental assumption that situational relationships and not universal principles should guide practice and research remains highly popular as an approach to the study of OB.

OB and Management

Before examining the current nature of OB, it is probably desirable to briefly address its relationship to the topic of management. Management subsumes OB but is not limited to it. In the real world, the management of people is part of a manager's or administrator's job. The management of work tasks, procedures, or projects are other parts, as is the management of capital. In many organizations the management of tasks and capital are emphasized over the management of people. Individuals are viewed only as the doers of the work, rather than as vital human resources that require effective management. The essential assumption in such organizations appears to be that individuals must adjust to existing organizational conditions and if they cannot or will not, they are free to leave the organization. Clearly, from the organization's perspective, this assumption results in missed opportunities for increased motivation.

Control rather than motivation is emphasized and, as a result, performance levels are often not likely to exceed the just acceptable or minimal levels, if they attain those. Management, it can be seen, is both a social and a technical process requiring interpersonal and organizational as well as technical skills.

It is in this vein that the field of OB has purported to have application over the years for management practice. Such implications have, however, sometimes been more difficult to realize than first conceived. In addition, even when the field's documentation has been clear, the applications have been attacked as 'unscientific', 'biased', or 'one-sided'. Later in this chapter we will examine these controversies.

ORGANIZATIONAL BEHAVIOUR: AN APPLIED BEHAVIOURAL SCIENCE

Organizational behaviour purports to be an applied behavioural science. This means that the knowledge upon which it is based should be both valid and useful. In other words, the research process by which knowledge is generated needs to be both scientifically acceptable and also useful to those concerned with the effectiveness of and satisfactions to be derived from organizations from either managerial or employee perspectives. How well does the field of OB meet its scientific and practical goals? Is it scientific? Is it practical? These are our concerns in this section.

OB as a Science

As a science, OB attempts to generate knowledge through scientific inquiry, a process originally developed within the natural sciences to enhance the probability of producing valid or true knowledge. The goals of scientific inquiry are description, prediction, and explanation (Babbie, 1979). Through logical theory and observation of empirical facts, scientists attempt to understand attributes, the proposed causal relations between the attributes and the conditions which may affect these phenomena. There are several important values and norms of science which define this approach and which we need to keep in mind. These include the following:

1. All concepts must be clearly defined.
2. Theory should guide the development of hypotheses which can be empirically tested.
3. Data should be collected via careful, precise measurement.
4. Confounding influences must be controlled; yet scientific research should be parsimonious.
5. Generalization beyond the circumstances of the particular data collection is necessary.

6. Replication of one study's results by other studies is required.
7. Scientists must be unbiased, avoid ego involvement, and accept peer criticism.

Of particular interest to understanding OB research are some assumptions underlying all scientific inquiry. Thus, science assumes that phenomena, including beings and events, can be ordered or classified. Other assumptions include both stability and determinism. That is, the phenomena being studied are presumed to possess sufficient stability so that we can examine their possible causes. Finally, the conduct of scientific inquiry rests on the belief that human beings can be trusted to be reasonably accurate in perceiving, remembering, and reporting (Lee, 1980). These are the characteristics of science in an ideal sense. How well does OB meet these ideals? In the following pages we will focus on some of the problems of the field. This will then lead us to make some suggestions for redirection.

OB as a Behavioural Science: Issues and Problems

OB as a behaviour science, with a focus on how people behave in organizations, has often found it difficult to meet these scientific criteria and guidelines as a result of both methodological and theoretical problems. Despite these problems, however, the goal and values of science remain important to OB.

Methodological issues

The collection of valid, useful data has been a continuing problem on several levels. Laboratory experiments are often limited in generalizability to real organizational settings because of the experiment's highly controlled environments, simple tasks, and frequent use of non-representative subjects; while field experiments (those done in real organizations) rarely allow random assignment of subjects or permit control of confounding influences. Controlling confounding influences refers to eliminating the effects of other variables when isolating the effects of a particular factor on performance or some other outcome. Surveys have been the most common form of data collection in OB research but unfortunately most surveys have been cross-sectional rather than longitudinal. (That is, data have been collected at a single point in time rather than repeatedly using the same individuals.) This, in conjunction with the lack of control of confounding influences, has often made causal inference impossible. Thus, while the existence of some relationships have been established through survey studies (e.g., considerate leadersihp behaviour is associated with subordinate job satisfaction) the causality of relationships has not been. In addition, survey studies in OB have often been limited by the lack of validity of perceptual measures, lack of conceptual or measurement differentiation among independent variables, and common method bias resulting from measuring independent and dependent variables with the same survey questionnaire or interview. Also, OB research has often not used identical measures for a given variable across studies or undertaken replication studies, both of which have prevented meaningful patterns of results from emerging. Another methodological problem concerns the fact that statistical analyses of data in OB research have often been limited to linear techniques, which may have prevented discovery of some meaningful results.

Organizational behaviour research has often been broad but not deep. That is, while the topical scope of research studies has sometimes included numerous variables, the variables in a given study have generally been similar in coming from a single unit of analysis. Sometimes, only individual perceptions and attitudes are incorporated within a particular study. Alternatively more macroscopically oriented researchers limit themselves to organizational and environmental variables, ignoring the individual level of analysis. Under such circumstances, more precise knowledge about increasingly narrow, limited matters is the result (Roberts, Hulin, and Rousseau, 1978). That is, instead of integrating frameworks, too often we obtain scattered knowledge, data bases that cannot be integrated, and overlapping models and theories. Clearly, the field of OB needs a more comprehensive understanding of networks of relationships within multi-tiered models incorporating more than one unit of analysis. For example, variables such as personality, leadership, group norms, organizational formalization, and inter-organizational uncertainty ought to be examined in a study focussing on individual, group, unit, and organizational performance. However, if such models are to be developed, two occurrences are probably necessary. First, researchers must be willing to conceptualize and collect data at diverse levels, a demand which requires most researchers to think at and to work with data at levels to which they are not accustomed. Second, if such models are to be developed, it is probably necessary, as well as otherwise desirable, to include the dimension of time. The study of how organizations function and how people behave in organizations requires more consideration of processes i.e., a sequence of events and their relationships. However, restricted funding and limited organizational co-operation discourage longitudinal studies.

OB research has also generally been more interested in internal than external validity. That is, researchers have emphasized controlling measurement, data collection, and data analysis procedures to conform to the scientific method rather than emphasizing generalizing a study's results from its sample to a large, meaningful population. Rather than sampling so as to assure representativeness to a significant population, sampling procedures have, at best, concentrated on avoiding bias by seeking representativeness between an actual and potential sample. Specifically, researchers have concentrated on avoiding non-respondent bias when they have surveyed an organization's members. They have attempted to ensure that those members who exercised their right to not participate in the research project were not systematically different than those who did participate.

While this concern is necessary, it is not sufficient if the research goal is to generate scientifically and practically valuable knowledge. Researchers must also sample so that their data are representative of a population larger than and outside of a given organization's or sub-unit's membership. Without generalizability of this scope, knowledge will not develop at a quick enough rate to constitute a meaningful contribution to either theory or practice. Roberts, Hulin, and Rousseau (1978) offer an interesting observation in connection with this issue of generalizability, indicating that most organizational behaviour studies have been done in organizations with more than 50 employees, a size which represents only about 10% of United States organizations.

This issue of generalizability is important not only because scientific and practical criteria require it, but also because theories may be bound to certain populations. These limitations cannot be determined if OB researches are not addressing the issue of generalizability. In addition, as OB research becomes a more accepted influence on public policy, the obligation to develop more sensitivity to the populations we can validly generalize to becomes greater. Roberts, Hulin, and Rousseau (1978) suggest instituting a mathematical index showing inter-organizational resemblance so as to better know the extent to which findings from one organization are applicable to another.

Theoretical issues

The theoretical and conceptual problems within OB research refer to the substantive treatment of organizational issues. As expected with a young, developing discipline, existing theory in OB is limited, fragmented, and non-integrated. For example, theories of leadership and theories of motivation have been constructed separately but have not been integrated. Also not integrated have been our theories of individual behaviour, groups and organizations. Theoretical synthesis is needed to integrate those separate frameworks and also the results of many empirical analyses so as to more meaningfully understand organizational life. Data collection in itself does not disclose ordered relations; real world complexity must be conceptually simplified through logically coherent, concise, predictive theories. OB requires theory that incorporates individual and organizational structures, processes and values (Kaplan, 1964; Dubin, 1976; Kelly, 1980).

The difficulty of developing synthesizing theory is evident in the problems encountered in the presumably simpler task of conceptualizing major constructs in OB. Lack of agreement and thus limited consistency has too often characterized the defining of topics such as organizational structure, environmental uncertainty, and interpersonal influence. Where some consistency has emerged, as in the case of task and person dimensions of leadership, the content tapped in these cases has been limited. If we have found it difficult to conceptualize the major topics in the field, it is not surprising that meaningful, synthesizing theories incorporating both individual attributes and social context have not been forthcoming.

A fundamental point to be made in an evaluation of OB research is that it has been dominated by a functional paradigm (Burrell and Morgan, 1979). The basic assumption that society is characterized by social order, consensus, and integration and that organizations are systematic production units within this societal context has influenced OB researchers to study organizational life in limited terms. Among these are that:

1. Individuals have been treated as essentially rational beings instead of complex psychological, social and economic beings.
2. Organizations have been viewed as technical instruments, emphasizing official goals, formal structure, technological core, and adaptation to environmental constraints rather than as institutions with a socializing culture of values and norms, informal structure, socio-technical processes, and an interactive relationship with an environment.

The combination of relying on the former framework, with its implicit managerial perspective, and adhering to scientific norms has resulted in limited qualitative, interpretive, longitudinal analysis in OB research. Simply put, OB researchers have not sufficiently immersed themselves in the lives of organizations and their employees to really understand the richness and complexity of organizational events and relationships. An important consequence of researching organizational life under the influence of this functional paradigm has been more limited understanding than we would like of individual psychological dynamics, interpersonal relations, organizational power and politics, and organizational influences on the structure and functioning of society.

Related to the question and the possible problems of using this type of dominant paradigm in the organizational sciences is the work of Lundberg (1981). He characterizes the dominant OB paradigm as assuming a passive model of man such that human behaviour is assumed to be a function of antecedent factors which operate according to laws. Lundberg further indicates that the OB paradigm is nomothetic, which means that researchers search for general laws and do so relying on mathematical analysis. A nomothetic discipline requires verification through replication, preferably by experiment, and it allows prediction. Inquiry opposite in nature to nomothetic research is idiographic. This approach to knowledge focusses on phenomena not as instances of universal laws, but as unique events. Emphasis in idiographic inquiry is on individual values and ideas and on the historical unfolding of some phenomenon. An interesting facet of the nomothetic approach is its advocacy of large samples. Large sample research, Lundberg (1981) suggests, often bypasses individual idiosyncrasies. Thus, the attempt to realize the advantages of statistical inference may lead to loss of a qualitative understanding of specific instances.

A third characteristic of the dominant OB paradigm according to Lundberg (1981), in addition to its passive model of man and its nomothetic orientation, is the presumption that organizations are bounded, rational, goal-seeking entities. These three characteristics of the field result in OB assuming a linear unidirectional pattern among variables in its research. This pattern is simply not realistic, and there is little question we need to explore other alternatives.

OB as a Generator of Management Guidelines

While it is clear that using scientific methodology to study how people behave in organizations and how organizations function has proved difficult, the attempt to generate managerially useful knowledge has been no less a problem. The factual question as to the extent of actual use of OB knowledge within private and public sector organizations remain unanswered. It is likely that profitable firms who have the resources and a knowledge base to use OB effectively have taken OB seriously. General Electric and IBM exemplify corporations which do use behavioural science knowledge, but much of that knowledge is generated internally by the companies' own behavioural scientists rather than by academic researchers. Academic OB studies, on the other hand, often cannot adequately account for the determinants of such important practitioner concerns as productivity, turnover, and absenteeism. Not being able to explain and help solve important organizational problems limits the acceptability and application of OB in the real world.

Reasons for OB research providing limited useful concrete knowledge are diverse. Problems of applicability arise in part because the need for scientific generalizability and replicability and the diverse, complex nature of the phenomena under study require conceptualization at an abstract level. This limits utility for practitioners since real world managers find knowledge useful to the extent that it is concrete. In addition, measurement usually demands the use of standard general instruments. This makes the data collected by researchers appear inapplicable to the particular circumstances of many practitioners. Similarly, because most OB data come from self-reported human perceptions, practising managers often remain sceptical, with good reasons, about the presence of bias. Also, economic constraints limit the nature of empirical studies for many researchers. Another reason for this limited practical orientation is the desire of OB as an emerging discipline to gain legitimacy within the academic profession, a group which historically has frowned upon practical, particularly commercial concerns. Most importantly though, academic researchers and real world practitioners possess different goals, the former seeking to study problems and the latter working to solve problems. Clearly, if researchers are not motivated to address and help find solutions for issues important to practising managers and workers, the utility of their research efforts is likely to be limited.

Despite these problems the promise of building a science of administration that can guide managerial action, as articulated by Thompson (1956) over 25 years ago, remains a hope and, sometimes, a reality. Practitioners make many assumptions in their management of people and work and OB theories and empirical research have value for clarifying assumptions and considering alternatives. Experience is valuable to the degree learning occurs and OB can allow an individual manager to learn more quickly from his experience, and from the experience of others. Without some conceptualization and alternative empirical knowledge, a single stream of experience, coupled with the individual's personal values and resultant subjective perceptions, will provide limited learning. It is here where the field of OB can be useful by providing and integrating knowledge in a systematic manner.

In this context, it ought to be recognized that sensitivity may be as important as knowledge in considering OB as an applied behavioural science. For example, OB has probably influenced practitioners to become more sensitive to managerial practices other than autocratic ones. Practitioners may have become more aware as a result of OB research of the benefits to themselves, to their organizations and to their subordinates of managerial styles incorporating consultation, participation, and autonomy.

Some Suggested Directions for the Field of OB

These, then, are some of the intrinsic problems of OB as a science, as an applied behavioural science and as a field of management application. As we have indicated, the problems are not insurmountable and we can make progress even if the ultimate goals that have defined the field eventually prove unattainable to the degree we would like.

In this section we offer some suggestions about possible directions for OB research. Our proposals are both of a content and methodological nature and are consistent with our previous discussion. Taken in context we think they may, if followed, help attain the theoretical and applied goals of OB within its constraints.

The need for problem-oriented research

Our earlier discussion suggests that we may have reached a limit in the values we are gaining from 'theory-oriented' research and in our enchantment with rigorous 'traditional science'. We think, therefore, that we need research that is less formally stated, more 'problem-oriented' and more of an 'I wonder if' nature. We also need a greater acceptance of less rigorous (in a traditional, experimental sense) but more content—meaningful research designs.

Besides the intrinsic problems of OB we have outlined earlier, there are other events which have been taking place in the last few years that we believe amply support this contention. One of these is that it has become apparent that the self-correcting characteristics of the scientific theory-hypothesis-testing model are simply not working. That is, theories that have little or no evidence still continue to dominate the literature, continue to be written about and continue to influence the thinking of both students and practitioners when they should not. Illustrations of this point abound, with the Maslow theory of the hierarchy of needs only being the most obvious. Another illustration is the most popular motivational theory, i.e., the expectancy-value model. Recent research reviews have all agreed as to the moderate (at best) predictive usefulness of the framework, as well as its circumscribed nature (cf. Campbell and Pritchard, 1976; Korman, Greenhaus, and Badin, 1977). Like Maslow's hierarchy, it continues to receive considerable research and teaching attention, although as a theory it simply is *not very good* (cf. Campbell and Pritchard, 1976).

Why is the self-corrective process for theory confirmation not working? There are, we believe, several reasons. One major reason is that what we have been calling theories are not really theories at all. They are really 'meta theories', i.e. assumptions about the nature of knowledge and the kinds of knowledge we are willing to accept in a science of behaviour (cf. Deci, 1975). Such meta theories are socially determined values and are not subject to empirical disconfirmation in the sense that traditional theories are supposed to be. For this reason, our so-called theoretical (but, really, value) arguments continue. Second, there is the fact that individual researchers become personally invested in their previous writings and, as a result, are less likely to accept disconfirmatory evidence. This lack of responsivity to disconfirmation is also aided by the very complexity of the research process in this field. That is, since research is (legitimately) complex, it becomes easier to question and discount the disconfirmatory findings of another and hold on to one's own pet theory longer than is warranted. Another reason for the continuing pervasiveness of theories beyond their evidential basis is that they provide ready-made vehicles for 'little studies' and 'quickie publications', a type of pressure with which most academics desirous of promotion are familiar. This has been discussed extensively both in the U.S. and the U.K. (cf. Boyd and Wall, 1974), and virtually all qualified observers believe it to be debilitating for the growth of any field of knowledge.

A second major influence which recommends the changes we suggest comes from our previous discussion. Briefly, the types of theory which seem interesting and challenging and also easy to use administratively after investigation turn out not to be so. The best examples of this are the contingency theories. These theories propose that the effect of one variable (e.g., type of leadership) on a second variable (such as performance) depend on a third variable (such as the type of workers involved. These theories seem only 'commonsense' at first glance and should be very valuable. Yet it has not worked out that way. Cronbach

(1975), for example, has pointed to the continuing failure of 'contingency' theories as viable, replicable models in research. One of the authors of this paper has also been somewhat involved in this question and has pointed out elsewhere that contingency models, despite their theoretical nicety and 'commonsense' character, are:

1. Almost impossible to test *a priori* because of the need to specify parameter values of the contingency variables and to measure them accurately.
2. Unreliable because of their reliance on extreme scores in the distribution of the contingency variable (when it is normally distributed).
3. Of minor value both theoretically and practically since they provide no guidelines for dealing with individuals falling in the (larger) mid-areas of the contingency variable when it is normally distributed (Korman and Tanofsky, 1975).

There is also the argument (cf. Payne, 1975) that the intrinsic characteristic of scientific theory upon which much of its value has been supposedly based (i.e., its value-free nature) is, at least in part, not so, and that our knowledge, our questions and our answers are, at least in part, as socially determined and as predictable as other phenomena. Furthermore, it is argued, the illusion of a 'value-free' science needs to be exorcised and the personal orientations of the investigator dealt with in a more open and explicit manner if his or her results are to be accurately interpreted.

It is for these reasons that we are not surprised by the calls of Argyris (1975), and Cronbach (1975), for research studies where the attitudes of the researcher are taken into account and assessed for their influence in planning research and in understanding findings. We think that such an approach is dictated by the nature of all that we have learned about 'scientific method' and 'theory' in recent years, that it is meaningful, that it is realistic and that it will lead to significant understanding of work behaviour *if* the research is carefully planned and well executed. It also does not mean that we should not experiment in a traditional way when we can and that we should not develop rigorous theories. Both of these should, we believe, remain. What we need to do is loosen the grasp of an overly naïve view of 'science' on our thoughts and our activities. We will deal with this argument later in our section on 'ethical problems'.

The need to expand our dependent variables

Traditionally, predicting work performance has been the major concern of OB. Researchers also studied job satisfaction for a long time, first for its possible effects on work performance and then, when this seemed quite difficult to establish, for its occurrence as an important dependent variable worth studying from the viewpoint of individuals, organizations, and society.

We think that we need to undertake a massive change in this area and that work performance and job satisfaction should be moved over, to make space for new variables with names like family problems, alcoholism, 'self-esteem', and 'personal and social alienation'. Our reasons are several. First, we need to recognize that work is a social experience that may affect people and we need to know the nature of this experience. In other words, we want to know when work meaningfully affects individual characteristics. We need to know, for example, the implications of different types of organizational leadership patterns for outcomes of societal significance. What is the implication for family life if the father spends his working life in an atmosphere marked by rigid authoritarianism or by routinized, simple work demands? We also believe that alienation and anxiety have considerable behavioural significance, both in and out of work situation. Since they can occur as a function of work experience (Warr and Wall, 1975), we need to understand them at least as much as we do job satisfaction, a job outcome whose conceptual meaning has recently come under serious question. Although this latter statement may seem a bit surprising to some, we believe that the consistent findings that 'the lower the expectations the higher the job satisfaction' implies that high levels of job satisfaction may be a function of two processes. First, it may be a function of meeting both personally and socially appropriate needs; second, it may also be found in individuals who, by most criteria of mental health, would be viewed quite negatively, i.e., they would be apathetic, expecting little, alienated, have low self-esteem, etc. (cf. Korman, Greenhaus, and Badin, 1977). For researchers in this field, a job satisfaction measure in and of itself may be of little value in assessing the mental health of that individual as a result of his work experience (or the health of the organization, for that matter). For some individuals, a high score on 'job satisfaction' might mean some very good things such as challenging work, psychological growth, satisfying coworkers, etc., for others, it might mean an acceptance of one's 'lot in life', an apathy and a dullness of negative consequences for individuals, organizations and society. (This might also explain why we sometimes get such high job satisfaction scores from the most surprising sources!) It is for these reasons, then, that we believe that job satisfaction needs to be moved over, to be joined by these other types of job outcomes.

Our other reasons for supplementing job performance, although obviously not eliminating it, are several. First, of course, there is the problem of measurement. The fact of the matter is that, too often (but, fortunately, not always) the only methods we can use for measuring performance are so ridden with error and subjectivity that the effort simply may not be worthwhile. Mixed in here also is the fact that, often, either the amount of variance in performance actually attributable to people (as opposed to technology, etc.) is so minimal that it may not be worth predicting, either theoretically or administratively, or the variability of performance may be so great over time that there may not be sufficient reliable variance at a given point in time to enable accurate prediction. Related to this is the diverse nature of the variables generating the administratively significant predictions. To illustrate, a manager may be effective because of planning skills, instructional capabilities, or technical decision-making skills, and there may be changes over time in his competence. What we might do, therefore, when studying behaviour is use these specific skills as dependent variables in our research studies rather than complex job performance measures. (We realize that this particular argument is not a new one but it needs to be repeated.)

The need to see 'people as process'

We think that we are beginning to see vast, significant changes in our views of the human organism as he (she) behaves in the work organization and that as useful as our previous theories of human motivation have been, we need and are, in fact, beginning to see changes. In order to understand more completely what these new perspectives on motivation might be, we need to first review what our traditional perspectives have been.

Basically, research in the field of OB has reflected four different views of motivation. These approaches have differed in several respects from one another in their basic assumptions but they have been similar in that they have all viewed motivation as essentially a choice process. In each of their views, motivated processes and motivational theories are concerned with examining the factors that influence the arousal of behaviour and the choice of the direction of behaviour. The idea behind all of this is to study these factors as they affect choice at a particular point in time. The difference between them is the factors they think are important in influencing such choices. Thus, anxiety theory says we make our behavioural choices on the basis of what will reduce our anxiety even though, sometimes, these choices might not meet 'commonsense'. For example, the research on 'fear of success' pointed out that women will sometimes choose *not* to achieve, even when it is available and possible because they may be anxious that they will lose their possibilities for marriage and family life. The second theory, the expectancy–value model, argues that we make choices on the basis of the 'value' to be obtained. The more value to be obtained, the more likely the choice and 'more is better'. This is, of course, a very popular theory of choice even though it has many weaknesses. For example, it can not account for self-destructive behaviour and, in its extreme case, suicide.

The same general comments can be made about the two other popular motivational theories found in the literature of OB. Equity-theory proposes that we make choices on the basis of what is fair and equitable for us and for the world around us. Of key importance here is the pre-existing views of ourselves and the world because, based on these views, we seek equitable outcomes. These outcomes may be good or bad, depending on whether we view ourselves and others positively or negatively. Equity theory is a theory of choice which has considerable value but, like anxiety theory and expectancy–value theory, there is much that it does not account for.

This is also the case with respect to self-actualization theory, the fourth approach. This is the famous 'hierarchy-of-needs' model of Maslow, a theory which became the rallying cry for a generation convinced of the basic upward striving of all people, people whose expression of self was only hampered by an overly restrictive world. Our more recent perspectives on this theory have, however, been more modest. We now believe that it is a useful theory of choice for some people but there is little reason to view it as a general model.

If we bring this brief review together, then, two conclusions seem warranted. All of these theories are useful but none of them are all-inclusive. Second, they are all theories which view motivational processes as 'choices' at particular points in time. They take little account of longitudinal processes. It is these perspectives that we need to change. Thus, we need a new perspective of man (and woman) as changing, achieving (sometimes), value-seeking (sometimes), equity-seeking (sometimes) beings who select and are influenced by their organizational experience. Useful as our expectancy–value theories have been, and our equity models, their frequent use as over-all theoretical frameworks needs to be revised as we now seek to understand the conditions when each is useful, how and when their usefulness may change over time and the types of work experience which may affect these changes in motivational processes (cf. Campbell and Pritchard, 1976; Korman, 1976). In brief, it is our belief that the study of work and organizational socialization processes, in conjunction with the more traditional motivation theories, need to become our dominant conceptual underpinning.

We think that the evidence for adopting a longitudinal, process perspective is by now too compelling to ignore. To begin with, there are the weaknesses of the contingency models we have noted above. The relevance for this here is that when we see a particular management practice not having the effect we have expected, a major reason is that we often assume a static, permanent quality to the individual whom we have previously classified or measured as being of a certain type. This assumption is not warranted according to Cronbach (1975). It is the latter's belief that it is, in fact, 'change' in human processes over time that is responsible for the failure of contingency theories (and management practices) to generate consistently positive outcomes. This conclusion is consistent with the general arguments of Mischel (1968) and the work of the attribution theorists (Korman, 1977). (Incidentally, we might note that, at first glance, there is an inconsistency in what we have said. On one hand, we suggest the limited utility of contingency models whereas, here and immediately below, we argue that some type of contingency understanding will be necessary. There is no inconsistency, we believe, since it is obvious that all theories eventually need some boundaries, i.e., no theory accounts for everything. The point is that contingency theories might be better built inductively. For the reasons we have outlined above, it may be too hard at this time to build them deductively.)

Our other reasons for suggesting that the different motivational frameworks we have been using will gradually fade into some more coherent, integrated frameworks with a longitudinal perspective is that this is the only conclusion which is warranted from the literature if we pay attention to it. We need to recognize that expectancy–value theory, the favourite framework of OB over the years, simply accounts for too little and too narrow a range of work behaviour for it to have the prominence that it does (cf. Campbell and Pritchard, 1976; Korman, Greenhaus, and Badin, 1977). We also need to recognize (we have not so far) that it is logically inadequate (Locke, 1975) and that its basic postulates are contradicted by the findings of Deci and others that incentives may not be additive (cf. Deci, 1975). In fact, adding incentives may detract from the likelihood of behaviour. Equity theory (Adams, 1963) has, we think, been challenging in its attack on 'rational man' and it has had considerable value. Yet, here also, we need to recognize that equity theory is often overly general with little attention paid to specific parameters; that it has logical problems in handling some types of change; and that it is incomplete since humans are obviously not always equitable. Since similar comments to these can be made for our content theories (e.g., N Ach theory and its lack of accounting for great amounts of variance), even more support exists for the necessity and desirability of a 'change' perspective in motivation, one that relies less on the permanency of individual characteristics and one that views 'people as process', rather than 'people as choice'.

In a related vein we note that we need to expand our study of the longitudinal effects of different leadership styles (e.g. consideration, emphasis on group decision-making, etc.). The research in attribution processes and the variability of the adult personality suggests that longitudinal changes in effects may be quite strong.

The need to train practitioners in methodology

OB needs to give more attention to how it can most assist practising managers. There are a number of viewpoints here but they are not necessarily contradictory. One way is to raise the sensitivity and sophistication of managers, as we have said elsewhere in this chapter. Another is to instruct organizational members in evaluation skills, (Staw, 1977). This latter suggestion is based on our belief that organizations themselves, rather than OB researchers, should play the central role in applying behavioural science knowledge. Organizations should experiment and evaluate different programmes and practices to discover what is most suitable for their particular circumstances. Thus, it is with programme evaluation and field experiments that OB experts should most concern themselves if they wish to provide useful knowledge to administrators.

While this is an intuitively appealing suggestion, we should recognize that the propensity of most organizations to conduct field experiments is limited. Staw

(1977) addresses some of the potential problems of organizational experimenting. One primary difficulty is the reluctance of organizations to allow random assignment of people to treatment and control groups. Yet, some conditions might encourage this assignment. For example, where some uncertainty about a programme outcome exists or where demand for a particular programme exceeds supply, random assignment of units to treatment and control categories may be organizationally desirable and acceptable.

Programme evaluation in organizations is unfortunately often subject to political problems. Some managers, believing that negative results reflect poorly on their performance, will increase investment in the programme, sometimes to the point of seeking to 'make it' at almost any cost. Other managers 'test the system'. This refers to allocating some resources to a programme and then looking for quick results which, if not forthcoming, causes them to abandon the project. As a response to these problems, Staw (1977) indicates that organizations should evaluate programmes without evaluating people associated with them and should loosen the link between specific programmes results and allocation of future resources to responsible units.

While these suggestions of Staw's are understandable, they ignore the fundamental managerial and organizational formal value system that emphasizes individual performance appraisal based on results. In other words, if organizations are going to begin experimentation, or at least evaluation, with behavioural science programmes, some suspension of customary managerial thinking may be necessary. This revised type of thinking will not be easily accomplished, nor is it always clear that it should be. We may conclude, then, that if Staw's (1977) suggestions for applying OB are to become a reality, managers must believe more than they do now that conducting experiments or evaluation programmes can constitute part of good performance, and that well selected interventions, subject to well designed implementation and evaluation, will contribute to organizational goals.

ETHICAL DILEMMAS OF ORGANIZATIONAL BEHAVIOUR

Organizational behaviour as a field of academic interest and applied practice has come under the same scrutiny as other fields in recent years as to its objectivity, its ethical characteristics and its effects, both intended and unintended. This is well and good. More traditional fields such as physics, chemistry, and biology have been asked to examine their possible contributions to the despoilation of the earth's atmosphere and the environments in which we live and we believe they are much the better for it. Organizational behaviour has not been and should not be exempt from the same type of self-examination.

In this section we will deal with some of the ethical issues that have been raised about organizational behaviour both as an academic area of research and theory and as an applied practice. We will first examine what some of these major questions have been. Following this we will discuss some responses to these ethical issues, including those that are already taking place and others that are possible in the future.

Is Organizational Behaviour a Servant of Power?

Perhaps the major overriding charge that has been made against the field of organizational behaviour has been that it operates as a servant of entrenched power interests rather than as the objective, impartial field of research and theory it professes to be. Before we examine exactly what this charge means, its significance and its validity, we might note that this complaint against organizational behaviour as a field is not the first time that behavioural scientists have been called to task in this manner. Over 20 years ago Baritz (1960) criticized the field of industrial psychology along very similar grounds arguing, in essence, that psychologists were serving as agents for existing power structures rather than examining questions and issues from an impartial objective perspective.

What exactly does this charge mean? Integrating the arguments of writers such as Nord (1977) and Scott and Hart (1979), among others, we can answer this question by considering four criticisms, as discussed below.

1. 'Organizational behaviour is overly preoccupied with the values of management and their definitions of organizational problems.' This charge reflects the belief that the field of organizational behaviour is overly concerned with such matters as productivity, turnover, and absenteeism, all management problems, while it has tended to ignore the study of behaviour in organizations as behaviour, regardless of its implications for management problems. An illustration of this argument concerns the study of such problems as turnover and absenteeism. It has been claimed that OB has examined these two matters as management problems but that the field has ignored thse phenomena as human problems affecting individuals.
2. 'Organizational behaviour, as a field, has assumed that there is a basic community of interests among all members and across all hierarchical levels of a work organization.' Nord (1977) has called this the 'integrative' assumption, an assumption which has led specialists in organizational behaviour to recommend such techniques for increasing work motivation and work commitment as job enrichment. These recommendations and applications by OB specialists assume that this is desirable (i.e., that it is in the interests of everybody that work motivation and work commitment be increased). But is it? This seems a strange question, considering our present concern with the productivity of American and British corporations and workers. Certainly, from a societal point of view, increasing productivity is in the interests of

everybody. Yet, it is important to recall the traditional 'fear of speed-up' without increased rewards among workers, and their related belief that increased productivity on an individual level leads to a loss of jobs for the work group as a whole. Why, then, should workers feel about increased productivity the way that management does?

The point here is that the assumption often made in the field of OB that all organizational employees would feel that increased work motivation would be desirable may be true for those who are in power but perhaps not as much so by those who are not.

3. 'Organizational behaviour has neglected the political realities of organizational life and failed to recognize the power motives and drives that dominate organizational leadership.' Basically, the charge here against the field of organizational behaviour is the one of naïvete. It is a claim that there has been a failure to realize that the leaders of our organizations may have strong power drives for themselves and that they are often not as committed to the good of the organization as they are to themselves. Hence, theories which have assumed such organizational commitment do not reflect the realities of organizational life and implicity serve to satisfy the needs and interests of the current power-holders by assuming their motives to be less self-enhancing than they actually are.

4. 'Organizational behaviour has over-emphasized the value of the organization in contemporary life and under-emphasized the value of the individual.' While now new, this argument has been made recently in a very effective and very forthright manner by Scott and Hart in their book *Organizational America* (1979). According to these authors we have in recent years seen the growth of the 'organizational imperative', an ideology which stresses the value of organizational goals over individual goals. There are two propositions which make up the organizational imperative:

   a. Proposition one: What is good for the individual can only come from the modern organization.
   b. Proposition two: Therefore, all employee behaviour must enhance the health of such organizations.

It is claimed that researchers and writers in organizational behaviour, as well as other organizationally employed professionals, have contributed to the growth of this imperative and therefore to supporting those individuals who have been given the responsibility and the power to administer organizations.

This issue is particularly significant when one considers the socio-political context in which organizations function in the U.K. and the U.S.A. Democratic societal ideals such as equality and freedom are not much present in most organizations, and judicial structures to ensure due process and protection of individual rights generally do not exist in organizations. In other words, organizations are usually allowed to function autocratically and arbitrarily within a larger societal context of proclaimed equality and liberty.

Employees' and the public's rights are protected only by government regulation of varying effectiveness. The result of these circumstances is that the organization's well-being is emphasized *vis à vis* the individual's and dominant power holders are not subject to control.

These are some of the components of the 'servants of power' critique. While these four statements do not cover all of the specifics of the criticisms that have been made, we believe they represent the essence of the argument.

Are the complaints valid? Is the field of organizational behaviour a 'servant of power'? And if so, is there anything we can or should do about it? The answers to these questions are complex and difficult to answer but we will make an attempt.

Basically, we believe that these complaints about the field of organizational behaviour have some validity but that, like most complaints of this nature, the arguments are overstated and too extreme. There is little question, for example, that much of the work of the field is defined in management terms and reflects the concerns of management rather than a desire for objective understanding of behavioural phenomena. Any examination of the academic journals relevant to organizational behaviour would quickly lead to such a conclusion. Yet, there are many individuals in the field who recognize this problem and are reacting to it. While most of our techniques for change assume a desirability of work commitment for all, some theorists in the field now view organizations and the practice of leadership as developing and maintaining bargaining relationships and agreements between groups and individuals whose goals may sometimes be antagonistic and sometimes similar. The 'industrial democracy' movement in Western Europe, consisting of attempts to develop co-operative relationships between groups with sometimes conflicting goals, has only begun to spread to the U.K. and the U.S.A., but we believe this movement will increase. The recent experiences in the U.S. of unions co-operating with management to prevent financial disaster in certain troubled industries may represent the initial step.

There are also new research programmes that suggest that the latter two complaints concerning the absence of power research and limited attention to the value of the individual in OB may also be overstated. Consider, on the one hand, such recent articles on power motivation in organizations as Vredenburgh and Maurer (1981) and, on the other, the growth of the career-development movement. The articles by Schein and Vredenburgh (1977) reflect the recognition by some researchers in the field of OB as to the inevitability of political processes in organizations and the significance of power drives that focus on personal needs as well as organizational requirements. Similarly, the popularity of organizational programmes in career-development and the seriousness with which they have been undertaken reflects the fact that some OB practitioners have tried to modify the impact of the organizational imperative proposed by Scott and Hart (1979).

Organizational Behaviour and the Conflict Between Organization and Society

Organizations exist in a societal context and they interact with that society in a number of ways. However, the goals and values of organizations may not be congruent with those of society. While they overlap to some extent, there are many areas where they are in considerable conflict. The question which has been raised for the field of organizational behaviour concerns its loyalty and commitment in this conflict. Should OB serve the organization *or* the larger society of which it is a part? This is the ethical issue that has been raised here, an issue that can be illustrated by a rapidly growing problem of our time, i.e., the work–family conflict.

Research during the past decade has shown increasingly that the contemporary demands of work and career, particularly at high levels, can operate to affect family life negatively. Factors such as long work hours, travel, geographic mobility, and stressful work demands are only some of the reasons cited for high levels of alienation and life dissatisfaction, according to a recent study of over 500 European managers and executives by Evans and Bartoleme (1981). Similarly, Korman and his coworkers (1981) have found that an emphasis on work responsibilities and requirements is a common cause of alienation among successful executives and professionals.

There is a dilemma here for the organizational behaviour scientist and/or practitioner. Should the focus be on encouraging work achievement and commitment on the part of the individual, knowing at the same time that he may be contributing to the break-up of the person's family? Should the scientist be absolved of responsibility for the latter? Can one be concerned with the family life of the manager when it is the organization that is the employer? Answers to these questions are not easy to develop.

Organizational Behaviour and Trade Unions

With few exceptions, the relationship between the field of organizational behaviour and the labour union movement in the U.S. has ranged from, at best, mistrust, to, at worst, outright hostility and antagonism. Such feelings are, we think, understandable. The field of organizational behaviour has been devoted, in great degree, to developing techniques designing to increase organizational effectiveness, as defined by management.

Such activities have not endeared the behavioural scientist to labour unions, which have viewed both these activities *and* the parallel efforts to increase job satisfaction as attempts to install speed-ups and to do away with the need for trade unions. There is considerable evidence to support the argument that job dissatisfaction may, in fact, lead to union organization (cf. Schreisheim, 1978). The distaste of unions for attempts to increase job satisfaction seem, therefore, understandable, particularly if one is committed to the belief that unions are important for the protection of organizational members.

The case of the job enrichment movement is another example. A basic tool developed by organizational behaviour researchers for increasing job variety, responsibility, and autonomy and, thereby, work motivation and satisfaction—job enrichment has become increasingly popular with management in recent years. At the same time, it has been attacked by many trade unions as a type of speed-up and a union-busting device.

Does it have to be this way? Perhaps not. We are seeing, increasingly, trade unions recognizing productivity changes as being in their interests also. Again, unions have worked with management in Western Europe in furthering the concept of 'industrial democracy'. Perhaps organizational behaviour and unions will start communicating in the U.K. and the U.S. as well. How to do this, however? This is one of the questions to which we now turn.

Overcoming the Ethical Dilemmas of Organizational Behaviour

There are basically three steps or changes we see taking place in the field of organizational behaviour over the next decade which will help in responding to some of the problems we have outlined here. First, we see an expanding number of clients for the field. We believe that these clients will include the trade unions and societal organizations that possess different goals and represent countervailing power to the private and public sector organizations that have overwhelmingly served as the major clients of the field up to now. Second, we see an increasing expansion in the dependent variables of the field. The concept of organizational effectiveness is being redefined and expanded in order to understand and comprehend more fully the significance of organizations in our society. Third, we will begin to be more flexible in how we define 'good' and 'bad' outcomes and we will begin to realize how they may both be occurring at the same time. Such recognition will lead researchers in the field of organizational behaviour to become generally more complex in their judgments and to be generally less quick to adopt the viewpoints of a single group, e.g., organizational management. In the following we will explore these matters further.

The need to expand the client basis in OB and, more generally, the study of different types of organizations is increasingly being recognized. The need to study and work with trade unions is of course crucial. The field also needs to examine organizations such as trade associations, lobbying groups, and labour organization coalitions both as organizations themselves and as organizations which interact with private companies and public sector agencies. The mechanisms of interaction need to be examined, both collaborative and conflicting ones, and the impact of different types of relationships investigated. Relatedly, OB researchers should focus on organizations with which both business organizations and/or trade unions interact (such as political organizations or consumer organizations) and determine the patterns of conflict and co-operation which exist and have impact. To cite an important illustration,

General Motors, the United Auto Workers, and Ralph Nader's consumer groups are all organizations and the field of organizational behaviour needs to examine all of them, both individually and in interaction with each other. We see this type of change coming.

Another significant development likely to occur in OB is an expansion of the dependent variables with which the field is concerned. Organizational outcome variables such as turnover, productivity, and growth are important. So also are the people who work for organizations and the society in which organizations and individuals interact. They also have criteria with which they evaluate organizations and these criteria deserve consideration.

Society is concerned, for example, with different kinds of pollution and with job losses because of their consequences for community services as well as family well-being. Society has an important stake in the family disintegration and societal anomie that might occur as a result of organizational policies and practices. Individuals are also interested in these matters and the field of organizational behaviour must develop greater awareness of these concerns. We believe it will.

Finally, we believe that the maturing of the field will also help to reduce the excessive management-mindedness which has dominated research, theory and practice up to now. Part of this new development has centred around the realization that no particular group and no particular decision has a particular claim on being 'right' or 'good'. Virtually all decisions in the organizational realm have *both* 'good' and 'bad' outcomes and the same is true for particular groups, e.g., management, labour, societal-pressure groups, etc. Each of these has a particular perspective toward the problems and processes of organizational functioning and each has a particular view of what is 'good' and what is 'bad'. As the researcher and student of organizational behaviour becomes increasingly aware of pertinent interests of particular groups and their decisions, we may expect to see theory and application in the future being more multi-dimensional and less tied to the management-oriented perspective of today. Such freedom will, of course, serve to minimize some of the ethical problems we have concerned ourselves with here.

REFERENCES

Adams, J. S. (1965) Inequity in social change, in: L. Berkowitz (ed.), *Advances in Experimental Social Psychology*, Volume 2, Academic Press, New York.

Argyris, C. (1975) Dangers in applying from experimental social psychology. *American Psychologist*, **30**, 469–485.

Babbie, E. R. (1979) *The Practice of Social Research*, Wadsworth Publishing, Belmont, California.

Baritz, L. (1960) *The Servants of Power*, Wesleyan University Press, Middletown, Conn.

Beckhard, R. (1969) *Organizational Development Strategies and Models*, Addison-Wesley, Reading, Mass.

Boyd, J. E., and Wall, T. D. (1974) *Encouraging scientific psychology.* Unpublished paper, Sheffield University.

Burrell, G., and Morgan, G. (1979) *Sociological Paradigms and Organizational Analysis,* Heinemann Educational Books, London.

Campbell, J. P., and Pritchard, R. D. (1976) Motivation theory in industrial and organizational psychology, in Dunnette, M. D. (ed.), *Handbook of Industrial and Organizational Psychology,* Rand-McNally, Chicago, Illinois, pp. 63–130.

Cronbach, D. J. (1975) Beyond the two disciplines of scientific psychology. *American Psychologist,* **30,** 116–127.

Deci, E. L. (1975) Notes on the theory and metatheory of intrinsic motivation. *Organizational Behavior and Human Performance,* **15,** 130–145.

Dubin, R. (1976) Theory building in applied areas, in Dunnette, M. D. (ed.), *Handbook of Industrial and Organizational Psychology,* Rand-McNally, Chicago, Illinois.

Evans, P., and Bartoleme, F. (1981) *Must Success Cost So Much?* Basic Books, Inc., New York.

Fayol, H. (1949) *General and Industrial Management.* Translated by Constance Staws, Pitman, London.

Glickman, A. S., Goodstadt, B. G., Foey, R. G., Jnr., Korman, A. K., and Romanczuk, A. P. (1974) *Navy career motivation programs in an all-volunteer condition.* American Institutes for Research, Final Report, Studies in Naval Career Motivation, New York.

Kaplan, A. (1964) *The Conduct of Inquiry,* Chandler Publishing, Scranton, Illinois.

Katz, D., and Kahn, R. L. (1978) *The Social Psychology of Organizations,* Wiley, New York.

Kelly, J. (1980) *Organizational Behavior: Its Data, First Principles, and Applications,* Irwin, Harewood, Illinois.

Khandwalla, P. (1977) *The Design of Organizations,* Harcourt Brace Jovanovich, New York.

Korman, A. K. (1976) Hypothesis of work behavior revisited and an extension. *Academy of Management Review,* **1,** 50–63.

Korman, A. K. (1977) *Organizational Behavior.* Prentice-Hall, Englewood Cliffs, N.J.

Korman, A. K., and Tanofsky, R. (1975) Statistical problems of contingency models in organizational behavior. *Academy of Management—Journal,* **18,** 393–397.

Korman, A. K., Greenhaus, J., and Badin, I. (1977) Personnel attitudes and motivation. *Annual Review of Psychology,* **28,** 175–196.

Korman, A. K., Lang, D., and Wittig-Berman, U. (1981) Career success and personal failure: Alienation in professionals and managers. *Academy of Management Journal,* **24,** 342–359.

Lee, J. A. (1980) *The Gold and the Garbage in Management Theories and Prescriptions,* Ohio University Press, Ohio.

Likert, R. (1961) *New Patterns of Management,* McGraw-Hill.

Locke, E. A. (1975) Personnel attitudes and motivation. *Annual Review of Psychology,* **26,** 457–480.

Lundberg, C. (1981) On the paradigm orthodoxy of the organizational sciences: Consequences for theory and research—toward an alternative strategy of inquiry. *Proceedings of the Eighteenth Annual Meeting,* The Eastern Academy of Management, pp. 61–66.

March, J., and Simon, H. (1958) *Organizations,* Wiley, New York.

Mischel, W. (1968) *Personality and assessment,* Wiley, New York.

Nord, W. (1977) Job satisfaction reconsidered, *American Psychologist,* **32,** 1026–1035.

Payne, R. L. (1975) *Epistemology and the study of behaviour in organizations.* Unpublished paper, Sheffield University.

Pfeffer, J. (1978) *Organizational Design*. AHM Publishing Corp., Arlington Heights, Illinois.

Pondy, L. (1980) The circle of inquiry, in Pinder, C., and Moore, L. F. (eds.), *Middle Range Theory and the Study of Organizations*, Nijhoff, Amsterdam.

Roberts, K. H., Hulin, C. L., and Rousseau, D. M. (1978) *Developing an Interdisciplinary Science of Organizations*, Jossey-Bass, Chicago.

Roethlisberger, F. J., and Dickson, W. J. (1939) *Management and the Worker*, Harvard University Press, Boston, Mass.

Schein, V. E. (1977) Individual power and political behaviors in organizations: An inadequately explored reality. *Academy of Management Review*, **2**, 64–72.

Schreisheim, C. (1978) Job satisfaction attitudes toward unions and voting in a union representation elections. *Journal of Applied Psychology*, **63(5)**, 548–552.

Scott, W., and Hart, D. K. (1979) *Organizational America*. Houghton-Mifflin Co., New York.

Slater, P. (1971) *The Pursuit of Loneliness*. Beacon, Boston, Massachusetts.

Staw, B. M. (1977) *Psychological Foundations of OB*, Goodyear, Santa Monica.

Taylor, F. W. (1911) *Principles of Scientific Management*, Harper and Row, New York.

Thompson, J. D. (1956) On building an administrative science. *Administrative Science Quarterly*, **1**, 102–111.

Vredenburgh, D. J., and Maurer, J. G. (1981) A process framework of organizational politics. *Academy of Management Proceedings*.

Warr, P. B. (1976) Aided experiments in social psychology. *Bulletin of the British Psychological Society*.

Warr, P. B., and Wall, T. D. (1975) *Work and well-being*. Penguin, Harmondsworth, Middlesex.

Weber, M. (1947) in Parsons, T. (ed.) *The Theory of Social and Economic Organizations*. Oxford University Press, Oxford.

Author Index

Subject Index